THE TIDE BETWEEN US

BESTSELLING AUTHOR OF THE MEMORY OF MUSIC

OLIVE COLLINS

This novel is entirely a work of fiction. The names, characters and incidents portrayed in it are the work of the author's imagination. Any resemblance to actual persons, living or dead, events or localities is entirely coincidental.

The moral right of the author has been asserted.

A catalogue record for this book is available from the British Library.

ISBN 978-1-83853-056-3

www.olivecollins.com

 Created with Vellum

ABOUT THE AUTHOR

Olive Collins grew up in Thurles, Tipperary, and now lives in Kildare. For the last sixteen years, she has worked in advertising in print media and radio. She has always loved the diversity of books and people. She has travelled extensively and still enjoys exploring other cultures and countries. Her inspiration is the ordinary everyday people who feed her little snippets of their lives. It's the unsaid and gaps in conversation that she finds most valuable. Her debut novel, *The Memory of Music*, was a bestseller. *The Tide Between Us* has continued to ride high in the charts since its release in 2019 attaining No. 1 in numerous categories in amazon.

ACKNOWLEDGMENTS

To Eileen Keane, for friendship, input and advice.

A special thanks to Pat O'Brien, for encouragement and reading the early drafts.

To Crooked House Writers Group whose early encouragement prompted me to continue.

Thanks for the help and horse-insight from Vern Carroll.

To Bertie O'Connor, for parting with his wealth of knowledge on the terrain and stories of North Kerry.

To Tom Ryan, for always encouraging me and reading early drafts.

To Mary Dollard who sat patiently through the many changing first-page rewrites.

To Olive Foran, Jacques and Jo – for the open invitation to Kerry and allowing me to sit at the window seat as I plotted the scene for my novel and imagined Art O'Neill's early years.

To Jacinta Matthews at The Creative Flow for encouragement when it was most needed.

To my friends and family for understanding my absence in the last year as I brought *The Tide Between Us* to life.

I would also like to extend my sincere thanks to Kildare Arts County Council for their generous support which enabled me to undertake detailed research for my novel.

And, finally, a heartfelt thanks to you, the reader.

This book is dedicated to the many Irish exiles and Jamaicans who celebrate their Irish heritage.

The Exile's Return (or Morning on the Irish Coast)
John Locke (1847–1889)

And my prayers would arise that some future date
All danger, doubting and scorning,
I might help to win for my native land
The light of young liberty's morning.

THE O'NEILL FAMILY

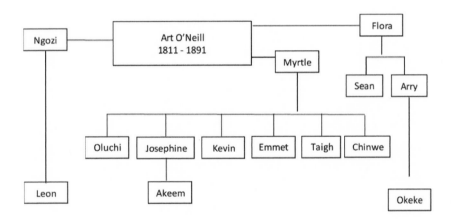

THE STRATFORD-RICE FAMILY

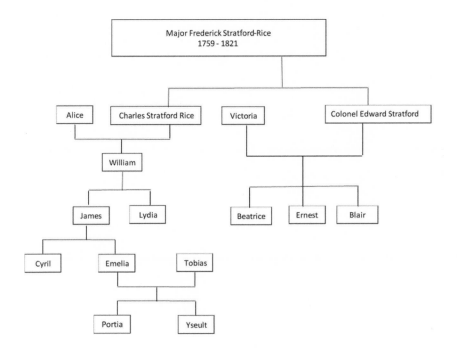

PROLOGUE

13th January 1991

Yseult kept her back to the man as he relayed the news. The time for decorum and manners had passed – it belonged to a younger woman from a different era. She stared out the window into the dark night.

The man spoke hesitatingly. "It was the storm on Tuesday night."

Yseult didn't turn to face him. It allowed her some strange privacy to absorb the details.

"The strongest winds in a decade were recorded," he continued.

In the window she saw their reflections. The man who spoke was a few feet behind her. He was wearing a uniform and, even in the distorted reflection of the window, it was imposing, the right attire to bring sombre news.

"We can only assume the tree toppled during the storm ..." his voice trailed off.

Yseult remained still as she listened.

"When the tree fell it dragged the roots and earth with it."

Yseult moved her eyes from his reflection to her own. Apart from her white hair, she was indistinguishable. She could have been anybody standing in the drawing room, listening to a strange account from a man of the law who was growing uncomfortable with her silence.

Yseult remained perfectly still, allowing him to continue and getting some perverse pleasure from his awkwardness.

"The bones were beneath the tree."

She imagined the skeleton, the skull, empty eye sockets and teeth, the long bones of the legs and arms entwined with the dirtied clay from the earth.

"I'm sorry to be the bearer of bad news … we need to establish a few facts." As he spoke he was looking to his left at the portrait of Alfred Stratford-Rice. It was painted almost 300 years ago. "I don't believe it's a murder mystery from today or even the last ten years," he continued. "It all depends on the age of the tree."

"Where is it?" Yseult broke her silence. "The skeleton?"

"It's beneath the tree," he said as if she had not been listening.

Yseult's voice rose impatiently. "On whose land? My land or my neighbour's land?"

He tilted his head sideways. "I don't know," he said as if he was surprised by his lack of information. "I haven't seen the tree myself."

She saw him quickly glance around the drawing room again. To a visitor, her stately home appeared ostentatious and eloquent. One of the rare estates that remained, it carried tradition and history on its sturdy ancient shoulders.

She was not surprised this day had come. She couldn't help thinking how the grace and elegance had slipped through the crevices of her home long before the gust of wind blew a tree down to reveal a skeleton on a wild patch of her kingdom.

PART I

CHAPTER ONE

1891, Jamaica

Long ago I learned to stop questioning my beginnings ... until my youngest son was born. A slave who spends fourteen hours a day working on a sugar plantation has little time for anything apart from servitude. Now I am old, my daily chores are light. I have time to sit on the fringes of the old plantation and gaze at the sun as it sinks into the Caribbean Sea. I notice my friends, the years etched on their faces, and suddenly realise I too am as aged as they are, although few are as old as I am. I notice children, I see how they mimic the adults with their games. They play at cutting sugar cane and then standing straight, flexing their backs as if they too endured the pain of hard labour. I notice resemblances in my children, grandchildren and great-grandchildren. I have a number of children. Some I know and others I was only briefly acquainted with. Some live a short distance from me and others are lost in the barbaric haze of slavery. But one ten-year-old boy in particular has spiralled me into the brutal abyss of recollection. At the sight of his lighter skin and aquatic green eyes in this land of darkies, I am assaulted with memory.

I FATHERED MY YOUNGEST SON LEON SIXTY-NINE YEARS AFTER MY own birth, yet I feel he has journeyed with me for my whole life. He has been blessed with better luck than most of my other children. Born in a time when the black man here was liberated, his back is not crisscrossed with scars and his children will bear his name, not that of his owners. He is able to read and write. He is an eager student and hardworking with his chores. He reminds me of myself when I was his age before I was transported across the great seas to serve a master in the cane fields of the Caribbean.

THERE WAS A TIME WHEN I WAS A HAPPY BOY IMMERSED IN A culture so vastly different to the plantations of Jamaica. Recently I find myself sitting too long in the quagmire of recollection. Faces and smells return. My mother's features become as vivid as my own in a mirror. In my dreams I see her wide alert eyes and round face framed with dark hair. I see my father and recall the beat of the music he preferred. Last night, I dreamed I was sitting with him on the bank of the river fishing. I could see his long lean body stretched out on the grass waiting for the fish to tug the bait. I could feel the wet blades of grass beneath my feet as I returned through the field to our home. On awakening, I called my father's name and woke disappointed to find my wife standing over me with her hands on her hips.

In recent months my wife has noticed my strange mood.

"Wat de matter?" she asks in her usual abrupt manner. "Yuh goin' mad wid dat sadness."

How could I begin to tell her that I was lost in memories of my old home? What became of those I left behind? Did they seek me out? Did they mourn for me for the rest of their lives? We exiled servants learn to fight recall. It is as fierce as our deadly hurricanes, except it kills us more slowly. It drains us of our remaining sanity and eventually takes us into the sea. Yet I defiantly sit in the shade of the redundant cotton trees remembering the months of voyage across the seas.

We were two hundred Irish boys and girls, taken from our country to cut sugar cane in the sweltering heat of Jamaica, this exotic little island. My home? My mulatto son's home? During our six-week voyage we were fed on strange food. I thought the devil had stolen me. It was my captor's job to deliver me to Satan where I would burn in the fires of hell. Then, when my eyes first saw the beauty of the island, in my childish mind I thought the devil had changed his mind and sent me to God instead. An awed silence descended as we gaped at the exotic splendour before us. It was like a colourful mystical land that burst from the quivering liquidated earth, inviting and magical. If it had been described to me as a boy, they would have called it paradise. The beaches of golden sand in the middle of a clear blue sea, and trees bearing fruit with as many colours as the rainbow. I remember my surprise at how sweet and succulent the watery melons were. The warm sun and trees that stretched to the clouds on long stems astonished me. As I was escorted from the boat, I remember the surprisingly warm sea as it splashed against my legs. It was further validation that God would appear and welcome me through the gates of heaven for all eternity. It was not heaven – however, the fact I believed a small piece of luck was on my side, it stopped me from rushing into the ocean to allow the mystic exotic sea quench my terror and take my ghost back to Ireland.

It is not yet bright. I walk up the hill and follow a path to a secluded river. I swim in the water and afterwards follow the path, taking the long route home. These past few months I have returned to prayer. The prayers in the Irish language came tumbling back to me. *Paidir an Tiarna* – The Lord's Prayer – flowed as if I had been reciting it *as Gaeilge* my whole life. Quietly I recite a decade of the rosary, still surprised I can recall each line of the prayers in a language I have not spoken in seventy years. The first morning it happened to me, I thought my mind had receded to my childhood. It happened to a man I knew many years ago. Elijah began to play like a child and hoist the seats in his cabin onto the table as if he was loading a boat. He called to the children to raise the anchor. Then he stood gazing solemnly at the wall as if waiting for the boat trip to end. After a while he told the children to drop anchor and he removed the seats from the table. Initially we thought it was the after-effects of too much rum. Then we held him down and checked him for cuts or marks, thinking he might have hit his head. When we found nothing, we kept it quiet, fearing he would be sold to another master who would flog him to death.

I say The Lord's Prayer *as Gaeilge* for Elijah who abandoned manhood to return to the wild antics of his childhood. I say another prayer for the Irishmen I've witnessed arriving on the piers of Jamaica. Some arrived in shackles and others came with the promise of land and a country far removed from the oppression of England. I would watch them step off the great ships after weeks at sea. The men carried one suitcase and wore their temperance medals with pride. Quickly they discarded their Irish clothes and, within a short time, life in Jamaica took the shine from their temperance medals.

I return to my cabin and sit outside, waiting for my wife to bring my breakfast. Over the breadfruit trees, I see the roof of the Big House. Blair Stratford-Rice lives there with his third wife. His great house is perched high on the hill overlooking his crumbling plantation. Since the abolition of slavery in Jamaica over fifty years ago, the great plantations and fortunes of the plantocracy have almost gone. Blair Stratford-Rice is not deserving even of the dwindling lands or the slaves he now must pay. I am pleased to say he is afraid of me yet he cannot do anything to hurt me. There was a time when his father could have sold me or strung me up from the hanging tree that adorned every plantation in Jamaica. Now the hanging tree has been felled, the stump a reminder of the sea of change. He is afraid I will turn the remaining workers against him, afraid of the rumour that I killed one of his kind – and those who seek answers only find silence. His fear pleases me but I do not lose sight of the fact that I am now an old man, easily overpowered by a snarling foe who wants retribution. The bad blood that flows between us is almost visible to the naked eye. Our hostility did not begin on this pretty island of Jamaica but many years before in a townland called Mein on the coast of Ireland.

Yet for years when Blair Stratford-Rice and I met we slotted into a charade of master and servant, each disguising his fear and loathing of the other man.

Only yesterday I and my wife chanced to meet him by the empty slave cabins in the bleakest part of his estate. The rotting wood and overgrowth is a reminder of what they had and what they lost. The monsoon rain tumbled down, adding to the desolation of the area.

He was riding his black mare and he demanded to know how I chanced to buy the land on which the old cabins stood.

"I thought James Inglott was the buyer – I only learned this morning it is you who bought it," he said, clearly annoyed I had got a third party to buy the four acres.

I waved my hand at the rotting wood. "Master, it was my good fortune to serve you, and your father the Colonel, and your grand-uncle Major Beaufort. I learned to farm this wonderful land from your good kin."

Although his mare moved restlessly he continued to look at me, aware of my hidden irony and contempt.

He visibly gathered himself together. "I'm glad you know it, O'Neill," he said with a forced voice.

"I'll be up to you for my gold at the end of the month," I added, just to irritate him, referring to a payment of seven gold coins due to me after my seven decades of service.

The bit in the horse's mouth was poorly lodged. She moved her head irritably. He couldn't even saddle his mare properly. He had trouble steadying her.

"Of course, the end of the month," he said loudly before riding away.

"One dese days him gonna kill yuh," my wife whispered as we watched him gallop off.

Nobody alive knows the truth. It goes back to the days in Ireland when his father was a Colonel in the English army.

I will never forget the day I first saw Colonel Stratford-Rice and his wife land on Jamaica's shores, armed with trunks of belongings and imperial ideas. I placed his luggage on the carriage and scrutinised his features to see if my eyes deceived me. When I heard him speak and saw his wife's small body next to his, it was confirmation he was the man who signed my father's death warrant in Ireland. For many years I was invisible to them. By the time the old Colonel Stratford-Rice recognised me it was too late.

On the table beside me are my paper and inkwell. Five years ago, I began to learn to read and write. Each evening when my son Leon and grandson Akeem returned from their hours of schooling they would write their new words in the clay. The other children would copy their squiggles. Like two little tutors, they would create words from the letters and explain their new lesson for the day. Gradually the neighbouring children grew bored with the game. However, I could not stop. I copied the curvy squiggles, marvelling how when put together they made words. I learned the alphabet, the small words and gradually the bigger words. During quiet times of the day I practised with charcoal on the bark of a tree. I spent a few hours a day reading and writing words, testing and retesting my knowledge.

As time passed, not only did I learn to read new words but I began to read stories. I learned that each sentence has a reason, the paragraph has a wider explanation and each chapter a purpose until eventually each book has a meaning.

"A beginning, a middle and an ending. Like life," I said, thinking aloud. "Maybe that is why we continue to live. We want to see how our life ends."

I bought my first book *The Moorland Cottage*, in Black River. I tried to read the words. For weeks Akeem and Leon and I followed the words with our fingers. It took us so long to read the book we had forgotten what the story was about when we came to the last page. There were plenty of words in *The Moorland Cottage* that we didn't know. We asked the teacher in the school, but neither did he know all the words.

Each month I go to Black River where I sell a book and buy another one. The only book I do not sell is *The Mooreland Cottage*. Now in a time of my life when there is little to do but grieve for my missing grandson, Akeem, I read. I escape to the foreign countries in the books and leave my porch to mingle with the characters for several hours each day.

My wife brings me my breakfast. She places her hand on my shoulder as she passes and sits beside me.

"Me man is good?" she cautiously asks.

"Not too bad."

The dead I see in my dreams do not trouble me so much. I have not dreamed of my family in Jamaica. It is Ireland I dream of – green, damp, sad and ever-present.

As usual she frowns with disapproval when she sees the book, paper and quill on the table. My wife thinks reading and writing is bad for my health.

"Is no surprise yuh shoutin' to yuh mama and papa wen yuh are fillin' yuh old head wid words," she chides. "It can't fit." She points at her head irritably.

"Of course it can fit," I reply, as I always do when she tackles me on this subject. "Some men know every word ever spoken in the world and they are not dead from packed heads."

"Me poor man!" She laughs as if I am an idiot. "Anyway, who gonna read yuh words? Nobody knows how."

"Enough," I say.

I know she is thinking only of my good. A stoic, hardworking, simple woman. She does not share that awful sadness that afflicts me and so many of my sons. Sometimes I think the sadness is more prevalent in the Irish. I don't discuss these thoughts with my wife.

She does not see the world as I see it.

"Maybe it is Akeem?" She looks at me cautiously.

Akeem, my grandson, the child I could not save. I am unable to say his name aloud.

"Maybe him is safe." Her voice grows quieter. "Or Okeke? Maybe him is sorry?" Clearly she does not want to mention this but feels compelled for my betterment.

I close my eyes against the memory of that most unspeakable act of treachery.

There is only the sound of the birds breaking our silence. I wait for them to quieten and flee as they sense my seething rage that I failed Akeem and am grandfather also to a monster like Okeke.

Ngozi inclines away from me, afraid of my response. She suddenly appears vulnerable.

I take my breakfast bowl in my hand and eat slowly. She gets up from the table and leaves me alone to eat.

Although Ngozi is thirty years my junior, somewhere in her early fifties, she remains a striking figure of beauty. She has light-brown skin and a gloriously curvy body. She has a large handsome face dotted with small black spidery freckles. Ngozi's father was Irish. She says she got her freckles and her singing voice from the Kirwans of Galway. She loves to sing. When she walks she sways as if moving to music. She is soft, soothing and generous. Equally she can be abrupt and angry. Many years ago I taught her grandmother how to speak English when she came from Africa in her slave ship. Ngozi is not legally my wife but the woman who came to my cabin over a decade ago and never left. She gave me one son, my youngest child. He came into my life at a time when my responsibilities were almost gone. The anger and Irish temper had abated over the decades. He got me at my best.

"Bring the coffee," I tell Ngozi. I want her to sit with me and hear her noisily sip coffee and sigh with satisfaction when she finishes the first cup. She has an air of contentment in the morning when she gently sways on the rocking chair, her sandals scratching the wood as she rocks hypnotically. There is something comforting about the early-morning sounds and sight of my Ngozi as she sways and hums. In silence we drink.

My son is slow in the morning. He joins me on the veranda. He will go to school for two hours and work with my mulatto son on the acres I own in the hills. Lazily he leans in close to me, and I sink into his large green eyes and forget the ailments of old age.

He eats his breakfast at a leisurely pace. He places his hand beside mine and spreads his fingers on the table. He is comparing the size of our hands. My son is ten years of age and cannot wait to grow to a man's full height. He is impressed with size: big hands, strong men, big ships, wild storms.

"Will we go to de Blue Lagoon today?" he says, referring to our favourite fishing post.

After living for eighty years, I thought I had felt every sensation known to man. Then my little Leon arrived and he gave me something so unexpected I thought I was growing younger. Like Oisín in the ancient Irish tale who finds his way to Tír na nÓg, the Land of Youth, my son has been my guide to bring me to my own Tír na nÓg.

"Yes, we will," I reply.

He rests his hand on mine, his clean pale fingers a contrast to my withered scarred hands. It is a reminder of our age difference. He taps my arm in a friendly manner as he gets up to leave us for the day. "I will find de best oyster wid de most pearls," he tries to tease me.

"Your oyster will not have as many pearls as mine," I say.

"No, Papa," he wiggles his finger mischievously, "me oyster will have a hundred round white pearls."

Ngozi and I smile.

I have been given one last chance to redeem myself. I am thankful his mother is comfortable enough to challenge me. I come from a time when this little island annihilated the meagre men, persecuted the brave and defiled the pretty. Propelled by fear for my children I tried to teach them. Once, I opened the back of one of my sons with a whip. He robbed from our community to buy rum. I have many regrets.

Ngozi bends over me to refill my coffee. Her breast rubs off my shoulder. It distracts from harsh regrets and bitter remembrances.

"Thank you," I say. "You're a good woman."

She looks at me pensively, her head tilted to one side. Seldom do I give her a compliment.

"Big month for yuh, Art – yuh gonna be rich," she says, looking down at me.

"I was always rich with a woman like you," I reply.

She laughs and returns to her chair to rock and scratch the wood with her sandals.

I close my eyes, fighting the sense of foreboding. At the end of this month, in twenty days' time, I will collect seven gold coins from Blair Stratford-Rice. A gold coin to represent each decade I have been of service to the Stratford-Rices. It was promised to me by Blair's mother for my loyalty when most ex-slaves were lynching their masters. At last I am a free man and will have the money to enact a promise I made to myself five years ago.

"Wat yuh gonna do wid de money?"

"I will give you money to buy whatever you want," I say.

"Yuh joke, old man, I don't need nothin'," she says, yet I can see she is flattered.

With the remaining coins I will find and buy my grandson Akeem who was sold to Morocco as a slave by my grandson Okeke. If my health continues, I will find Okeke and, if forgiveness does not find me first, I will kill him. I will buy more land and make my sons proud masters of their lives. Each year we will cherish the distance between slavery and freedom until memory is no more. The gold coins will replenish my dignity and hopefully take me from this crippling melancholy. Those coins will give me hope, like the promise of land gave me hope when I was a gangly eleven-year-old boy arriving on these shores. That is, if Blair Stratford-Rice will give me my due.

I will also take the time to leave my sons something more than land. In order to help them understand, I must take them back. I will leave an account of the events that shaped my life and, in turn, shaped their lives. Someday when they are old men, possibly gripped by melancholy or cornered by life, they will understand humanity and accept my achievements and understand my wrong-doings. I will begin at the start and take them back to the rolling hills and green valleys of Ireland with my quill and my paper.

CHAPTER TWO

I was born in a parish called Mein. In Irish, *Min*. It means a smooth grassy patch on the slope of a hill. My cottage was high in the mountains overlooking the wild Atlantic Ocean. As far as the eye could see were rolling hills of various shapes. The mountains ran west to east and formed rugged peninsulas that had dangerous mountain passes to reach the shore. Only we natives of that corner of Ireland knew the terrain of those deceiving highlands. With each shift in the sun the view changed – colours shifted from greens to orange to brown to pink from the heather, and sometimes the shape of the mountains changed as well. They appeared to roll like enormous incoming waves.

The only piece of nature that did not change was the oak tree at the bottom of the mountain. Sprouting from the fertile clay was the largest oak tree I'd ever seen. They said it was there since Jesus was a child. There were hundreds of sturdy branches inclining towards the sky. From each branch were smaller branches, and smaller branches again until finally there were hundreds of twigs. In the wind they'd quiver like withered fingers pleading to the heavens for respite. Each time I passed the tree I tried to avert my gaze. It was the hanging tree where my grandfather and two uncles met their deaths. It remained a great looming symbol of oppression, a constant reminder of the Crown's presence in every parish and townland in Ireland. For some of us in the parish of Mein, it was preordained that we'd join the ranks of those who went before us.

We too would add to the wearing of the bark of the great oak and die dangling on the branches of the hanging tree.

AN INCIDENT IN 1821 PREVENTED ME FROM GROWING TO MANHOOD in my own country and also spared me the hanging tree. A man was murdered. The echo from the sound of the gun rippled through the valley, reaching our cottage. The murdered man was Major Frederick Stratford-Rice, an English landowner with over 2,000 acres. Over the following days my father and every peasant man in the area fled to the hills, accused of being members of the clandestine organisation, the United Irishmen, which in fact was all but defunct since the failure of the 1798 rebellion and Robert Emmet's rebellion in 1803. The men knew there would be deadly repercussions. Within a week they were hunted down, arrested and tried in a court where the deceased man's son, Colonel Edward Stratford-Rice, acted as magistrate. Intent on avenging his father's death and fearing he too would find his head at the end of a loaded barrel, he cleared out our little community of able-bodied men. Some were deported to the other side of the world and the remainder were sent to the hanging tree at the foot of Mein Hill.

Colonel Stratford-Rice did not have a voice that suited his body. For one full day I stood at the side entrance to the courthouse, unable to get through the packed crowd to see the proceedings. In a loud clear English accent, he delivered sentences ranging from hangings to deportations "beyond the sea, either within His Majesty's dominions or elsewhere outside His Majesty's dominions". In my child's mind, I tried to imagine the land at the end of the sea journey outside His Majesty's dominions. Some said there was such heat you could fry an egg in the sun, others disagreed and said it snowed all year round and would freeze a man to death if he stood still. In the packed porch of the courthouse, I felt my small body go hot and cold with each image of sun and snow.

During the court proceedings, the adults came to believe that the healthy men with lesser charges were sent "beyond the seas" and the weaker men were hanged. As the day dragged on I found some of the proceedings boring. I pictured Colonel Stratford-Rice as a large man with a stern face sitting upright in a comfortable chair at the top of the courthouse. To pass time I studied the tweed pattern on the back of the Widow McAuliffe's shawl and counted lice crawling on my neighbour's neck. There were only so many death sentences and deportations an eleven-year-old boy could listen to.

The Widow McAuliffe was the only woman who did not murmur desolate objections when her son was sentenced to deportation. Her piercing shrill silenced the courthouse, her words incomprehensible her rage was so intense. She fled from the court, swearing she'd curse the Colonel and all belonging to him. At the end of the day, my father's name was finally called.

"Killian O'Neill."

The tears sprang to my eyes, betraying the man I wanted to be. The sea of people before me parted, allowing me into the courthouse to see my father. The charge was read: "Killian O'Neill of Mein. Charged with membership of United Irishmen."

My father was standing up, his wrists in chains. He looked the same as he did five days ago before his arrest. I had taken food to his hiding place in the heather and sat with him and his friends while they ate.

I sought out the man to match the voice.

Colonel Stratford-Rice was too small and insignificant for his voice. He was positioned on an elevated stand at the top of the courthouse flanked by officers in the red coats of the soldiers' uniforms. Despite what their uniforms represented, they made a handsome sight compared to my father and his friends. Their clothes were coarse with mud and their unshaven faces looked animalistic.

My father was escorted to the front of the court. He walked with a limp, an injury he sustained as a boy when his leg was broken in a man-trap on Lugdale Estate. I pictured his wilted red leg beneath his trousers. The tooth-marks of the trap had left a circle of large dotted even scars above his knee. His limp gave him a peculiar lopsided shape. When he stood still he looked taller, his good leg carrying the weight of his body. Colonel Stratford-Rice studied my father's lame gait and sized him up as he came to his full height when he stood still.

"Three swings on the gallows," the Colonel said calmly.

It was the sound of my father's shoes with the irregular clop that I later recalled most. He was pulled by the guard and stumbled slightly before being led away with a look of bewilderment on his face. There was a surge of talk by the door where we, my father's family and friends, were positioned. I stood staring at Colonel Stratford-Rice, feeling as if everything I had in life had been suddenly snatched from me. My hopes and little happiness scurried after my father to perish with him on the hanging tree.

Colonel Stratford-Rice sounded the hammer on the bench. "Next!"

I noted the Colonel's every feature: the pointed nose, the receding chin, and long arched eyebrows.

For years and years when my mind returned to the weeks following my father's death, I clawed at anything to avoid dwelling on that time. As a young man in Jamaica I spent a decade of my life bathing in the cauldrons of rum to flee from the memory. When I recalled my mother and brother, Hugh being forcibly removed from our cottage, I turned my thoughts to Colonel Stratford-Rice's expression. I imagined the merciless death I would like to give him. It was easier to focus on hate than to dwell on the boy whose mother was forcibly taken with my younger brothers when I was stalking the Colonel. When the soldiers returned to our cottage again, I fled from them and escaped to the mountains, using the same hiding place as my father and the rebels had used. None could tell me where my mother had been taken.

On the day of my father's execution I called to the Widow McAuliffe. Some said she was a witch who had the power to inflict eternal unhappiness on any man she wished.

I asked her where my mother had been taken. "You won't see her again," she said dismissively.

I stood watching the Widow as her hands worked busily, knotting the innards of animals together. She'd sworn she'd curse the Colonel and his offspring.

"What curse are you making?" I asked.

"The worst kind," she said as her strong capable hands knotted the entrails of animals around the heart of a goat. "Each of the Colonel's heirs will die by the hand of his own offspring."

I left her alone with her rage and magic and her bleeding intestines of animals.

THE NEXT DAY I SAW THE COLONEL LEAVING HIS ESTATE IN HIS carriage with his lady friend, Victoria Hemsworth. I followed them to town and walked behind them, feeling the sharp edge of my father's knife in the palm of my hand. The Colonel and his female companion were dressed in their finery. He was so frumpy and old, she was so young and pretty.

I saw her balk with wild terror when the Widow McAuliffe accosted them.

She rushed toward them and blocked their path.

"*May you and each of your heirs die by the hand of their own offspring!*" she cried out. She took from her shawl the innards of the animal and threw them at the Colonel.

In the melee that followed, I noticed the Colonel's companion stagger backward with disbelief at the sight of the bloodied heart at her feet.

THAT SAME DAY I WAS CAPTURED. WHEN THE AUTHORITIES imprisoned me, at night I hummed aloud to drown out all that had happened. I was sent to Kinsale, the last landfall on the Atlantic crossing to the Caribbean. There, children from every orphanage, workhouse and institution were loaded onto a ship and sent to the other side of the world.

CHAPTER THREE

The first time that I saw flying fish I remember being awestruck with terror and excitement all at once. I remained to the spot, gaping at them. A few of the children scampered below deck at the outlandish sight of fish with fluttering wings springing from the sea and soaring over our heads. Fairies, leprechauns, angels, and the devil himself, I had heard of all of them but had never heard of flying fish.

When a few landed on deck, I rushed to see if they were really fish with wings or a bird that resembled a fish.

"'Tis evil spirits," my new friend Ned Doyle from Kildare said.

We gathered round the fish as it flapped at our feet. Those of us brave enough poked it and kicked it towards the fearful. Infected by our childish wonderment, our captors laughed.

From then on, each day we looked towards the water, hoping the flying fish would burst from the sea and mesmerise us once more.

Some of the children had never seen the sea before.

They spent their first few outings on deck, mutely gaping at the water. Unable to bear the uncertainty, three children jumped overboard. Only one resurfaced from below the water. We watched from the deck to see how far he'd swim, willing him to fly like the fish and tell our families what we'd seen. The ship sailed away from his bobbing black head, feeding some with a little hope that he'd carry a message to those we left behind.

Some of the children refused to leave the cabin. A few died where they lay. Their bodies thrown into the sea for the flying fish and the predators they flew from. Other were afraid that, if they moved, their small bodies would topple the boat.

"How does it stay up?" Liam Clifford asked. "It's so heavy."

Liam was from my parish of Mein, and our fathers and grandfathers had been friends. When we met on the ship we slotted in together, finding comfort in the familiar. We slept beside each other and used to whisper through the darkness at night as we listened to the swishing sound of the water as it rolled off the rudder.

"It's built to stay up," I said, not knowing the mechanics of shipbuilding. I had been to Fenit Pier only once where I saw great ships with flapping sails.

"It's made of planks of wood," Liam said, touching the panel above his head. Lightly he tapped it. "Planks can float but not a huge load of planks tied together."

"It's special wood," I said.

"Wood from the fairy forts?"

"No, just wood for making big ships that can carry loads of people and can sail for weeks and weeks and even months without sinking."

He nodded, accepting my simple uninformed explanation.

LIAM LEFT THE STENCH OF THE HOLD AND CAME OUT OF THE DARK and joined me. He stood on the deck, looking at the sails and surveying the ocean.

"They say we're going to a roasting hot country," he said.

"I think so."

I had overheard some of our captors discuss us children like my father and I would discuss the weakest pup of the litter that would die within a few days.

"That redhead don't stand a chance in 'ell of survivin'," they said when they spotted Liam. "He shouldn't have been brought."

Our captors spoke with strange accents, cutting the words in half, and sprinkled their conversation with curses.

"The captain will still get his money's worth, bleedin' 'ungry devil. Even if the red-tops only last a few weeks."

The men agreed.

They smoked their pipes and considered it.

"They're better at this age. At least they can get used to the 'eat the way the older ones can't."

"In no time most of 'em will look like Africans when the sun browns 'em."

"The sun and the rum murder the Irish."

"Aye."

They nodded in unison.

I didn't know what rum was but took some consolation from the fact that there were Irish inhabiting the land where we were destined to live.

As time passed we slotted into our routine. We looked forward to the peculiar food. It was rice, Pablo told us. He had long grey hair tied in a woman's plait and yellow skin. He was unlike anything I'd ever seen. He told us rice grows in hot countries like potatoes grow in Ireland. Pablo was the kindest – he gave us extra portions of food and water despite the captain bellowing at him to take it easy.

The crying tapered off except for a few who were utterly lost to their past. The crew ignored the crying children.

"In time they'll see their bawlin' won't make an 'ought bit o' difference."

While some could not stop crying, there was one boy who could not stop singing. They called him Cal. He was a fat boy from Meath with a high-pitched beautiful voice. At night he sang terribly lonesome songs. One of our captors, Augusta, hated to hear Cal singing. He'd come below deck with his ears covered as if he was in pain, then he'd shout at Cal to stop singing.

"If you don't stop that racket I'll bloody kill you!" Augusta sounded as if he was about to cry.

Cal would stop for a while, then resume singing more quietly. Gradually his voice would reach a crescendo and Augusta would return and hit him. Cal was the strangest boy of all. He never cried. Even when he was hit hard on the mouth and his tooth was broken, he didn't look angry or sad.

"That boy gives me the heebie-jeebies," Augusta complained to his companions.

The other men told him they liked his singing – one called it pretty.

One night Augusta dragged Cal away while he was singing and he never reappeared.

AT NIGHT I'D SLEEP BESIDE LIAM, WHISPERING ABOUT OUR HOME and our possible future which seemed infinite on those nights. In our grief for our parents and the country we'd left, we offered strength and alleviated each other's worries. Liam was all I had from my home on the side of a marshy mountain.

"What do you think our new country will be like?" he asked.

There were nights when we fed each other's dreams that we were being whisked to another country where we'd be kings with all the land we could want and all the food we could eat.

Several times I tried to imagine it. The kind man with the long grey hair, Pablo, told us it would be hot and we'd be sold and work in the fields. One of the boys asked if we were slaves. We were told we would not be slaves all of our lives. If we were lucky we'd own a bit of land eventually.

"At least it'll be warm," Liam said. "The English won't be so close either."

I agreed with him.

"Just nice men like Pablo with long hair like a girl's. Maybe my hair will grow as long as his. And I can brush it and tie it up."

As the weeks passed Liam's pale face and hands became dotted with freckles. In the glaring sun we counted our freckles each day. The first day I counted twelve, the next fifteen. Each day I added another five to my count. We'd stand together and soak up the salted ocean breeze and cling to a little hope that we'd grow to be men in our new country and have land we'd call our own and children who would eventually be kings of all they owned.

CHAPTER FOUR

The day we first saw land the crew applauded. Through the haze of heat I could see the distant outline. Quickly, I looked over my shoulder into the vast sea, imagining the distance to Ireland. Before ever docking at Black River Pier, a vague plan began to form in my boyish mind, a dream I returned to in the following years during every moment my mind was not occupied with work. I imagined the returning. I was happy to endure a storm every night of my voyage and any amount of hardship – only to return to Ireland. Like so many, I would remain torn between two countries for many decades.

When we landed at the pier we were like stunned animals in the dazzling sun as men of every colour talked in strange accents. One by one we were taken out and examined in a hurried manner. We were asked our name and the county we hailed from by a red-coat soldier who made a note of it. So accustomed to hearing my elders lying to the Crown's military, I gave Ned Doyle's address – Prosperous, County Kildare – and warned Liam to do the same. It was a place that sounded hopeful.

We were ushered into a hall. One by one we were taken to a desk where a man examined us. We were ordered to strip and hop on one leg. He made a note and told us to point to our eyes, then hop on the other leg and point to our ears. By the time my turn came, the humiliation was overcome by our competitiveness to see who could hop the fastest and highest.

Ned Doyle from Prosperous, Kildare, Liam Clifford and I were escorted onto a cart where an enormous black man and a black boy were waiting. Sitting up top, driving the cart, was a white man who identified himself as Sexton. He was a young man with a strange drawl.

"You'll be working on Major Beaufort's plantation – Mangrove Plantation at Black River," he told us.

It was irrelevant as we'd never heard of Major Beaufort nor knew what a plantation was.

I don't remember much of the cart ride except for a fleet of hundreds of crabs which crossed our path and the enormous black man who sat beside me. For all his monstrous size and ferocious appearance, he was the one who seemed more frightened of our gaping eyes. He looked shyly away from us at the rising dust left in our wake. His cotton trousers only came to his knees. I guessed there were no pants in Jamaica to fit his great legs. I looked at his hands resting on his knees – the skin appeared inhuman, like a leather glove. My finger hovered near his hand – I'd like to have touched it, to feel it. I looked at the crease over his knuckles and saw where the skin was hardened. Tempted as I was to feel the texture of his skin, I didn't dare touch him.

The black boy was not as frightened by our wide eyes. Instead he seemed curious. He looked from one of us to the other and then smiled and nodded when we made eye contact.

"Weh yuh from?" he asked.

Terrified, none of us spoke.

"Yuh English? Weh yuh from?"

When he repeated the question I realised he was asking where we were from.

He tried again. "France?"

He looked disappointed that none of us answered.

"Ireland," I said.

He smiled and nudged the black giant who suddenly spoke.

"Ireland?" He seemed surprised.

Liam, who was sitting across from me, began to whimper.

"Me wife, she be Irish." He spoke in a voice so deep it sounded as if it came from the bowels of the earth.

Liam began to bawl.

Although comforted that we would live among our own, we were perplexed at the giant who claimed an Irish wife.

Everything was inconceivable, even the fleet of crabs that crunched as the wheels of our carriage rolled over their shells. We rode along the coast, itchy and hot in our clothes.

FOR MONTHS I WATCHED MY NEW COMMUNITY, STRUCK WITH wonderment and terror. I lived by the Black River in south-west Jamaica. There were approximately one hundred and fifty slaves living in cabins huddled together towards the bottom of a hill and hidden from view with large trees. Ned Doyle was sent to a separate cabin which he shared with three slaves while Liam and I lived in another cabin with two slaves. One was the nice boy who accompanied us on the ride from the boat – he was called Tariq and he was a couple of years older than us though he wasn't quite sure of his age. The other boy, called Burdan, was much older than us. He had lighter-coloured skin than Tariq and was hostile towards Liam and me.

"White boys – wat dey doin' sendin' us white boys?" he said, angrier with our colour than with our presence.

Tariq treated us like new toys and was eager to please.

"Yuh new home!" he announced, showing us our cabin which consisted of one room with a cooking area in the corner. He told us that at night we would sleep on the floor. "Come!"

He took us out the back of the cabin.

"Dis a weh we grow de food. Sell it at de markit and have money for ourselves. Yuh too!" He pointed enthusiastically at Liam and me.

There was an array of sprouting bulbs and vegetables. Reds, yellows, and greens, purple and white, golds and pinks.

It was an enormous garden. I'd no idea of the value of the produce and quietly wondered how much we'd make.

I asked where were the potatoes.

"Potato?" Tariq looked at the ground as if a potato might appear.

"Spuds," Liam said, thinking he'd understand that, and then mimicked eating.

Tariq just shook his head. He indicated a giant green circular ball. "Look at dis!" he said, picking it up with his hands. Burdan watched us from the side of the cabin without speaking.

At the very bottom of the hill was the warm sea and at the top of the hill was the Big House. When I stood on the roof of my cabin I could see the roof of the Big House over the trees. I had no idea who lived there – the slaves only referred to him as Masta. Masta, according to Tariq, owned the plantation and was so old, "Him gettin' ready for de nex' life."

During daylight hours I worked in the fields. I remember the first time I saw the black men and women cutting the huge sugarcane plant. Their machetes rose and fell in unison, the women every bit as able as the men. I noticed their infinite strength as they hacked through the cane from sunrise to sunset with the glint of the sun on their black bodies giving them a mystical quality.

Our job was not cutting cane – we were part of the "weeding gang" with Tariq. I rooted my small fingers into the earth and ripped every weed with a fury to stave off the crippling homesickness that would arrest me several times a day. My fingers were coarse from pulling weeds and eyes swollen from the rising dust were rinsed by my tears a few times a day. I cannot say how many times I cried – suffice it to say, if sugar cane sprouted from my falling tears the planter could have fed every slave from the patch of earth where I worked.

After our days' weeding Tariq showed us the magnificent delights of Jamaica. He showed us how to catch birds and snakes and how to hold them. We trapped and ate crocodiles from the river. He showed us the delights the sea contained and took us to the best fishing posts that offered the most plentiful and succulent fish. At another location we swam among schools of fish with luminous colours. There were fish the colour of our bumblebee, fish with teeth, fish with spiralling fans of tentacles. There were fish that appeared to be rocks – a blinking eye startled me as much as my presence startled them – and the docile sea cows grazing beneath the water with their large bulbous noses appeared as misplaced as the blinking rocks. Tariq warned us against the dangerous fish – the lionfish and sea snakes. Then he showed me gems that continued to mesmerise me into old age: the oysters that contained pearls. Their large hard rugged shells and hidden stones thrilled me. Their varying shapes and many colours fascinated me.

Not only did the treasure beneath the sea enthral me, but there was solace beneath the water with the sound and smell of nothing – only the sensation of our limbs swimming deeper with a dream-like effect. While beneath the water the last few months were removed, I was temporarily indifferent to this strange country and people, my grief was washed away and the sadness that encased me was no more. For those few moments beneath the water with the docile sea-cows and the sound of water in our ears, there was nothing, a glorious sense of nothingness until my breath reneged. Finally I'd rush to the surface and breathlessly spring from the stillness.

I earned my first money from the pearls I plucked from the sea-bed and rivers. Tariq, Ned and I attended the market with the other slaves in Black River town. We showed the buyer our entire collection. He only plucked the few round shiny pearls and discarded the rest. Then he tossed us a few coins. Tariq and Ned were pleased with the exchange. I was not. The pearls were worth more to me than the few coins he threw us. We didn't spend our money – instead we mingled freely with the slaves from Black River, feeling like men with the weight of our money in our hands.

As the weeks passed Liam grew listless and despondent. For a period he worked in the weeding gang but got so burned in the sun they moved him to the big house as a domestic servant to serve drinks and dinner. Even indoors the mosquitoes found his flesh. He was bitten so badly his face swelled up. Despite Tariq burning dried orange peel to keep the mosquitoes away, they continued to feast on Liam. His appearance became so unsightly they moved him to the kitchen. Regardless of where they placed him he was not able for the heat or conditions. At night he returned to the cabin and lay in the dark while Ned, Tariq and I escaped to the outdoors.

Despite so many Seáns, Patricks, and Michaels claiming to be Irish, there were very few born on the island of Ireland. Those who called themselves Irish had parents who hailed from every county of my old country, their heritage evident in their peculiar brogue. Some spoke with an Irish lilt as strong as our own. Us three Irish boys were further stunned into silence when they sang Irish songs. They made flutes from bamboo stems which accompanied the singers. They were familiar with our legends from folklore. They talked about Cú Chulainn's strength and skill, Fionn mac Cumhaill and his band of soldiers, and some of my new black friends sang "The Battle of Benburb".

Ned and I looked at the brown man singing our songs, taking great pride in the fact that our little country's plight had reached the slave villages of Jamaica. Only then did we feel at home, listening to our songs as the fireflies glowed brilliantly and seemed to cover the walls of the cabin with gold spangles.

ONE NIGHT, ONE OF THE FIELD SLAVES WAS DRAGGED FROM HIS CABIN by two white men. The fear on the adults' faces was as frightening as the arrested man's pleas for mercy. Later I heard that he had stolen a machete. He and two other men were planning to kill the overseer. The slave was hanged, his head removed and placed on a spike in the home pasture as a lesson to the rest of us. I staggered with disbelief when I saw it. The other slaves paused to look, then shook their heads and continued. The slave's decaying head remained there for several weeks as a warning to the rest of us. The other two men were tied to a tree and given two hundred lashes.

We were made stand and watch. As the whip cracked their skin I looked away. Burdan stood beside me, his face puckered with hate.

LIAM SPENT A FEW DAYS IN THE CABIN, CLAIMING HE WAS UNABLE TO get up. I came home to find Burdan trying to get him to drink tea.

"Is dogwood tea, come on, Liam," Burdan said, holding a spoon to Liam's mouth. "Yuh will feel betta, man."

It was one of the rare times I saw Burdan being kind.

Liam tried to remove the blanket that Burdan had wrapped around him. "I want to go home," he said.

A few of the slaves visited him. "Get betta, Rat Face," one said.

When the slaves are sick, their friends give them ugly new names which they think may deter their god from taking them. Liam knew what they were doing.

His watery blue eyes looked pleadingly into mine. "Call me a pretty name, Art – I want God to take me."

I was startled at his words.

The following morning when we woke Liam was dead. His face was illuminated by the shaft of light from the half-opened door. His last sight was the violent red-and-purple sky.

Phoebe, the girl who looked after the children during the day, washed the clothes that Liam wore on his boat trip from Ireland and then dressed him in his warm Irish trousers and jersey. Like so many of us, Liam had kept the warm clothes, believing he would need them for the return journey.

The slaves buried the dead with objects or clothing which would identify the dead person to their relatives in the afterlife.

They told Doyle and me that we must be happy because Liam was being buried with all of his limbs attached. Without all of his body parts they believed his spirit would never return to his home after death.

"Him be floatin' around here for eva more," Tariq said, adding an air of theatrics to the funeral, "like all de Duppy who not happy and playin' tricks on us."

A Duppy was an evil spirit or ghost.

Before burying him Phoebe packed food into the coffin. Then she stood back to admire the corpse. "Now him will have enough food for de journey and him people will know him."

Secretly I tucked a shiny white pearl into his coffin. Just in case Phoebe was right, Liam would have a gift from Jamaica for his people on the other side.

EACH DAY WHEN MY MIND WAS NOT OCCUPIED, I IMAGINED MY return to Ireland and telling my friends about my travels and that the English were as brutal in this foreign land. I'd tell them about Tariq and me trapping a snake and eating it, the crocodiles and the depth of the clear ocean where I'd swum and the great treasures it contained. I'd tell them about the heavy rain – nothing like our own mist but a torrential downpour – and how the sun and heat soaked up the rain so quickly. I'd tell them at home that it wasn't wet and damp but refreshing. There was no priest bellowing from the pulpit in my new country, only men and women of all shades of brown who believed in their own ghosts and spirits. They called them Duppy or Abarra, evil spirits who lured people to their death. At night they'd tell stories about the Duppy who revisited some of their tribe and drove them mad. One man was so terrified he ate salt and wore his clothes inside out to chase away the Duppy he feared was coming for him. I told Tariq about our fairies – good fairies and evil fairies who were capable of awful doings. We had the unlucky single magpie, they had the carrion crow. If a crow was injured in the eye you'd never be at peace until the crow was well or dead. As they told me, I looked at the carrion crow perched on the tree. Slowly it edged its way towards the slave's decaying head on the spike. I thought about the many crows my father and I had killed for pecking at the potatoes. As we discussed the carrion crow, I said a prayer to God that all of the carrion crows whom I had injured were now well or dead. I wanted to return to Ireland, and so left nothing to chance, even if it meant a prayer to God to save a crow maimed by my hand.

CHAPTER FIVE

The slaves and employees on the plantation were divided into classes. The field slaves, the domestic slaves, the skilled slaves like Burdan who was a boiler in the sugar mill, and then the managerial employees like McCovey, Sexton and Acklen, the overseers – they were an altogether different class. They were white and privileged, at the top of the ladder, and lived in cabins removed from our quarters. We, the field slaves, were the lowest class. The domestic slaves felt they were superior to us field slaves. They were better dressed and better fed. Occasionally they were lighter-skinned mulattos. The skilled slaves like Burdan were very well valued and fed even better than domestic slaves.

It was easy to distinguish each class of slave except for Cian Donnell.

"Irish like yuh," Tariq informed me and Ned.

Cian Donnell was a coloured old man with the small pointed features of a white man and the lighter brown colour of a mulatto.

He dressed in the good clothes of a gentleman and walked with the aid of cane.

"Him de oldest man in Jamaica," Tariq said in the hushed voice he used when he felt he was telling me something of great importance. Correcting himself, he added dramatically, his eyes widening, "Oldest man in de world!"

I waited for Burdan's reaction. He was cooking his food and looked over his shoulder with an intolerant expression.

"Yuh know how old him?" Tariq asked us.

I shook my head.

Burdan paused from cooking to hear what Tariq was about to say. Tariq was always eager to impress Ned and me with his knowledge of the local area and often got carried away with his stories. Ned and I thought his tall tales were hilarious while Burdan couldn't tolerate them.

"Dat man one hundred and thirty-one years old." Tariq's face froze as if Mr. Donnell's age was a shock to himself. "Him have anotha secret to him big age." Tariq looked from me to Ned before continuing. He loved an audience and he himself believed everything he said. "De gods bless him wid age cuz him born Christmas Day – de same day as Jesus Christ. De gods give to him special powas to live foreva."

Burdan shook his head in exasperation and resumed cooking.

"Cian Donnell is a free slave. Him have de best job a black man can have. He sits wid us." Tariq pointed to the lone bench by the door. "Him be here wid us," he whispered as if he was referring to Jesus Christ. Knowing I was a captive audience, he continued, inflated by his sense of importance. "He eat wid us. Him a man of de people. Eat from our hands."

"Him did neva eat from yuh hands," Burdan interjected as if he'd had enough of Tariq's nonsense. "We have bowls for food."

"Yeah, him did," Tariq said in anger before reverting to his simple voice. "Him sit in dat very seat and speak to me."

"If dat happen yuh would neva stop chatting bout it," Burdan contradicted him.

"It happen," Tariq retorted.

"So why am I only hearin' bout it now?"

"It's between Cian and me," Tariq said, pointing to his chest gently. "Cian come to me to chat alone."

"Yuh expect me to believe de Almighty Cian Donnell want to

tell him secrets to Tariq from de weeding gang?" Burdan threw his head back, laughing.

"Anyway, yuh cook yuh food and mind yuh own bizniz," Tariq said, reverting to his normal voice. "I'm chattin' to Art and Ned, not yuh."

He turned back to us.

"Him comes to me cabin," he pointed to the door, "and talks to me." He waved his hand around. "He knows me name – and me only in de weeding gang." He looked pointedly at Burdan.

When I asked Tariq what class of a slave was Cian Donnell, he held his hand high above his head.

"De highest black man in any plantation in de world."

Burdan threw him a glance.

"Him sits in him good clothes among de field slaves and asks how we doin'. Him knows everythin' and everybody. Him knows who is good worka, him knows who should be whip, and who should be hung."

The truth was that Cian Donnell was indeed a freed slave, well respected and valuable in keeping the peace between the slaves and whites. He had no children and lived alone in one of the good cabins reserved for the overseers and bookkeepers of the plantation.

There were several stories about him and his longevity, although I doubted he was really one hundred and thirty-one years of age. Each day he bathed in the stream by the rocks. They claimed the water cured all sicknesses and kept old men young. Another contribution to his age was his diet of herbs. Even as a young boy he used the herbs. Some of the herbs were for his body, his knees and legs, others for his eyes and ears and the rest for his head and his brain and to help him remember.

CIAN SAT WITH HIS POLISHED WALKING STICK BETWEEN HIS LEGS AND his hands resting on the head. The men were talking about the harvesting season and the months of hard work ahead of them.

"There will probably be a few Europeans this year too." Cian spoke good English. "A few Irish."

"Irish boy from yuh country," Tariq said to Cian and pointed at me.

The old man asked my name.

"Art O'Neill," I said.

"Where you from?" he asked.

I hesitated before giving Ned Doyle's address. "Prosperous, County Kildare."

"The O'Neills – The Red Hand of Ireland," he said, referring to the O'Neill symbol on their coat of arms.

Everybody remained quiet after he spoke.

"You think I know everything because I know that?" He had a gamey smirk.

I nodded.

"My grandmother's name was O'Neill – she came from Sligo," he continued. "My grandfather came from a small parish in Limerick. Like all the Irish, they never stopped talking and pining for their old country. I know as much about Ireland as I know about Jamaica."

There was silence as the gathering listened.

"My grandfather came to Jamaica during Cromwell's time. Cromwell cleaned us out of Ireland. He stripped the forests of oak to build the English fleet and furnish their parliament." Cian rested the walking cane against his leg – it was dark oak like the wood he referred to. "Cromwell halved the population. He killed us, sold us, and those who remained were left to starve. You know how my grandfather came to this island?"

I shook my head.

"When England took over this island, they needed some fresh white blood. Cromwell sold 2,000 children between the ages of ten and fourteen. He sent a letter to a planter telling him to do with them what he wished. My granddaddy was one of those children. My granddaddy's father's crime was to harbour a priest. For that crime he was sent to prison and his three daughters and one son were sent to Jamaica. The English didn't want the new slaves to form their own communities so when they got here they were broken up and sold in separate lots. That's why we have this higgledy-piggledy language here in Jamaica." He grinned when he said that. "We're all a bit of something else."

A FEW DAYS AFTER MY FIRST ENCOUNTER WITH CIAN DONNELL, I was summoned to his cabin.

Tariq thought Cian's request meant a whipping. "Or maybe him sell yuh," he said.

Nervously Tariq showed me the way with beads of sweat on his upper lip. The Big House was at the top of the hill with steps leading through a large lawn with ornaments and a waterfall in the centre.

Although Tariq was terrified at its close proximity, he couldn't resist adding his own knowledge, "Yuh eva see a house like it? De biggest house in de world."

In fact, its imposing location and size reminded me of Lugdale House in Ireland.

When Cian's cabin came into view, Tariq pointed it out and fled. "I be whipped if dey see a weedin' boy here."

The cabins for the managerial staff and overseers were located higher on the hill – a cluster of five white-painted cabins with fences and flowers around the edging. It was a prettier sight than our dilapidated hidden dwellings.

Cian was sitting on the porch drinking juice, his long legs stretched out before him and his hands joined on his chest. For a man who was about to whip me, he did not appear angry.

He indicated a bundle of clean clothes with his long, withered fingers. "Take these. Soak in the sea until you are white again, and then come back to me. You're going to work in the gardens. We need you looking clean and sprightly."

As I was about to leave, he raised his head. "Art O'Neill from Prosperous," he sighed. "Art who might yet become prosperous if he plays his cards right."

I blushed, conscious of my lie, yet felt it necessary until I knew which side he was on.

"Yes, sir," I said before galloping off, relieved I would not be tied to the tree and flogged.

CHAPTER SIX

The interior of the Big House unsettled me with the vast rooms, polished furnishings and large paintings of stern British soldiers on the walls. I tiptoed beneath their shadowy eyes, intimidated by their stern gaze and the formality of the regal house. Reminding myself of Tariq who was afraid of all white men, I returned the intimidating stare of the British redcoats' portraits. There was a painting of Major Beaufort, the plantation owner, when he was a younger man, and beside that his father's portrait and his father before him – and finally the first owner of Mangrove Plantation, Major Beaufort's great-grandfather, who bought the plantation over one hundred and fifty years ago.

Cian Donnell's grandfather was one of the first slaves sent to Jamaica in the 1660's at the age of ten. I thought about Cian's grandfather who arrived with 2,000 children as I went about my daily chores and realised my own plight was not unique.

Twice a week I had to water the flowers in all of the downstairs rooms of the big house. Each room had its own name: the blue room because it was blue, the yellow room, the dining room, the study, the veranda. Each day the domestic slaves cleaned and polished all of the rooms although nobody used them. I was warned not to go upstairs where Major Beaufort was resting. As the weeks passed, I heard he was not resting but dying, albeit dying slowly.

One month after I began my new post, I heard the doctor tell the white overseer, Mr. McCovey, "He's a miracle man – he wants to sit in the gardens today."

There was a great fuss made. I had to sweep the area where he'd sit. Two slaves brought out the enormous chair which was positioned facing the ocean. Nkechinyere, the housekeeper, cleaned the chair and covered it with a blanket. I watched as four slaves carried the Major downstairs on his bed. The housekeeper and his nurse, Nancy, helped him into the chair. Nurse Nancy sat beside him, another slave stood at the other side holding a parasol to shield his face from the sun.

Through ancient beady eyes for an hour he surveyed all he owned: the pristine garden with statues, the acres of land and sugar-cane fields, the panoramic sea view from his house and the trees at the bottom of the hill which hid his slave village. For one week the same routine was repeated each day.

While watering my flowers, I passed him closely and looked at him. I doubted he had the ability to see through his small lost eyes in a pallid milky face.

He grunted as if he was distressed and flicked his head ever so slightly.

"Move, boy," Nancy the nurse said.

ONE OF MY DUTIES WAS TO MAINTAIN THE FLOWERS BY CIAN'S CABIN. If he was on the veranda he would offer me orange juice.

He told me he liked the original Irish accent. He knew a great many Irish who had come to Jamaica.

"Some never lost their accents. It was one of the few ways they could defy their master. Keep as much as Ireland in them as they could." Suddenly he asked again, "Where you from?"

"Kildare."

"Where's the other boy from?" he asked. "The Irish boy in the weeding gang?"

"Ned is from Prosperous in Kildare too."

He nodded slowly. He poured boiling water into a cup, tore a leaf and added it to the water. He saw me watching. "Guinea-hen weed, keeps me young and pretty," he chuckled, and then added, "Long time since I was pretty." He sat back into his seat and gave a long sigh. "Good for the soul too."

I'd seen him using different leaves, weeds and bulbs at different times of the day. Some he drank in his tea, others he crushed and made a paste for his bones. At the side of his cabin were a few neat rows of plants, and each had a purpose. The slaves also brought him weeds from the fields. Some were unsightly and smelled like nothing you could put into your mouth, but each had a purpose. Cian told me that he was raised on a mixture of Jamaican food and herbs and Irish folklore. "The best of both worlds."

Regularly he gave medicinal advice to the slaves. During an outbreak of yaws, a nasty contagious skin and bone infection, Cian cured them with an old remedy he had learned. Each night for nine days the slaves sat around with their feet immersed in buckets of water and hog-plum-tree bark. He had such authority that each slave obeyed his orders. During the nine days he checked on their progress and scolded those who were not cured, believing they had not adhered to his remedy and fearing they would spread the disease further.

"A new master is coming," Cian told me. "Old Major Beaufort isn't going to last much longer. We need to make a few changes. The new master is his nephew from Ireland."

I waited for him to elaborate.

"I sit with the major when his nephew writes letters."

Eager to hear news from home, I asked what the letters said.

"He talks about the Irish who still fight. Although sometimes I wonder what they're fighting for." He sighed as if exhausted at the prospect. "It's all hopeless – the Irish have been fighting the English for hundreds of years and getting nowhere."

I wanted to tell him he was wrong. Ireland would never stop fighting until they won. If I had not been put on a ship, I too would be fighting.

"You'll have a better life here."

How could he think I'd be better off in this foreign country?

"I don't know one white man who was hanged in this country," Cian said. "The white man in Jamaica is what the Englishman is in Ireland. Do you know one Englishman hanged on a tree in Ireland?"

I didn't answer.

"Every year I see the Irish arrive – their stories never change."

My dismay must have registered.

"The letters from Ireland are filled with stories of hangings and failed uprisings. Same as we got here," he said, pointing towards the Cockpit Country. "The Maroons fight like the Irish."

The Maroons were slaves who ran away and formed independent settlements in the mountains. There was a constant threat of Maroons preparing for an uprising or raiding plantations and killing any white man who stood in their way.

"Those you left behind will etch out enough crops to barely feed their families. Here you will have a little opportunity that will never present itself in Ireland." He pointed towards the cane fields. "The black man will never be free. You will be free and earn your own money and lease your own little patch to grow tobacco or cocoa or whatever you want. The poor black man will have nothing at the end of his days but a beat-up body good for nothing but dying slowly."

Only then did I understand what Burdan resented about me being a white boy.

This was confirmation of what we had been told on the ship and afterwards – I felt I could trust Cian's word.

"You'll be free eventually."

"When will I be free?" I asked, suddenly walking to his side.

"Maybe fourteen years' time when you've paid for your passage and board. Then they'll let you lease some land or work for pay. It all depends on Major Beaufort's nephew. He will decide."

My imagination spiralled. I could own land of my own, not leased to landlords who varied the rents but own my own land. Someday I would go home and tell them about my travels. The idea made me tremendously happy. I didn't ask Cian how much the boat to Ireland cost because I knew he'd get annoyed. Already he had told me that the quicker I forgot the idea of going home, the happier I'd be.

He added, "Play your cards right and you'll never again want to go home."

Cian had an easy way of talking. There were times when I could have sat all night and listened to him. He knew so much about my home country. His talk was sprinkled with Gaelic, African and English.

FINALLY MAJOR GEORGE BEAUFORT EXPIRED. AS THE FIRST RAINS OF the monsoon bounced off the windows, some of the domestic staff were in tears.

"Best masta I eva did have," Molly said.

"Good man in de end," Nkechinyere said.

They talked about local masters who mercilessly beat their slaves, some beatings resulting in death, and some masters who were not content with sex with women but wanted something darker to sate their peculiar cruel cravings. At the mention of one master's name, they stopped talking, their silence speaking the brutality they were unable to say.

"Wat will de new masta' be like?" one asked.

They looked at Nkechinyere, the older black housekeeper who was born on the plantation. "I think it be Masta Edward," she said.

"Him be English. Him used to visit here a long time ago. Not a bad man but yuh neva know."

THAT NIGHT I TOLD NED, TARIQ AND BURDAN THAT MASTA WAS dead.

Tariq said he knew that was going to happen – he claimed he saw it in Major George's eyes last Christmas. "George said to me," Tariq said, leaning in close to me, re-enacting what the Masta had done. "Him touched me hand and say, 'Could be me last Christmas'."

"Yuh don't need to be Death Spirit to know dat," Burdan said as he made a paste to massage onto the burns that dotted his arms from his job in the boiling house.

I relayed part of what the women in the kitchen said. "They say he was one of the best masters to serve."

Tariq confirmed that was true. He was a great master, the best in Jamaica.

Burdan was quick to disagree. "Him wasn't always old. Him de same as all de masta and all de white man."

"How?" I asked.

"Why yuh ask?" Burdan said with anger. "Yuh white boy – it doesn't matter to yuh!"

Tariq broke the silence that followed, glancing covertly at Burdan. "Burdan's mother knew de Masta wen him was a younger man."

"Younger man who beat the slaves like every other white man," Burdan interjected angrily, "and take from de women wat him want."

"Why didn't they stop him?" I innocently asked. "Or why didn't their fathers or husbands stop him?"

Burdan scoffed at my question. "Yuh white boy know nothin' bout de life of a slave."

Tariq shrugged with an air of acceptance. "De white man take it – if de woman fights de white man will take it anyway."

I tried to comprehend it.

"Slaves can't stop de white men." Tariq shrugged. "We him property so him does as him want."

Burdan looked at me with abhorrence before leaving. Only then did I understand his lighter skin and recognise his white parentage.

"It shoulda be more easy wen yuh papa be white," Tariq said as he watched Burdan walk down the hill towards the sea, "but maybe is not dat easy."

"Why doesn't the Major do something for Burdan?" I asked Tariq. "If he's his papa?"

"Major George not his papa," Tariq said. "George's nephew is the papa. But he in England."

"Maybe George doesn't know?" I said, sounding like Tariq as I used Major's Christian name. "Maybe none of them know?"

"Dey know – das why dey make Burdan boiler," Tariq explained. "Big job – boiler one of de best jobs."

"I think you're right," I said to Tariq.

Several times that night and the following day I thought of Burdan. I thought of his detestation of the white man, the same white colour of his father's skin, and half the colour of his own skin, except the colour that Jamaica saw was his dark skin, the colour of a slave.

The more I saw of the island, the less I understood. Why didn't they do something? Where were the fighters? Why was there no black uprising?

"Where are the rebels?" I asked Cian.

"Dead," Cian told me. "Any slave who does not want to wipe the dirt from the Masta's feet will not be a domestic slave. Any slave who fights against the Masta will have his back broken in the fields or his head on a spike." He added quietly, "The slaves fight in their own way. At least now we got freedom to pray to whoever we want."

Cian told me that his grandfather had hoped Jamaica would offer him freedoms that he couldn't have in Ireland, like practising the Catholic faith in a time when it was banned in Ireland. When Cian's grandfather arrived in the colonies the Irish were dismayed to discover that the suppression of their language and religion was replicated in the transatlantic colonies. But secretly they continued to keep their religion alive.

"I know all my prayers in the English language and the Irish language," he chuckled. "I know how to keep the devil away with my prayers, and keep my old bones moving with the weeds. Jamaica has it all. I even know a few strange prayers for a man like Major Beaufort." He winked mischievously when he said that.

CHAPTER SEVEN

O n the morning of the arrival of the new heir to Mangrove
Plantation, Birky and I were dispatched with the overseers to
help with their luggage. Birky was not young and didn't move as fast
as he once did, but he was large and strong. He was ideal for the
garden work. He could plant large trees and uproot trees alone
which normally took the effort of two men.

"Help me wid dis and stop starin' at de pretty ladies," Birky
teased. "Yuh will scare dem away from me."

Black River Pier was always a thrilling place for a young boy, not
only because of the ships but also the assortment of people. It was
filled with expectation, a maze of new arrivals and sad farewells.

"Quick!" Birky hissed. "McCovey is comin' wid de new masta."

We began to load the trunks onto the carriage. There were
several trunks. They'd also sent luggage earlier in the month which
was in the Big House awaiting their arrival. I couldn't fathom what
the trunks contained – surely Mangrove's Big House had all they
needed?

As we tried to manoeuvre an awkward large trunk onto the
carriage, it almost slipped from my grasp.

"Do be careful," a female voice said over my shoulder. "That contains our silverware."

I looked up, wanting to match the voice to the woman. When I saw her, I just assumed most white girls in bonnets and long dresses looked similar. She had black hair visible under a bonnet and pale skin.

"Yes, Mistress," Birky said as he struggled under the weight of the trunk.

She looked at me as if she was surprised at the sight of me. "Look, Edward," she said to the man beside her, "it's a white boy!"

The sight of her husband stunned me. His small frame and pointed nose, his undershot mouth and arched eyebrows. I was unable to move, transfixed with the memory of the courthouse. The Colonel's features were the same yet I gaped, doubting my own recollection.

"Something the matter, boy?" he asked.

And his voice completed the set.

The trunk slipped from my grasp.

"Careful, boy!"

I slowly turned back to the fallen trunk. With trembling arms I helped Birky lift it onto the carriage. Suddenly it seemed much heavier.

OUR DAYS OF POLISHING AND CLEANING A HOUSE IN BLISSFUL quietness were gone. The new master and his wife swept through the house dumping furniture, ripping down curtains, redecorating rooms and renaming the domestic slaves.

"Nkec ...Nkec ... chin ..." Mistress attempted to pronounce Nkechinyere's name as she watched a man measuring the windows for new curtains. "Am I pronouncing it incorrectly? Nee-catcha-near?"

"Dat is fine," Nkechinyere said.

"No, it's not. This will never do," she said over her shoulder. "From now on you will be called Anna. We had a lovely maid in Ireland called Anna."

Nkechinyere looked at me when Mistress made a reference to Ireland. I averted my eyes. Since their arrival I had done my best to remain invisible.

"It's a nice light name – Anna – that will be your new name," Mistress concluded cheerily as she left the room.

Nkechinyere curtsied as she passed then whispered to me, "Wah de matter wid Nkechinyere? Wat Anna mean?" She had told me her name meant "What God has given".

I shrugged. I'd been hardly able to focus on any task since the Colonel and his wife arrived. Each day I watched her sweep through the house, intent on changing so much so quickly. She was a tiny woman who wore long flouncy dresses with so much material that it rustled loudly. Her noisy dresses were her calling card. When the domestics were enjoying an idle moment, they'd jump-to at the sound of her approaching swishing sound. Although she was usually busily giving orders to put, as she said, "the house in order once and for all," she insisted on supervising every task until she felt it was done to her liking.

"No, no, get into the corner," she clapped her hands, "the corner! Use your finger." She was standing over Nkechinyere and Lucy as they washed the floor.

"Yes, Mistress," they chimed, increasing their pace.

AN ENGLISH CAPTAIN CALLED TO SEE THE COLONEL. THE COLONEL addressed him as Mathews. Like old friends they sat in the cool library discussing Jamaica as I listened from outside the window.

The Colonel told him of his plans for the estate.

"I will not be another absentee planter," he said. "This is my home. Jamaica and the sugar industry are my future." He said he was fascinated with the sugar industry. "It's not as lucrative as it once was – however, it remains a wonderful means of getting rich." He paused and added, "Each time the King of England sips his tea sweetened with sugar, or a little old lady sprinkles sugar on her tart, it comes from this lovely oasis."

"You'll find the Jamaican life similar in ways to the life of a Colonel in Ireland," Captain Mathews said.

"Yes, it's really about managing volatile people. There is very little difference between the Irish and the darkies."

"Incidentally, Johnson is very pleased with the Irish children you sent him. A good many survived."

"I'm glad to hear it," the Colonel said. "It's a risk – the heat doesn't suit the Irish. They'd be better in New Zealand. Wetter climate."

From outside the window I could smell their cigars.

"Are you not a little unnerved that some of the boys you sent from Ireland might well be on your plantation? As you know, the Irish can be a vicious vindictive lot, especially with a feed of rum."

"No, not worried at all. Every child from Ireland is asked their address. There are none from Munster on this side of the island. They go to Lord Hawthorn's estate outside Kingston."

"Very clever," the captain said.

"As soon as the house and gardens are ready, we'll round up some of the old stock for a knees-up."

"Smashing idea. In the meantime, if you need anything, you know where I am."

EACH DAY THE COLONEL RODE AROUND THE PLANTATION WITH THE overseer, McCovey, and the deputy overseers, Acklen and Sexton. According to Tariq, the overseer was teaching the Colonel about the sugar industry. Tariq told me the Colonel dismounted from his horse in the cane field and spent an hour with the slaves cutting cane.

One evening he arrived into our living quarters with Acklen and inspected some of the cabins. With white men and women, there are some clean and some content to live in squalor. The black man is no different.

When he saw a cabin belonging to a family who worked from sunrise to sunset, he held a hankie over his mouth. "How can they live like this? Animals."

I lurked in the thick overgrowth behind the cabins, watching and listening.

Then I saw Burdan. He, too, was hiding, and watching the colonel closely.

Burdan was the only other person who seemed as perturbed as I was with the arrival of the new master and, as time went on, there was a shift in him, something I couldn't identify. It was a strange angry stillness that unnerved me. The angry Burdan who resented my presence and insulted me was easier than the new calm rage. It was as if he was about to do something awful. He was whipped for shirking work, and whipped again for disobedience. Even as he was whipped, the same raging defiance remained and, unlike the other slaves, he didn't look over his shoulder or appear frightened. He clung to the tree, arched his back with each lash but didn't cry out or plead for mercy.

Later that night while Nkechinyere put paste on his back to ease the pain, I heard her say, "Yuh betta get used to seein' him." She begged him to go back to the way he was before the Colonel arrived. "When Masta is scared him sell or kill de slave – it make no difference dat he yuh papa."

IN THE LIBRARY THE COLONEL HUNG A HUGE MAP OF THE WORLD. IT was two circular balls side by side with a series of lines running from top to bottom and across the middle. Each day, when I thought I was alone, I'd spend a few minutes studying the map. There was a similar one on the wall of the courthouse back in Ireland and I had spent time gazing at it on that terrible day when my father was condemned. A man beside me in the crowd had told me what it was and had pointed out certain features, including little Ireland with England lurking over its shoulder. Now I found them again. But I didn't know where Jamaica was. I could see some islands across the great blue expanse that was the Atlantic Ocean and the huge land mass to the left of it that was America. Was Jamaica one of those?

Sometimes I felt sadder after looking at the map and promised myself I would not look at it again. Yet I couldn't resist – like a dog scratching its wound, my eyes always fell on the map if I was alone.

One day Cian suddenly appeared behind me.

"We are here." His long bony finger pointed to a cluster of islands. "We are this one."

We were a little speck beneath a larger island.

"That is Cuba," he said, pointing to the bigger island. "We are below it, here," and then slowly he dragged his finger across the Atlantic Ocean, "here is Ireland where you came from … and here is Kerry where the Colonel's home is."

I traced my finger across the sea and held it on Ireland, over Kerry and the mountains that sheltered Mein.

I stood back to look at the gulf dividing me from my home.

"More than 4000 miles," Cian said.

It was one single big mass of water. It was one single tide between us.

"Forget it," Cian said, placing his hand on my shoulder. "You'll never know a happy day if you dwell on it."

That evening when I watered his plants Cian was sitting on the veranda. He told me I didn't have to like the Colonel.

"But it is important he does not know that."

I nodded, unsure why he was saying it.

"I am the only negro who survived to my age because I learned how to hide how I feel from those I most hate."

I remained standing outside his veranda, holding my water canister.

"If the Colonel thinks you are trouble he will send you back to the fields. If he thinks you are willing, he will trust you." Cian was sitting back on his chair, his long legs crossed. It was as if he was speaking to himself. "Use this time wisely. You survived so far. If you are clever you will survive to see happiness on this island. Remember, you work for him now, and if you are wise someday you will work for yourself. For a white boy, everything can change."

. . .

AFTER TWO MONTHS OF REMAINING INVISIBLE, THE COLONEL AND HIS wife finally came striding across the garden of the house and asked me my name. I had been pruning a yellow rose bush.

"Art," I said with a broad smile hiding my abhorrence.

"Jolly good, Arthur," the Colonel said. "Now, this garden has been an eyesore long enough. You and I are going to do a lot of work on this godforsaken wilderness."

Mistress Victoria followed him, and Lucy followed her, holding a parasol over her head. They stood by his side surveying the garden. They were so taken with the focus of their attention that I too looked around the garden as if seeing it for the first time.

"There's so much to be done," the Colonel said. "Uncle George was never adventurous with the garden design. No imagination."

"You must admit the views are stunning, darling," Mistress said.

"Indeed. Although that had nothing to do with Uncle George. His grandfather built the house on this spot." He turned towards the land and pointed. "When I was a boy this was all tobacco, before that it was cotton and then Uncle George turned his attention to sugar. He was tasteless but clever." He looked at the garden. "There is no order to the flowerbeds. So primitive."

"Maybe they're wild," Mistress said, bending down to examine them with Lucy lowering the umbrella to keep her sheltered.

"I suppose – what can one expect when one never travels outside one's domain? Uncle George had no interest in seeing the splendid gardens of London or Paris. He'd rather remain here, more at ease with his darkies."

They stood in silence for a few moments, a little awkwardness between them. We could hear the birds and in the distance see a ship approach the pier.

"Darling, the board," she prompted him.

As if remembering their purpose, he said, "Yes, the board." He leaned over my barrow of tools and took a scythe. "This will do the job. Come with me, Arthur."

I didn't correct him when he called me by the wrong name again – instead I followed him, rubbing my finger off the sharp point on the pruner. He was a small dapper little man with a tiny boyish frame. Narrow shoulders and small legs that befitted his small torso. At thirteen years of age, I was as tall as him.

With determined strides he walked towards the end of the garden.

"Come along, Victoria – if memory serves me, our wonderful game is somewhere over here."

His wife giggled as she struggled to keep up with him and Lucy struggled to keep the umbrella over her head.

He stopped at the end of the garden, facing several layers of shrubs and trees, and behind them a high wall separating the house and gardens from the cane fields.

"As far as I remember it was about here." He pointed into a purple and lilac Bougainvillea tree.

"It sounds preposterous, darling," she said in her high-pitched voice. "I won't believe it until I see it."

I watched him wade through the bushes and overgrowth. He flattened the smaller flowers with his boots as if he was looking for something hidden beneath them. Then, with the scythe, he started hacking at the smaller bushes.

"I knew it was a tall tale," she pretended to scold.

Ignoring her, he looked at the house then looked at his position as if measuring something. "Maybe it was a little to the right."

She giggled again as he slashed his way through the flowers with the scythe.

"I think I've found it!" he said, clearing more plants and flowers. "We're going to bring a little glamour back into Mangrove Plantation."

I waited on the edge of the lawn and peered between the flowers to see what he was looking at.

"That's the Rook's square, then the Knight's, then …" he cleared more flowers, "the Bishop's. Uncle George appears to have planted the Bougainvillea tree in the King's place."

"Darling, this is wonderful!"

"Stupid damned flowers. Uncle George was content to allow these ghastly wild flowers consume one of the feature points of the house – a human-sized chess court."

"Nonetheless, darling, we'll build our own chess court right here," she consoled him.

As newly-weds they were not yet at ease in each other's company. The effort to adjust to their new roles was evident in her tense voice.

"I want the original chess court," he said. "If we cleared this tree it would give you a better idea." He placed his hand on the trunk of the Bougainvillea tree and pushed, as if testing to see if he could knock it with his hand.

He began to hit the tree with the scythe.

"Oh Edward, such a beautiful tree! Must you cut it down?"

He didn't respond, only kept hitting the tree trunk with the scythe.

Beneath the midday sun and faced with the impossible task of cutting down a tree with a scythe, he continued to hack at it. His face glistened with sweat while he grunted loudly.

Birky, the older gardener, passed by with his barrow of tools. Disbelievingly he stopped dead and stared at the Colonel as he wildly swung the scythe at the bark.

Mistress's giggling grew forced.

"This damn blasted …" he swore as the effort became too much.

As I watched him I toyed with the pruner in my hand. I'd like to have pierced his eye with it. Discreetly I again pricked my finger on the point of the blade. Each night I imagined how I'd kill him, his screams serenading me. The unfairness of life kept me awake long after he bled every drop of blood from his body. Sadly, no imagined death ever brought me prolonged relief.

The beads of sweat trickled down his face and neck, dampening his shirt. "God damn you, George, you nitwit!"

In anger he turned the scythe wildly on the branches. The petals freed and cascaded upon us like a shower of bright pink-and-purple raindrops. The head of one single flower landed at Mistress's feet. She hummed slightly, pretending not to notice his rage. She picked up the lone flower at her feet and smelled it.

I took an axe from Birky's barrow and stepped into the

flowerbed beside him. He stood behind me, breathless and spent. I began cutting the tree for him. Each time the axe hit the bark of the tree, I felt a surge of relief. I focused on each blow, relishing the chippings that sprang from the bark.

For all my hatred, I had placed Edward Stratford-Rice as a man higher in rank than a meagre mountain peasant such as I was. I was intimidated by his inherited position and power. I deemed him superior then despised myself for the thought. Now the spectacle I had witnessed pleased me. He was foolish, childish, boorish and, more importantly, he was human. A man who tries to impress his wife by cutting down a tree with a scythe during the hottest time of the day has many failings. I would stay close to him from now on, I would hide my abhorrence, and I would survive in this hotspot of the Caribbean.

When the tree inclined I handed him the axe to finish it off. "Master," I said in a new deferential tone.

He took the axe. In three blows it toppled.

His wife applauded.

CHAPTER EIGHT

The Colonel was intent on, as he called it, "designing a garden befitting a king." Each morning he met Birky and Max, the two gardeners, and me in the tack room and gave us clear instructions. He had large drawings of the garden with measurements and ruler marks. Enthusiastically he would discuss our plans for the day. He bandied about words like gazebo, iron plant-holders, Aphrodite's Statue, wall monuments and so on. Birky would nod as if he understood the Colonel's drawings.

The slaves continued to scrutinise him to determine his character. After the episode with the scythe and Bougainvillea tree, Birky and Max were terrified of him.

"Him no good wid him hands – and part of him head not too good," Birky said.

"Angry man like dat, him make bad masta," Max said.

I became fixated on him. During the day, when he was on the plantation, I knew where he was and who he spent time with. I stalked him as cautiously as Tariq and I stalked the crocodiles. I noted how he changed his shirt each day, wore different boots, grew tired and often irritable during the afternoon. I heard how he liked to linger in the bath at the end of each day. I thought about the ideal place to kill him, I imagined his red blood seeping into his bathing water. In the garden I would stand beside him and compare my size to his.

"I want everything uprooted. Take every flower and shrub. Take the clay from the back garden and raise the height on the front lawn to make a level lawn."

"Yes, Masta," the men would chime.

As he rode off to spend his day in the sugar mill, he'd say, "I want the best garden in Jamaica."

"Yes, Masta!"

Calling him "Master" stuck in my throat, I did not have a master and did not want to call any man my master. Colonel was as underserving a title. I deemed 'sir' the best of a bad lot. "Yes, sir," I'd say. And, adapting the Jamaican tongue, "Yuh knows de best, sir." As time passed I became more comfortable in his presence although his past never slipped from my sight.

When he removed Birky as head gardener and gave me the position of boss, I thanked him and said, "Yuh de master, yuh knows best."

Cian told me the sooner I stopped speaking the black man's language and used my own tongue, the sooner the Colonel would respect me.

I lived with the coloured men in our slave village, I continued to hunt and fish with Tariq and many more Negroes. I was a Negro in almost every aspect except colour.

"You're white," Cian said. "Use it to your advantage or you'll be watering plants for the rest of your days."

Then I spoke my own English and adapted to the changes. With my new role I gained trust from the Colonel and listened to all Cian's words of advice.

"Let him think you are his servant. And, most important, let him think you are from Kildare."

I was going protest and remind Cian that I *was* from Kildare.

Cian stopped me. "I saw you several times looking at that map in the Master's library. Your finger was over the same part of the country as the Colonel's home and your face revealed your feelings for that place."

My silence confirmed my guilt.

He shrugged his shoulders. "The English think they know where the best slaves in the world come from. They've long talks about the ages and countries of their cane-cutters and skilled slaves but they haven't realised that the slaves lie about their origins. The Englishman is mistrusted not only by the Irish but by the Africans and Europeans."

I knew my secret was safe with Cian.

As time passed Cian aged very slowly. The subtle changes were his extended naps on his porch. Yet very little happened on the plantation without his knowledge.

I STOPPED GLARING AT THE MAP OF THE WORLD IN THE COLONEL'S study. Gradually the gap widened between Ireland and me. The dream of returning and telling my uncles about masters and slaves and the heat of the sun faded but never entirely left. Jamaica was no longer new to my acclimatised eyes. There were deaths, hangings, whippings, and severe punishments. The Colonel was not shy about using his whip or building a sweat-hole where the slaves were locked without food or water and allowed to bake and repent. When the Colonel was particularly agitated he'd rub their whipped backs with pepper, salt and lime juice. His punishments were so severe that several times he worried about his own safety. Once he was ill for three days and, fearing he'd been poisoned, he removed the cook from the kitchen and sent her to the fields.

At some stage I would know freedom, but there was no such respite for the lives of my slave friends. Some slaves who lost all hope tried to poison themselves by eating clay. When the "dirt-eaters" were detected by the overseers their faces were locked in a dirt-eating mask. It was only removed for eating food when super-vised by the overseer. As a last resort, the unfixable slaves were sold. Women and children were sold. In rare cases, mothers were sold without their children. New slaves arrived, we made new friends. The new recruits were branded, they no longer belonged to God but their owner, the Colonel. We taught them how to speak English. The sweat dripped from their stunned faces and in time their tongues managed a little at a time. There were survivors but plenty died. The only slave that silenced us was the lone child-slave who arrived crying for its mama. The women were charitable – they'd offer a little consolation but never replaced the lost mama.

Mistress never tired of cleaning or redecorating the walls of the Big House. It was unnecessary as she had a fleet of servants – however, it seemed to give her an objective in her life. When the room was finished she'd move to another room, and another and another. Her terror of insects and the ever-present geckos diminished but never disappeared. Her round eyes followed the darting small lizard-like geckos across the walls. The only times she appeared overjoyed was when her letters arrived from England and Ireland. She'd sit in the Green Room reading them. Almost immediately she would respond. I'd see her pausing, then she'd gaze out the window for a while before dipping the quill into her inkwell to continue. There were other times when she wrote quickly, as if she could not contain what needed to be said.

In the evenings when the sun was less torturous, Mistress joined her husband in the garden where she'd read the letters aloud to him. Although she continued to gloss over his many angry outbursts, she stopped applauding his every movement. She became more comfortable with him. The newness of life in Jamaica and their marriage settled. There were many more Bougainvillea outbursts – some he would take out on a hapless slave with his whip. Unlike the overseers he was too small to make an impact with his weak blows. The bull-whip did the job. Mistress couldn't bear to see violence used against the slaves yet felt it was as necessary as feeding them.

"The whip is guidance," she said to me as we passed a woman tied to a tree while Sexton warmed the whip with a crack.

Mistress fascinated me and I hated myself for thinking about her. Occasionally she'd say a few kind words to me, compliment my work or suggest I work indoors when the sun was hottest. It would have been easier if she were as unkind to me as she was to the other

slaves. It was easier to hate than find the enemy endearing. Each day
I saw her inspect the house. She'd check the corners of the room to
ensure the domestic slaves were doing a good job.

The only time she did not appear in control was during the
earth-tremors. When the doors opened and closed violently, she
asked me to sit with her.

"This damn country!" she cried as her commanding veneer
slipped.

Once, to stop her crying, I gifted her five pearls. They were the
valuable pearls – round, white and shiny. Afterwards I regretted it.
She asked about the pearls and was intrigued when I told her I took
them from an oyster. She asked for more. I felt foolish, conflicted
and unmanly when I saw her wearing a bracelet made from my
pearls.

When she found a rat in her bedroom, she screamed so loudly
that Lucy ran out of the house. Mistress beckoned me into the
green room. She confessed she wasn't comfortable with the other
men in her chamber yet the job required a man. Eager to see her
chamber I obeyed. I noticed the bed with a net draping over the
four posters. Her bell was on the locker beside a stack of books.
Then I noticed a door leading into another bedroom. That bed was
also draped with a mosquito net. I saw the Colonel's boots on the
floor and books on the locker. I realised they had separate
bedrooms.

When there was an influx of mice I brought a blacksnake to her
in a sack. Gently I took it out and told her how harmless it was for
humans but it would kill every rodent in the house. She didn't balk
but watched it closely as it slithered along my arm.

"The poison has been removed, it will do you no harm," I
explained.

She leaned in closer. "I suppose it is the lesser of two evils." She
sighed. "Oh dear, this is my life now. God be with the days in
Ireland when the most dangerous threat of nature was a bumblebee." Her humour prevailed. "Shall we give it a name?" She
appeared younger when she was playful. She pretended to converse
with the blacksnake by peering closely at its head. "You're welcome

to Mangrove Plantation, Blacksnake."

The black snake's tongue flicked in and out as if responding.

Despite my guardedness with her, I found myself laughing.

"Yes, we must give it a name!" she said. "Is it a boy or a girl?"

I admitted I didn't know.

She considered it before speaking. "We shall call you Hapi," she said decidedly, "after the Egyptian God of fertility who is both male and female." Then she grew serious and regarded the snake in a thoughtful way. "I don't want to be frightened of it."

When she concentrated she had a little line in the middle of her eyebrows. Since her arrival two years ago her round healthy cheeks had grown thinner. She had light blue eyes and black hair that was barely visible beneath her bonnet. She was pretty and pale, her small hands and face so white they appeared powdered. My mind drifted. I thought of her bedroom, the bed draped with the net – it seemed erotic and sacred. I felt a stirring in my trousers, a daily occurrence at that stage.

"Let me hold Hapi. I'd better get used to him, or her," she said.

I passed the snake to her and showed her how to hold it.

The contrast in the colour of the black snake and her pale fingers struck me. She held the neck in one hand, her other hand held the spine.

"Maybe I'll rub it as one would rub a dog."

Her fingers were loose on the spine as she toyed with it. Gently she rubbed it up and down several times. I leaned forward, hiding the growing bulge of my manhood. Was she experienced enough with the Colonel to know the effect of her tentative caressing of the snake? Slowly she cupped it with her thumb and forefinger, and stroked it. When I could not bear it any longer I took the snake from her and placed it in the corner of the room.

Hapi the Blacksnake moved around the house gobbling rats and other stray rodents while I found a woman in the cabins who relieved me of my seed. She was older and everyone's.

. . .

THE GARDEN TOOK LONGER TO CREATE THAN ANTICIPATED. THE Colonel insisted on planting trees similar to his friends' gardens in London. The Caribbean earth rejected his English plants regardless of the amount of water we poured onto their parched roots. Over two years the Colonel drafted drawings, until finally he hired a man from Kingston to advise him on the plants. Then the Colonel changed from his English-style garden to a Jamaican garden where the flowers he imported from India and China would thrive. He built a three-tiered garden with steps leading down. There were statues of women dancing and lions guarding the secret alcoves within the garden. He knocked down the dividing wall, extended the garden and hired a man from England to build a wall with special carvings. Within the walls he placed statues: Zeus, God of the Sky, Poseidon, God of the Sea, and Janus, God of Beginnings. He installed a gazebo close to the human-sized chess court. When Mistress saw the completed chess court, she applauded at length and loudly. She and her husband sat on the bench, admiring the vast sweeping colours of their garden and made great plans for games and parties.

True to their word, they filled up the house with guests every weekend. They served the best food – black crab, ring-tailed pigeon, calipever, mountain mullet, and a roasted peacock with the feathers of the tail left intact as a decoration. The feathers were spread so naturally that I expected to see the peacock rise and strut off the table.

They got hours of enjoyment from the chess court. Thirty-two black slaves of similar height were required to stand on the board wearing black and white robes and the headdresses of the chess piece they represented.

"Pawn 3. Forward 2." The player called his move from an elevated chair, giving him a bird's-eye view of the game.

"Rook. Right."

My job during their parties was to oversee the maids who served in the garden. I hovered about listening as their guests greeted each other. Attending their parties were dukes and lords, high-ranking military, clergymen, poets and politicians. Everyone sounded as if he or she were a person of great importance.

During the introductions, they all appeared to be familiar with each other.

"I believe we met at the Earl of Rossmore's New Year's Ball," one said to the Colonel.

"Of course we did."

"Splendid surroundings."

"Thank you," the Colonel said. "It's been in my family for over 150 years."

The men discussed Jamaica while they played billiards and casino. They talked about the difficulties of the sugar industry and constant threat of an uprising.

"There are ten black slaves to every one white person. We are in a perilous situation," they said. "If uncertain, shoot."

They were united in their abhorrence for the anti-slavery movement from England.

"The abolitionists are naïve idealists who know nothing about slavery. They are not acquainted with our country," the Colonel said.

Captain Hedley agreed. "Slavery, like poverty, death and other calamities are part of a God-given plan and nothing can be done to eradicate them."

"The middle passage was not such an ordeal as many anti-slavery campaigners make it out to be and the mortality rates were lower than they thought."

They acknowledged that certain planters behaved in an inhumane way.

"Most planters are in fact kind, compassionate to their slaves and treat them well. Even if there is evidence of cruelty and ill-treatment on some plantations, it does not mean that the whole slave system is flawed."

Some congratulated the Colonel on staying in Jamaica when he could have been another absentee landlord like most of Jamaican planters.

"I want to have the best plantation in Jamaica. That is an impossible feat when living thousands of miles away."

"*Hear, hear!*" They raised their glasses.

Lady Hedley appeared to be Mistress's closest confidante. She was married to Captain Hedley who was stationed in Ireland during the 1798 Rebellion. She regularly talked about missing England, saying that her sense of duty to her country prevailed however.

"I miss the climate. I will never complain about a wet English day again," she confessed, "but I must remember, I am wed to a soldier and must have no will of my own."

Another woman joined in. "Pity the Irish can't accept their lot so easily. Surely their small minds should accept that they are better governed by the English."

They talked about the slaves.

"The biggest cruelty we are doing to our slaves is to deprive them of Christianity," Lady Hedley said.

She offered advice to Mistress on how to survive as a white woman in Jamaica. "You must undertake projects like gardening or painting because you'll find it an utterly boring time. There is nothing for a white woman to do in Jamaica – even the household management is taken care of."

Another female guest agreed. "We are surplus to requirement."

"Jamaica is the most uncivilised of the islands. Religion is non-existent and in some cases all forms of formality and manners are forgotten," Lady Hedley said. "It is our duty to uphold sliding etiquette and maintain standards."

An image returned in my mind from the previous night with the Colonel's naked thrusting buttocks. He had Lucy bent forward as he entered her like a dog beneath the statue of Hera, Goddess of Marriage, Motherhood and Families.

CHAPTER NINE

One year after their arrival in 1823, Mistress Victoria gave birth to a son. They called him Blair George Charles Andrew Louis.

"Why dey give him five names?" Burdan asked, always ready to air his disdain at the British traditions. "What de matter wid one name?"

"A few names for de beginnin of de week and other names for de end of de week," Tariq said informatively.

A year later, Mistress delivered a second son called Ernest Mathew James Phillip.

"De second son not dat important," Tariq said. "Him only got four names."

Major Beaufort's nurse was reinstated and, when the children had established their routine, Mistress found time on her hands again. She spent a few years turning her attention to different aspects of the plantation. She spent hours in the evenings in the garden, with Lucy holding the parasol. She went to Kingston and bought trunks of material for dresses and she ordered books from France. The Colonel would sit with her in the evenings and watch the sun sink while she read and translated French poetry. When there was no more work to be done in the house or gardens, she turned her attention to the spiritual welfare of her slaves.

Quoting Lady Hedley, she said to one of her new guests, a minister from Antigua, "It is our duty by the Slave Code to baptise our slaves into our Christian Church."

"And no better time than now," the minister agreed. "The practice of Obeah remains widespread. The only way to counteract it is to convert the pagan blackies to Christianity."

Although the practice of Obeah was banned, most of the slaves consulted the Obeah men and women for spiritual help, spells for love, spiritual protection and messages from their dead. The whites believed it was a form of voodoo and witchcraft, and there were stories about the Obeah casting spells on cruel masters.

The minister gave an account of a couple he had heard of. "An English husband and wife both lost their mind in Negril. The husband began complaining of pains in his head. One afternoon he removed all of his clothes and jumped from the roof of his house and landed on his head, killing himself instantly."

Mistress raised her hand to her mouth. "My Lord, how awful!"

The colonel had an amused expression.

The minister continued in a sinister tone, "Exactly one year later his wife did the same thing."

At that the colonel put his hand to his mouth to hide his smile.

"She too lost her mind," the minister said. "She removed her clothes, jumped off the roof of their home and died on the exact same spot as her husband."

The colonel was unable to contain himself any longer, he erupted into hysterical laughter. "I'm sorry," he said regaining his composure. The Colonel didn't give as much credence to religion as his wife did. "Maybe it was the heat or some peculiar sickness?"

"No, it was not," the minister said categorically. "Afterwards, the authorities found an Obeah ring and stick when they raided the slave cabins. Two Obeah women and one man were hanged. The slaves were converted to Christianity and the deceased couple's children live quite happily on their plantation today."

"I doubt the children are anything but happy after both of their parents jumped naked to their death from the roof of their house," the colonel added still giddy from his outburst.

"Well, as happy as possible," the minister added.

"Without Christianity there is only room for the devil," Mistress said, clearly uncomfortable with the account of the Negril couple. "Our slaves have been saved, brought from a pagan land to a Christian one. I want the slaves to be encouraged to cultivate religious feeling and morality and punished for inhumanity to their children or for profanity, lying and stealing. It is our duty."

She spent a few hours each day giving instructions to the "converts" and more than once said she was delighted with their behaviour.

"The blackies are quite enthusiastic. They behaved so properly during instruction today."

She never mentioned the whip that was waiting in the wings.

There was a date appointed when every slave would be baptised. Mistress made the event appear like a celebration. She killed a few hogs and offered meals and rum to those who accepted the baptismal offer. Most of the slaves agreed. A few like Burdan refused and were made work on Sundays. Others said it made no difference while Tariq and Phoebe pretended to submit to the mistress's wishes. The night before the baptismal, the Obeah man visited their cabins. He sang and chanted to deter the entry of the mistress's unknown Christian god.

With the success of the baptisms, Mistress turned her attention to the introduction of a Sunday service for the slaves. She asked the minister where she'd hold the service.

"Some plantations have their service at the front door of their house, some build small chapels," the minister explained.

"On the front lawn?" she interrupted him. Incredulously she glanced out the window at her perfect garden. "We couldn't possibly have it on the steps of the house. Some of our flowers have been imported from Asia. We have one hundred and fifty slaves. Imagine a hundred and fifty pairs of feet on our lawns!"

The Colonel interrupted them. "And we cannot have it during

harvesting when we need every pair of our one hundred and fifty hands to work every hour God gives us."

The Protestant service was in any case simpler than the ritual of the Catholic Mass and so I listened to the Antiguan minister's service beneath the largest tree in the slave quarters.

"A Christian slave makes a better cog in the wheel for his master," the minister preached to the slaves. "We make a better island for our master which makes a better commonwealth. When you are well behaved and carry out a diligent day's work, we are happier people in a happier country making a happier commonwealth."

Silently the slaves stood looking at the Antiguan.

"God meant for you to work in the Empire's fields of Jamaica. We are part of God's great plan to be part of the greatest Empire in the World."

The slaves did not believe the minister's preaching about a god who made them slaves. They kept alive their African culture, they consulted the Obeah man and followed his instructions. They gave their children African names, they continued their own African customs and preserved their identity.

Afterwards I heard Mistress say, "A wonderful reading, Minister. We are doing so much for our blackies."

She continued to gently coax the unconverted to join the Sunday gatherings. She appeared charitable and kind yet she was devoid of any empathy towards the slaves.

When Aliza, a field slave, gave birth to a boy who died three days later, Aliza did not appear to grieve according to Mistress Victoria.

"They are lesser than animals," she said. "Even a wild boar would cry for its young if it died. These women have children with various men and abandon the children as quickly. It's no great wonder so many die."

She didn't understand that for the first nine days of an infant's life, the African women did not believe a baby is part of this world. It was thought to be a wandering spirit or a visitor from the underworld. If a baby died during this time it was considered not to have existed.

Occasionally the Mistress treated me like a little plaything.

"Art, it's so pleasant to work with you. The other gardeners don't follow instruction as you do."

"Thank you, Mistress."

"Hapi is still keeping the house clear of horrid rats and spiders," she said to me. "The Colonel is equally as pleased as I am."

She asked me if I'd found any pearls. I lied and told her I'd lost interest in pearls. I hated my moments of foolishness when I thought Mistress was fond of me and enjoyed our time alone in the garden. Each day I reminded myself of who this couple was. I would not take my eye off them. My relationship with them reminded me of my fascination with the crocodile.

At night Tariq and I stalked the swamp to trap crocodiles. We drifted through the river on a raft, dragging a piece of meat. The floating crocodile's back was like a ripple of water barely visible beneath the surface. The sight of its blinking eyes excited and terrified me. Although I admired its gnashing teeth and ferocious strength, with one wrong move it could spring from the calm water and viciously pierce me with its sharp incisors before dragging me to the bottom of the swamp.

Watering plants in the pretty green room with Mistress and the Colonel talking to the minister, I thought of the crocodile. Someday I could be the crocodile and they the vulnerable boy.

CHAPTER TEN

In 1828, one man's loss became my fortune. The Colonel summoned me to his study at the height of the harvesting season.

He removed a logbook from his desk and opened it. "How old are you now, O'Neill?"

"Eighteen, sir," I said.

He noted it in the book. "I took the opportunity to look at your papers tonight and thought I'd enlighten you as we have a little emergency. I'll get to that in just a jiffy." He spoke in a hurried manner. "As you've served seven years with us, in seven years' time you will get your freedom which covers fourteen years of servitude. As an indentured servant you must pay for your passage from Ireland to Jamaica, then pay for your board and keep for the fourteen years." He spoke as if he had done me a favour by keeping me. "After that time you are free to leave, or remain with me as a paid overseer."

He closed the logbook and returned it to the drawer.

"I don't know if you're aware, but Acklen died tonight. Poor chap. This deceitful climate shows no mercy. He complained yesterday of feeling unwell."

Acklen was English. He'd worked on the Mangrove Plantation for the last four years. So now he was dead. Although I'd seen him only a few days previously, at that stage I'd seen so many die it was no longer a surprise.

"I'll need you to take his place as boss over the cane-cutters in the morning."

"Yes, sir," I said.

"In the morning McCovey will teach you what he knows. You can have Acklen's horse, his whip, his cabin and his garden of vegetables."

Acklen's vegetables were ready for sale at the market which was a great windfall. But I didn't want Acklen's cabin. I enjoyed living with Tariq and there were times I enjoyed Burdan's sullen moods. Most of all, I did not want Acklen's whip.

"Thank you, sir," I said again.

"There are some men who make bad overseers – take care you're not one of those," he warned. "In any case, you will have your freedom in seven years' time to do as you wish."

On the wall behind him was the map of the world. As he spoke about my terms of employment and freedom I looked towards Ireland, then I looked for the dot that was Jamaica. The tide between us was shifting.

WHEN I TOLD CIAN ABOUT MY NEW OVERSEER'S POSITION, HE LIFTED his hat and smiled at me. "I'm so glad the Lord let me live to see you get ahead before I die."

With every conversation, Cian made a reference to dying, yet he remained watching the plantation from his porch. Admittedly, with each passing month he grew weaker. He rarely left his veranda, his sight failed and he became tired after a brief conversation.

Now he had trouble getting around on his cane. The slaves built him a chair with wheels. Each Friday night I'd wheel him to the Big House for dinner.

"Did they give you a whip for your new role?" he asked.

I admitted they did and that I was reluctant to use it.

He nodded his head. "The life of an overseer is not an easy task. Remember, it is you who will pass judgement on the quality of your friends' work. You who will give the signal for the day's work to begin and end. You who must punish the slaves who rebel, even for minor discrepancies. Use your whip wisely."

I kept the whip affixed to my horse, unlike the other overseers and drivers. There were men who enjoyed using it – it was exciting, as thrilling for them as the moment before a man releases his seed into a woman.

"I hear you visit the cabin of the girl called Flora?" Cian said to me.

"Yes, I visit Flora," I admitted.

At eighteen years of age, I became a father.

Cian cautioned me. "You must not get attached. It'll break your heart when your child is gone. And she will be gone. Your child is coloured so she is the master's property. Your colour or rising status will not save your daughter."

I tried not to listen to him.

And despite Cian's warnings I got used to seeing the little girl called Arry. Her mother Flora, a beautiful mulatto slave, lived on the neighbouring plantation. Flora's mother was also a slave on the same plantation and renowned for the flutes she made from bamboo shoots. Flora was not like her quiet ingenious mother. She was fiery, and sometimes her wildness terrified and aroused me all at once. Occasionally she was kind and rational.

"The girl Flora was twice a runaway," Cian cautioned.

I'd heard the same and I'd seen the whip marks on her back.

"That's all changed now," I said. "She has a daughter – she is happy, she tells me."

"What is your child's name?" he asked.

"Arry," I replied.

She was three months old. Small and chubby and utterly trusting.

"You smile when you say her name." He sighed loudly. "Maybe

it's not such a bad thing to have a mulatto child anymore. Things might change. Your child has far more concessions than a Negro. If the abolitionists have their way, your little Arry will know freedom during her lifetime. Maybe you will become so rich you'll buy Flora and Arry's freedom."

Each time I visited Flora and Arry's cabin that thought occurred to me. Despite trying to keep my distance, I felt the pull each night to ride to them. I reminded myself that they were not mine, and never would be. I had done without so much I could do without their comforts again. I had known dreadful loneliness and told myself, if they were sold, there would be other Floras and other children. Although no child could replace my little Arry.

MIDWAY THROUGH HARVESTING SEASON I WAS MOVED TO THE SUGAR mill. McCovey told me to expect no more than five hours sleep a night. Our freshly cut cane had to be processed within four hours or it would rot. The cane was immediately fed into a crushing mill which squeezed the juices.

McCovey warned me to keep an eye on the slaves feeding the sugar cane to the crusher, "It's fed by hand and it's dangerous. If a mill-feeder gets caught by the little finger, his whole body is drawn in, and he is squeezed to pieces." He pointed to an axe at the base of the crusher. "Use this. Hopefully you'll only need to chop off a hand or an arm. If he's sucked in any further leave him."

"Can't we stop the mill?" I asked.

"Too costly – at the risk of the cane going bad and the juices spoiling, it'd be best to use the axe."

The dark brown juice from the crusher would flow by gravity through a trough directly into the boiling house. Only when I saw the boiling house did I understand Burdan's anger and scars. The heat was terrible and the task immensely specialised. Furnaces blazed around the clock in order to process the raw cane juice as fast as it could be harvested and crushed. The juice arrived directly into the first pan of a boiling train. Burdan and the other boilers would ladle the clarified juice into the first of a series of copper pans above the furnaces that never ceased burning until harvested ended in May. It was Burdan's job, as one of the boilers, to constantly skim impurities off the surface, and ladle the remaining liquid into the next copper pan. As the juice passed from one pan to the next, each pan was smaller in size and hotter than the last. With constant skimming and evaporation, the juice would turn into a dark brown, thick, ropey mass. At this point, the boiler, whose skill, experience, and timing were of paramount importance, dampened the fire and ladled the taffy-like substance into large cooling cisterns where it crystallised.

"As soon as one slave is injured or maimed, always have another ready to take his place," McCovey explained as he instructed me in the last phase of sugar-making.

The brown sugar was packed into barrels which were loaded onto racks in the curing house. Perforations in the cask bottoms allowed molasses to slowly drip out, where it was collected in a cistern or similar storage vat. After curing for a few weeks, the raw brown sugar was ready to be stored in a warehouse, ultimately being loaded onto sailing ships for transport to the metropolis.

McCovey picked up a handful of sugar. "Look – ready to be poured into the king's tea and drunk six thousand miles away."

Every piece of the sugar cane was used. The spent cane was used to keep the furnaces burning and the drippings from the processing sugar was fermented and distilled to make rum. Molasses and skimmings or other boiling residue, along with water, were allowed to sit in a fermenting vat for between two to twelve days.

"Longer than twelve days if you like your liquor stronger," McCovey said with a wink.

Even the vermin played their part. The vat was an open cistern so that cockroaches and rats would fall in, aiding the fermentation.

"One more thing," McCovey said, reverting to the stern voice he used with the slaves, "I want you out of those Negro clothes and that cabin tonight."

It was the second time he'd told me to take Acklen's cabin. I was still reluctant to leave Tariq and Burdan.

"It don't do well to live with the slaves and dress the same as them. Tonight," he repeated.

TARIQ AND BURDAN WERE THERE WHEN I GOT BACK THAT NIGHT. There wasn't a great deal of possessions to collect, only my assortment of pearls which were hidden in the garden. My only other possessions were the clothes I wore when I travelled to Jamaica. I don't know why I kept the Irish clothes because they didn't fit anymore. It was the texture of the wool that used to bring me comfort.

"Once this harvesting is over we'll go fishing," I said to Tariq.

Burdan looked over his shoulder and Tariq returned an uneasy glance. He nodded and regarded me quietly.

I told Tariq about the parrots I'd seen that day, chattering as they flew by. It was one of the first birds that Tariq trapped and cooked when I arrived. "There were loads of them," I told him. "Only this morning I was thinking about the soup we'd have when we trap them."

With the harvest and lack of sleep, I missed the simple pleasures I'd grown to love. I'd love to swim in the lagoon, and afterwards drink the parrot soup with Tariq.

"Yes," he said aloud, then added quietly, "Yes, sir."

My new role divided us, I had become "sir", the man who would call them to rise, send them to work and whip them.

Saddened, I left.

As I passed the lit fire in the slave quarters, I added my Irish clothes to the flames and smelled the smouldering wool as it burned another small link to my home.

CHAPTER ELEVEN

As an overseer, each Friday night I ate dinner with the Colonel, the overseers, Cian Donnell, Nurse Nancy, Mistress and any visitors.

Mistress sat beside me during those dinners.

"We miss you about the house now that you're an overseer," she said.

Once she confided in me that she found it difficult to eat beside McCovey. "He makes such noises, it's disturbing."

I saw her inspecting the cleanliness of the plates.

"Lucy is not washing the plates properly," she said loudly.

Regardless of what Lucy did, Mistress would find fault with it.

She was the Colonel's favoured slave. At least once a week he ordered her to the tack room and occasionally he visited her cabin.

Lucy had been removed but later reinstated. I knew from Mistress's voice she would be removed again.

During those dinners the Colonel would sit at the top of the table airing his opinions loudly. He discussed everything from his minor preferences to the politics of the day. He was most vocal when he discussed slavery and Irish politics. "The Irish are the most ungrateful race in the world, O'Neill – you had a lucky escape," he said to me. "The Act of

Union marked the Irish as a single people under a single king. The Irish don't see the honour in that Saint Patrick's flag has been added to Saint Andrew's. I'll bet Jimmy would be grateful to be a white Irishman." The Colonel was referring to the slave Jimmy who had received eighty lashes and was locked in the hot hole. He had attempted to run away.

Quietly I seethed, my hatred intensifying with each utterance that left his lips.

"The supreme system of English justice has been extended to cover all of His Majesty's subjects, including the subordinate Irish. The Irish receive the benefits of the most advanced culture in the world yet they continue to rebel."

On and on he talked while everyone nodded politely except McCovey. When there was lull in the conversation, the only noise was McCovey noisily eating. His face rarely lifted until he was finished. Then he'd loudly belch before gulping wine and smoking cigars. He was so overweight his eyes were squeezed between fat cheeks and overhanging eyelids.

Sexton was the second overseer. He was sent to Jamaica by his uncle to see how the Caribbean plantations were run. He too found the Colonel a bore. "That bastard loves the sound of his own voice," he regularly whispered to me. Like a lot of white men living in Jamaica, Sexton was a conflicted man.

"This country has a way of getting into your head," he regularly said.

Mostly he lived a quiet life for weeks on end. During his time off he could be seen on his porch reading and was rumoured to attend a church in Black River on Sundays. It was difficult to believe a man with such a nature could take the hot irons to a slave and brand them with such little feeling. Occasionally Sexton would become restless, he'd begin drinking and take a few slave women before departing to town for few more days of debauchery. After his escapade he'd return to his old pious self, loathing everything in his sight but mainly his own behaviour.

"These darkie women and their luscious bodies should be locked away," Sexton moaned. "These women shave the hair from their genitals – how's a man supposed to behave morally with that kind of knowledge?'"

I didn't have the answers he sought.

"In South Carolina they're locked up from sunset to sunrise," he said. "These darkies in Jamaica have it easy. They go fishing and hunting and can make a few dollars on their gardens of vegetable and fruit."

DESPITE THE TALK OF ABOLITIONISTS GAINING GROUND, THE Colonel continued to buy slaves. As an overseer I accompanied him and Sexton to the sales.

"Many years ago, when I came out here as a boy, I would accompany my grandfather to the slave auctions," the Colonel said the first time. "I learned the worst slaves to buy are the ones directly off the ships. The breaking-in period can be problematic. The best slaves are those bred on the plantation. Seasoning those slaves takes time, and time is money. Out of four slaves bought off the ship, do you know how many survive?" The Colonel looked from Sexton to me.

"One," Sexton said.

The Colonel held up his finger. "That's right, one out of every four survives to be a good slave. It's a costly business. It's more diffi-cult to tame a slave than an animal. Although Twinton, our dear neighbour, is shipping most of his slaves to America, which is not legal yet some men continue to flout the law. Twinton isn't as afraid of the law as he is of the abolitionists. Slaves have the capacity to hate in a way an animal is not capable of. They can be vindictive. They are inclined to have predatory and manipulative instincts that are foreign to an animal."

"The abolitionists are making waves," Sexton said. "They disagree with the whip. They say the legal number of strokes is thirty-nine." He looked towards me and winked.

"Nonsense," the Colonel retorted. "It is only deluded men who set thirty-nine strokes as the maximum. They do not know what it is to live in this hostile country. The do-gooders in London are not risking life and limb as we are."

During the auctions, the Colonel looked for men-boys and girls not exceeding eighteen years of age.

"Full-grown men and women seldom turn out well and, besides, the men are so well polished by the seller that it's impossible to gauge their age. Some Negroes appear solid and sleek but can fall away to nothing with misery."

There were two types of slave sales: organised auctions and scrambles. The scrambles were brutal. It was a free-for-all where the planters scrambled and fought for the slaves they wanted. The slaves would scream as they were dragged from their families and their buyers fought like sailors. Some saw it as a sport.

The auctions were more civilised. The Colonel would walk among the slaves before the sale, pulling their mouths open and pinching their limbs to find how muscular they were. He walked them up and down to detect any sign of lameness, making them stoop and bend in different ways to be certain there was no concealed rupture or wound.

The return journey to the plantation with the new slaves was a conflicting trip. Their oppressed silence was overwhelming. Their suspicious eyes darted from Colonel to me and Sexton. I'd be lying if I said there weren't times when I was impressed with my new role as overseer. The whip fastened to my belt made them see me as a man of authority.

IT WAS NOT ALL WORK. SUNDAYS WERE MINE. AFTER SUNDAY service, Ned Doyle and I rode out of the plantation, bursting with gaiety, hot on the scent of rum and ale houses. Our drinking companions were white overseers from other plantations, soldiers and the clients of the rum houses of Black River and neighbouring towns. We were at the age when we were impressed with our own masculinity. We pursued women, rum, song and dance, and realised we were men with a future closed to all of our coloured friends. I explored the locality and learned about the local plantations. I ventured into the hills and drank with the Maroons who hid in the forests.

Occasionally I'd go to the pier and see the Irish arrive in their droves. They came as indentured servants. Most had sold their souls and didn't realise it until it was too late. I'd ask them where they came from – Limerick, Sligo, Tipperary. When I'd meet the men from Kerry, I'd buy them a drink and trade stories from home. I was dismayed to learn my country remained as battered as the day I left. They fled the hunger and oppression of Ireland for work and the promise of land and, ultimately, survival. They worked hard and drank when they could. During those years I realised that Jamaica was a paradise only for a white man with a little money.

For them, it offered the best hunting, fishing and women in a country without judgement.

There were plenty of women, but none offered the sanctuary of Flora's little cabin. Flora's belly was big with another child and her behaviour increasingly troubling. Flora ran away with Arry, then she left Arry and ran away again. She was whipped, then whipped again. She told me she'd be free yet. She'd be free in the mountains with the Maroons. Each time I held Arry tighter.

As time passed I rebuked myself for growing so fond of Arry. Each night when she'd lie into my chest I was ashamed I loved her as I did. While so many white men fathered children and watched them at a distance or favoured them slightly, I adored my daughter. The sight of her toothless grin and her hazel eyes looking into mine melted everything else into a nothingness.

But Flora was a problem that seemed to worsen as time passed.

CHAPTER TWELVE

In mid-November 1829 as a hurricane approached and we rushed in frenzied attempts to prepare, I noticed Cian remained seated on his porch, making no effort to take cover. Gently I shook him. His arm flopped and swayed at his side. I carried him into his cabin and laid him on the bed. I wiped the rain from his face and the tears from mine.

Despite the roads turning to small streams from the monsoons, Cian's mourners arrived in their droves. There were black, white and mulatto mourners. Even two Maroons came out of hiding in the mountains with gifts of a pig and fowl. They moved freely among the grievers and went unrecognised as the Colonel and his wife came to pay their respects. There was wine, rum and food flowing for twenty-four hours. The mourners sprinkled rum and left out a glass of water for his spirit as they danced and sang by his body all day and night.

They talked at length about his life. Some argued he was actually a hundred and fifty years of age. Cian's birthday on the 25th December was much discussed, as were the herbs he took for every ailment which gave him longevity, and his Irish and African ancestry.

As I watched his body being buried in the slave cemetery, Flora gave birth to my son. I called him Seán.

"Me have picked Delia for yuh wen I'm nursin Seán," Flora informed me.

During breastfeeding, in order to avoid a new pregnancy which would interfere with the nourishment of the first child, it was permissible for men to lie with a sweetheart chosen by our women.

I'd left Ireland as a child, too young to become acquainted with some Irish customs – like the idea that a man lying with any woman apart from his wife was an abomination.

"Only lay wid Delia," Flora warned, "or me tell de Obeah man to put a spell on yuh."

I was amused by her jealousy.

"Obeah man will make yuh manhood fall off," she teased me.

I accepted the offer and did visit Delia's cabin, and those of many more women who were not chosen by Flora.

On Friday night during our weekly dinner with the Colonel, we discussed the week's yield and Cian's true age.

"They weren't fit for a great deal after Cian's burial," Colonel said when he heard about the poor week's work. "I never heard such singing and carousing in my life."

"Some say he was 100 years of age," I said, hoping he'd shed a little light on the true figure. I didn't dare mention Tariq's suggestion about his age.

"He was eighty-nine years old, the oldest man I ever knew," the Colonel proclaimed. "I rooted out the old logbook that my great-grandfather kept. He was a methodical old boy who logged everything."

The Colonel retrieved the book and scanned through the entries.

"There we are," he said, his finger tapping the entry. "Cian Donnell, born 25th December 1740. Longevity appears to run in his family." He flicked to the front of the logbook. "His grandfather, also Cian Donnell, came to this island as a boy. He was approximately ten years of age in 1658 when my great-grandfather acquired this plantation. He was one of the first batch of slaves to arrive. He lived to the grand age of eighty-four. An unheard age in the 1730s when he died. And Cian's eighty-nine years is a new lifespan in this era."

"Strong as horses," McCovey said.

"I must make a note of his age and use it in my next article to the *London Times*," the Colonel said. "This week I submitted an article to it lest the men of parliament think we're lolling here on our posteriors in the sun."

He constantly referred to articles he'd submitted to journals and newspapers.

"In my article I told them how much a slave cost, the likelihood of survival and their yield of work. I've paid fifty pounds for that new carpenter from the Palatial Plantation." He was referring to the plantation where Flora and Arry and my new son lived. "I need to invest in new slaves to increase the profits."

When McCovey had finished eating and drinking, he got up from the table and wiped his mouth with the back of his hand.

"Incidentally, that runaway girl slave we found on the fringes of Luana belonged to Palatial Plantation."

"What girl?" I asked.

"She was a mulatto with a little child at her breast. She'd covered good ground – apparently she'd only been gone two hours."

"What the Negros lack in intellect, they have in strength," Sexton said.

While they deliberated over the strength of slave women compared to white women, I thought about Flora and hoped she had not returned to her old ways. My skin prickled at the thought, not for her but for Arry.

"Was she alone?" I asked. "Apart from the infant?"

"Yes, she was alone and very determined wherever she was going."

. . .

THAT NIGHT I GALLOPED TO FLORA'S CABIN. I SAW HER LYING ON her belly. There were a few women gathered round rubbing paste onto her wounds. Little Arry's face was wet from crying. I picked her up in my arms and looked into her hazel eyes. Cian was right: my children would never be mine. They were at the mercy of their masters – and their mothers. I had lost so much at a young age. I could not recall what my own mother looked like. It was my father's step during the court hearing I heard, his long beard and dishevelled appearance, and occasionally his voice in song returned to me. So many intimate details from the past had faded. It was increasingly likely that Arry and my son Seán would also vanish from my life. They too would never recall my features or peculiarities. It was only a matter of time before they were sold. It would be easier to walk away now. I would allow their god to direct their lives.

I put Arry out of my arms and looked at Flora. She moaned in pain.

"Mama got whipped," Arry said. "She runned away."

I looked at Flora.

"Make Mama bettar," Arry said.

I doubted the Lord himself could make Mama better.

CHAPTER THIRTEEN

There is a moment before a slave is whipped when everything seems to stop. There is no conversation about the fruit in their garden or Sunday's market. Even the children stop talking, instinctively sensing the brutality about to befall one of their own. The day after Flora ran away I rounded up the slaves to witness a whipping.

The only sound was Birky, the gardener, as his feet shuffled. He was tied to a peach tree on raised ground with his back exposed. His breath was heavy with terrified anticipation. Frantically he twisted, trying to look over his shoulder. Birky was suspected of stealing some of the garden tools. I knew he'd borrowed them to work on his own garden. He'd return them the following day.

Sexton was about to whip him when McCovey took the whip from him and passed it to me.

"Fifty lashes, O'Neill," McCovey ordered me.

I hesitated. Birky was my old friend who worked on the gardens with me.

McCovey stepped aside to watch as if it were sport.

I looked into the crowd and saw Tariq looking at me under his eyebrows. Burdan was standing at the front, his arms folded as if daring me to begin.

I cracked the whip, putting off the inevitable. I looked at Birky's exposed black shiny back. There were several criss-crossed raised scars from previous whippings. I was loath to reopen his old wounds. When I heard his feet shuffling again and saw him trying to look over his shoulder, I knew it was more torturous to delay. I struck him once. His back arched with pain. I repeated it, and I whipped him again and a fourth time. Birky released a long loud cry.

"We're going to be here all day if you don't hurry up," McCovey said. "Fifty times, O'Neill, not one lash less."

A country that practices such cruelties against one colour of people becomes heartless to all tender feelings. We can reject anything that dignifies our nature, including my daughter Arry's sudden kiss. Any man that does not learn to flog without mercy will lose his authority. I was aware of this. The whip I used placed me in a new category.

"Twelve," McCovey was counting. "Hurry up, O'Neill – you're not doing him any favour by dragging it out."

I increased the pace and ignored Birky's cries for mercy.

I had to believe then that the normal rules of behaviour did not apply in Jamaica. It went against everything I felt yet I continued. Who had I become?

"Eighteen."

A boy from an impoverished tenant farm in a country that enslaves another. A man who whips his friend to spare his own back? Would my father have thrived in this lawless country? My mother would not look. Like Phoebe and the other women, she'd wait for the ordeal to end and clean Birky's sores and help them heal with kindness.

"Twenty," McCovey continued counting.

My uncles would lie in wait for me and not think twice about killing me if I was doling out a whipping to any of the men from Mein.

"Twenty-five."

The sweat dripped down my face and wet my shirt.

"Thirty."

Had any man who shared my blood ever done something as

criminal to his old friend? How many men handed their daughters back to their mothers to spare them the pain of inevitably losing them? But if they lived in this unforgiving cruel land where the coloured man was treated as inhumanely as if he were a beast, they might do as I did.

"Thirty-five."

Did it matter what my Irish family thought? They lived in a green island where they were the black man, they were the oppressed majority. I had become the oppressive minority.

"Forty."

I had passed great seas and must survive to tell my own tale. With each lash I was widening the great ocean that separated us. The whip I used had transformed me into another breed of another man in another country. This scorched colony that God had not yet found. An island adrift where the norm did not apply, a country that wanted to Christianise, but plundered, chastised and demonised a dignified people. Jamaica, the dot of an island, was now my only home.

"Fifty." McCovey was at my side.

DESPITE MY BEST INTENTIONS TO STAY AWAY FROM FLORA, I WAS unable.

Hubert, the overseer on Flora's plantation, promised me he would do what he could to protect her which in turn would protect Arry and Sean.

"Flora is a nuisance," he said angrily. "She makes my job harder and she is a problem I could do without."

I no longer cared about Flora. Her fieriness was no longer attractive, it was worrisome. I knew she would run away again. I'd seen it on my own plantation. The systematic runaways rarely stopped unless the overseer removed a limb. Only then did their craziness become more contained but it never entirely died.

"I will keep Flora because she will breed again and she's a good worker but I don't want problems," Hubert said pointedly and looked at me. "I will do what I can to ensure she remains."

Each day I visited Flora. I brought weeds and flowers that were beneficial to babies.

"Yuh goin' on like a woman," Flora said. "Soon yuh will let Seán suckle yuh breast."

At night Flora cooked the fish that I caught. Arry would sit on my knee and eat out of my hands. I'd sing little songs I'd learned as a boy and songs I heard the slaves sing to their children. I took Flora, Arry and Seán to the springs by the rocks to help her recover and to indoctrinate my children into the habit that brought Cian a long healthy life. I took such secret delight in watching Arry splash and roll in the stream. I watched Flora in a different way. Although her references to running away were rare, she still spoke of escaping to the Maroons in the mountains. I told her they were too far away and she'd be captured and whipped again, maybe even sold. She shrugged indifferently while I held Arry.

"If you run away again, you will be sold, so will Arry and so will Seán. At the slave auction your children will be sold separately. You will never see them again."

Flora remained impassive. She was beautiful, maybe too beautiful.

"They might not sell you," I said, lowering my voice. "They might hang you and sell Arry and Seán. The slaves sold last week were sent abroad. In the cotton fields of America you are locked up from evening till morning. You have the liberty to go to the market or bathe in the springs in this country. America is different. What will they do to Arry?" I repeated our daughter's name, more terrified of the reality than I cared to admit. "Arry will be treated like an animal and they will do to her what a man cannot do to an animal." I spoke slowly, wanting her to understand. "Do you hear me?"

She didn't respond. I looked at her downcast eyes and acknowledged that some people found enslavement more difficult than others. Flora was one of those who would risk humiliation and the cruellest of punishments and even death to find freedom. It was that indomitable spirit I loved, the spirit that eventually tired me. In another country or as anything but a Negro slave her spirit would have been praised.

Then the angry edges to her face faded and she appeared remorseful and accepting. She didn't speak but nodded quietly.

CHAPTER FOURTEEN

For a few years life ambled along in an uneventful way. There were births, deaths and marriages. There were whippings and hangings, slave auctions, new recruits and more deaths, some living as if disease would consume them that very hour.

The Colonel told me he was satisfied with my work and gave me five acres of land to use. During my spare time I worked on my land. I kept pigs and poultry and grew mangoes, plantain, ackee, okra and yam. I began to accumulate money and thought of the land I would buy. At times like that I was pleased I'd spared the Colonel.

Ned Doyle did not have the vengeful veins that coursed through my body. He was more inclined to accept his life and found joy in the simple offerings. He became head driver in the sugar-cane fields and was given three acres of land to use as he pleased. When he became a father he gave his firstborn son an Igbo name.

There was little change in the Colonel or the Mistress's life. Their friends continued to visit, their children grew, they had their parties and time passed. The Colonel had the plantation to keep him occupied and Lucy, his favoured slave. Mistress kept busy with her flowers and paintings or instructing the slaves how to clean.

When we met she always seemed pleased to see me.

"How are you, Art?" she asked one such day.

"Very well, Mistress."

"Isn't this weather just horrid?" she said, fanning her face. "I can't bear to go outside until night."

I agreed.

She had one eye on me and another on Betty who was polishing the stairs. Lucy had been sent to the fields again. According to Mistress she could not follow basic cleaning instructions. It was pointless where they put Lucy – the Colonel would always seek her out.

"Not like that, Betty!" Mistress clapped her hands impatiently. "Push your nail into the groove!"

Mistress complained about the domestic slaves, complained about the weather, her house, the country. The years had hardened her, with circumstances that were as crushing and immovable as slavery. There was little for her to do, except to think about dust in the corners of her house and ridicule the slaves.

"I can't imagine the state of their cabins," she said. "These slaves are a slovenly dirty breed."

A few days later I mentioned Phoebe, the girl who cleaned my cabin. I told mistress how Phoebe looked after the babies and none had died since she took responsibility.

"She washes everything," I said.

"She could only be better than the current slave," Mistress sighed.

Although Phoebe could not speak as well as the domestic staff and had never carried a tray, I knew she'd learn quickly. The moment Mistress saw her she knew her husband would not be inclined to take a fancy to her voluptuous frame – he preferred the petite slaves. Phoebe was a stout, earnest, capable young woman, and a great confidante of mine. Everything that happened in the slave quarters during the day she relayed to me. My need to know as much as I could about the Colonel and his wife was a sickness, akin to a monster I fed. The more I learned, the more I wanted to know. I was comfortable with my detestation of them. I needed to see their failings and hear their horrid normalities. I scolded myself for this urgency to find out as much as I could. I wanted to rid myself of the need to know, yet I could only survive by exhausting myself with snippets of information about their lives.

Phoebe met me at my cabin. "De mistress say I'm gonna work in de Big House."

She was surprised and eager.

I warned Phoebe that she must never divulge any gossip or anything newsworthy from the Big House to anyone. I warned her about the petty jealousies among the domestic slaves and if one word of talk left her mouth it would get back to the Mistress and she'd be returned to minding the small children in the slave quarters.

Her earnest eyes listened as I instructed her.

"News from the Big House must remain between you," I spoke slowly so she'd understand, "between the Colonel and the Mistress," I pointed at my chest, "and me. You must tell me everything."

Before she began I instructed her how to clean Mistress's room, how she must use her forefinger to clean every corner of the room and get her nails into the groves in the stairs.

Phoebe listened before nodding once.

A week later when I met Mistress, she was cheerful and grateful.

"She's the ideal slave," Mistress declared. "Aside from my Irish maids, Phoebe is perfect."

Mistress told me this as we stood in the Blue Room. Phoebe was standing on a ladder with a blue patterned material draped over the window.

"Not only is Phoebe amenable, she has a natural flair for cleaning."

Phoebe fed my obsession for the Mistress and fuelled my hatred for the Colonel. She told me how Mistress rose each morning at seven and began her day by reading her prayers. She told me when Mistress and the Colonel shared a bed.

"Wen me brought Mistress breakfast, me see wid me own eyes de Masta did not sleep in his bed last night," Phoebe relayed in a loud whisper at the back of her cabin. "Two nights dis week de Masta sleep in Mistress bed."

I thanked her for telling me and reminded her again not to discuss it with anyone.

WITH EACH PASSING MONTH MY RESPONSIBILITIES AS AN OVERSEER increased. I grew confident in my role. Whipping the slaves was never pleasant. It was the only task I did reluctantly although I never showed my averseness.

Sexton remained conflicted and continued the same pattern of living. He worked diligently for several weeks before his need to hit the grog overwhelmed him. In 1831 Sexton went on a six-day drinking bender. I worked from sunrise to sunset covering his job and my own. On the sixth day when Sexton appeared for work McCovey relieved me from my duties for the day. I bathed in the sea for a while and afterwards I sat on the rocks and allowed the sun to dry me slowly.

It had been a long few days. As I rode my horse at an easy pace I remember thinking my six days' absence from Flora was possibly beneficial. I hoped it had frightened her into believing that I was not prepared to tolerate her behaviour. Flora never doubted my dependability. It was not her who raised my spirits but Arry who was now three. Seán was too young to fill me with the warmth that Arry did. My beautiful wonderful Arry. Some evenings I'd bring her a pearl from the sea. Her small fingers would examine it on the palm of my hand, her face uncharacteristically still as she inspected it.

"Dis is me treasure," she'd finally say and add it to the other pearls she'd gathered.

Occasionally she was bold. When I'd ask for one hug too many, she was direct in her refusal. "Get away, me too busy for yuh today."

I loved it – even the boldness was endearing.

Maybe Cian was right and my daughter and son would know freedom. I planned to buy their freedom. When I thought about our future it did not involve Flora. I knew Flora would never see old age.

In my fanciful daydreams only Arry and Seán were present. I indulged in foolish little moments when I imagined taking them to Ireland. I imagined the sea and telling them about my first voyage as a boy, mesmerised with the flying fish. Of course I kept those farfetched notions to myself.

On that day I travelled through the woods to their cabin and approached it from a height. It resembled the villages in Ireland with a cluster of houses built around a small square. Opposite Flora's house lived an old slave called Pompey. He was sitting on the porch and went into his house when he saw me arrive. Sensing something was wrong, I stood at the threshold of Flora's cabin and pushed open the door. I waited to hear their voices and the patter of Arry's feet as she ran to greet me. It was soundless. Slowly I stepped inside. A lone mouse scurried across the cabin, then as if changing its mind it doubled back. I stood in the empty cabin before rushing over to Pompey's.

He cowered away from me. "Me not want any trouble."

"Where is Flora?" I demanded.

"Yuh Flora, she run away."

I left Pompey and found Hubert, the overseer.

"She left the two children behind. I went looking for you for the last two days. I couldn't do anything. I had to sell them."

I lunged at him.

"You couldn't have done anything either!" he yelled at me as we struggled. "You don't have the money to buy them and we can't keep them! Flora cost money and now she's gone!"

Hubert told me the children had been sent to Savanna la Mar. I knew of one slave trader in Savanna – Irish Ignatius. Most slaves passed through his hands.

I left immediately, hoping Ignatius still had the children.

"If you see the girl Flora, tell her I'll cut her leg off this time!" Hubert shouted after me. "That should fix her!"

CHAPTER FIFTEEN

There is a time in every man's life when he walks into a storm and risks life and limb for something he can't explain. Something forces him through the storm. It might be duty, or love, or hate or necessity to find the fragments of peace that allow him to live. For six months I sat with men I loathed. I bought them drink to coax information from them about my children's whereabouts.

That first day the Irish slave trader Ignatius Duffy said he remembered the children but swore he didn't have them and hadn't bought or sold them. He thought it strange I should be looking for my mulatto child.

"She's not white," he stated the obvious.

"She's mine," I said.

He told me there was a scramble three days before.

"Can't rightly remember what happened to them. I would have bought the girl but she was gone. I grabbed what I could and sailed to America the same day."

I closed my eyes at the thought of men rushing to snatch Arry during the scramble. I imagined her terror.

"The Americans have no plans to end slavery," Ignatius continued. "Might buy myself a little holding and move there."

I bought him a drink and listened to him, hoping he'd reveal some specific details. Anything other than not knowing.

He talked about America. "Different people. Country is different too." He looked at his reflection in the mirror behind the bar. When his eyes moved to my despairing face, he promised he'd do what he could.

"She'll be a real beauty in a few years," he said, "a pretty girl like that …" He didn't finish what he was saying.

From that day, every free moment I had I spent on my horse travelling to every plantation describing Arry and Seán. Occasionally Ned Doyle accompanied me, mostly I preferred to be alone. At night I would fall on my bed drunk from grief and rum. When I imagined Arry's terror at the scramble I swallowed more rum to chase away the thoughts. Each day I'd work and in the evenings I'd climb on my horse and begin again.

There were times when I felt they were gone from me forever and my efforts were futile but movement kept the terrible thoughts at bay. I was too frightened to sit still and allow the cascade of horrors to tumble upon me. While I saddled my horse for the evening ahead I was occupied and, with each menial task I did for those moments, the thought of Seán and Arry left me.

The last hour of daylight was the most valuable time of day, when the slaves were working on their gardens or gathered in their quarters at ease after the day's work. It was the time of day when the overseer had more time to talk. I went to the Maroons for their help. I offered them my bags of pearls which they looked at with indifference – bartering them would be too difficult for the distrusted maroons. I said I could not offer money now for Arry or Seán's reward but swore I would be indebted to them forever and would somehow pay them for their help.

Memories of my late evenings with Arry pushed me harder. When I closed my eyes I recalled her touch, how she'd fit into the groove of my arm and eat her meals with her fingers from my bowl. I kept her treasure of pearls. At night I'd roll them in my hands, sense their coldness and finger the ridges. Their texture had a calming effect.

I rode through all kinds of weather and strangely the most comforting weather was the early windy mornings. There was a welcome relief in the storm as it torpedoed around me. In some way I hoped it would take me away with it, suck me into its gullies and cast me to the ocean to drown.

I hallucinated from rum and exhaustion. In the horrors from drink I thought I saw people and animals sitting at the foot of my bed feasting on my feet. When I reached out to touch them, there was nothing there only my trembling hand sinking through my mirage of chattering people.

My role as overseer was not fulfilled. There were times when McCovey came to my cabin. He arrived once while I was dozing. I kept my eyes closed. I was too miserable to rouse myself from my despairing state. I expected him to drag me from my bed – instead he placed food and water by my bed before leaving again.

During those months I attended slave auctions and scrutinised every child. I listened as the Colonel talked about his plantation and ideas.

"I have faith in the Empire – slavery is far from over."

Despite the talk of abolitionists, the Colonel continued to buy slaves. On the return journey from the auctions, it was my daughter's eyes I saw. I smiled at the new slaves and hid my whip.

It was three months after their disappearance when they found Flora in a disused barn in Santa Cruz.

The same afternoon, McCovey's faithful dog broke its back. It lay whimpering on the ground. McCovey bent down to inspect the dog. "She's knackered," he said and took a shotgun from his cabin.

He bent and stroked the dog before holding the gun to its head and firing. I would gladly have lain down beside the dog and asked McCovey to give me a moment's kindness and then shoot me. "They reckon that slave woman who was found in the barn was

Flora," McCovey informed me as he picked up the dead dog to bury it. "Same height as your girl, same colour and age."

Flora's death was "occasioned by the visitation of God". So said her death certificate.

My love of rum finally overrode my desire for everything else. No matter how hard I tried, I always found my mouth around the neck of a bottle within a few days, not knowing why or how I could have succumbed to temptation. There were days I didn't miss it, then suddenly I would be overcome with the need to guzzle a bottle of rum. There were times when I'd drop what was in my hand and chase the scent of rum. I'd welcome the warm liquid as I poured it down my neck, the sense of relief sweeping into every part of my body and finally bringing me oblivion. Stupefied on rum, I'd forget. I had no cares or worries until I opened my eyes the following morning.

Finally I returned to my cabin with five bottles of rum and a remedy I hoped would see my soul pass over Ireland one more time as it fled to its eternal resting place.

Five days later when I woke, Ned, Phoebe and Tariq were by my side. I could hear them coughing at the smell in my cabin. Everything inside me had poured out of my orifices, soiling the bed where I lay. The stench that had gathered while I lay in my bed was intolerable.

I could hear Phoebe's voice. "I boil him's clothes and clean him's cabin."

"Is alright, man," Tariq's voice said.

They were moving me from the bed.

During the following few days I drifted in and out of sleep. The Obeah man came to me in my dreams, so too did my youngest brother, Hugh. In my dreams I saw him at the front of our cabin chasing the frogs. When I woke I thought I was in Ireland.

"Him raving," I heard a woman say.

"He'll be fine in a few days." I recognised Ned's voice.

I finally woke alone in my cabin. I walked from the bed to my veranda. Like an animal unsteady on its feet after the mother of all fights, I moved cautiously. Slowly I walked down to the slave quarters, through the village and stood at the foot of the hill with the mountains behind me. I sat on a rock and watched a grass snake slowly meander through the long blades. Sensing my presence, it stopped and raised its head before moving slowly forward.

It was not yet bright, that time of day when we are suspended between darkness and light. Some slaves believe the spirits are most active then. I watched the day break and realised I had one chance of survival. That morning I spoke to God. I asked the African God, the Igbo, the Protestant Christian God, the Catholic God and the many gods I'd heard the slaves implore, I begged each for help to stay away from the rum and survive.

That morning as the sun pushed its way over the sea, I thought of the boy I was, the boy who stepped onto this island, and the man I became. Mostly a fearless man yet one who allowed rum to become my infinite master.

I prayed for Arry and Seán, and I even prayed for poor crazy Flora.

At the sound of the bell to rouse the slaves from their beds I got to my feet and looked towards the skies.

"Help me begin again."

CHAPTER SIXTEEN

I got on with my life, I worked and lived and survived. I worked on my own five acres. There were times when I'd think incessantly about Arry and Seán. I'd ride out of the plantation in the hope of hearing something. As time passed I began to believe I'd never again see my children. To banish these thoughts I worked harder, only stopping when my body could not continue. With the same determination, I'd fight off the temptation of the rum and ale houses. It was a daily battle fought each minute at a time.

I found temporary solace beneath the water. I'd pick oysters, open them and search their tissue for pearls. Reluctant to give up hope, I set aside the best pearls for Arry. Gradually the rum and ale houses moved out of my line of vision and little pleasantries replaced them.

My oldest friends pushed me forward without me noticing. Ned Doyle and I worked together, his presence and our shared past offered me a strange sense of security. Tariq and I resumed fishing and hunting together. He appeared at times when I found myself aimlessly wandering about the plantation fighting the urges to flee to the nearest alehouse.

I began to call to Myrtle's cabin, a slave who was everything Flora was not. She was solid and accepting.

Sexton left the plantation. He claimed he'd had enough of Jamaica, the luscious tempting women and his decadent lifestyle. He returned to America.

"I'll find myself a nice bride and marry," he said.

I shook his hand on the pier and wished him well.

The Colonel gave me the five acres of land Sexton had been using. In addition I had my own crops on my land and I was paid sixty pounds a year as an overseer. I became second in command to McCovey, and Ned Doyle became the third overseer.

Despite gaining so much from the Colonel my hatred never subsided. My desire to kill him was constant although there were times it was not so intense. Like the rum and ale houses, it drifted like a ship into the sea until there was nothing but the vague outline on the distant horizon. It never went completely out of sight but remained, an obscure murderous notion that could raise me from my bed as if the ship had anchored outside my window and had blown its horn into my cabin.

THE COLONEL'S FLOCK GREW. I WATCHED HIS CHEST SWELL WITH pride at the sight of his growing boys, and his last child, a daughter called Beatrice.

Little Beatrice with her mass of blonde hair was so like Blair in appearance. Then, at two years of age, when they thought Beatrice had passed the perilous age, she succumbed to dysentery and died. I was unable to feel sorry for the Colonel when he delayed the burial for one day to sit with his dead child. In some perverse way it brought me pleasure, his grief reminding me he was not immune to losing his children.

There were times I was sick with hate.

Fleetingly, I hoped the Widow McAuliffe's curse would work. I wished the Colonel's life was slowly progressing towards the hour that one of his offspring would kill him. I looked at Blair and

Ernest. Although endearing at that age, their appeal could not last. They too would grow into arrogant self-serving men like their father.

THEN BURDAN, MY OLD CABIN MATE, TRIED TO THROW THE COLONEL into the vat of boiling molasses. He didn't succeed in killing him but left him with excruciating burns on his back and arms. He was unable to leave his chamber for three weeks. I'd watch him squirm in agony when I visited once a week to discuss plantation business.

After the incident Burdan fled. Through gritted teeth the Colonel gave murderous instructions on how I was to round up a search party and find Burdan. I was to keep him alive and torture him. I was to remove all of his limbs to deny him any hope of meeting his ancestors in the next life. He regretted not whipping Burdan weekly.

"I should have sold that boy. I knew his mother. Those vengeful darkies!" he cried.

Imagining the scene in the boiling house when the Colonel's flesh sizzled brought me endless pleasure.

I FOUND BURDAN WITHOUT THE SEARCH PARTY. HE WAS SLEEPING BY the lagoon. I brought him food and a horse. I rode with him to the foot of the Cockpit Country Mountains. He would find refuge with the Maroons. With such fervent talk of abolition and the imminent slave uprisings, Burdan would be a good addition to the insurgents.

"Yuh not too bad for a white boy," were his parting words to me.

ONCE A WEEK I ATE WITH THE COLONEL AT THE PLANTATION. OUR guests varied – some died or moved on, others joined us but none stayed as long as I did. The Colonel remained at the top of the table dominating the conversation. He talked endlessly about his fruitful plantation, his capable children, his cane fields and his productive slaves. As time passed his words did not carry the conviction they once had.

His anger at the abolitionists never waned. "Let them live out here as we do or let their sons join the English forces and hear about our death-defying lives."

Every few years there were new concerns. In the early 1830s there was growing concern for any white man in authority. The insurgents were gaining sympathy and their star was rising rapidly. The sound of a shotgun late at night would make the Colonel call for extra security.

He was equally as vocal in his detestation of the new mission-aries who were accused of feeding hopes of freedom to the blacks.

"They should be rounded up, placed on a ship and dispatched from the Jamaican shores as quick as be damned."

McCovey dropped dead over dinner. He was so enormous it took six men to carry him out of the house. I was sorry that McCovey had died, as were many of the slaves.

Mistress sighed. "I'd grown fond of McCovey. At times I didn't hear him eat anymore. My ears must have grown immune to his noisy table manners."

At twenty-one years of age, I was made head overseer. Ned Doyle was my deputy.

The falling prices of sugar cane and competition from other islands dented the Colonel's profits. There was no longer any need for a third overseer.

"I might not remain in this chaotic little paradise much longer," the Colonel said.

It was the first time he had mentioned leaving.

The possibility of a revolt was imminent. That week the slaves in several plantations including Mangrove Plantation dropped their tools and refused to work. It was a strike led by the enslaved Baptist preacher Samuel Sharpe. They wanted more freedom and payment for their work. They had heard false rumours that they were free but that their masters refused to liberate them.

"I've given this country all I have," he sighed in dejection. "The well is dry."

At times like that I was pleased I'd allowed him live for the simple pleasure of watching his new despondency.

CHAPTER SEVENTEEN

December 1831 was the beginning of the end for the Colonel and his ilk. We heard the first shots of the rebellion on Christmas Day.

Mistress and the children were sent to the secret chamber below the floors in the study.

The Colonel fled from the mill and ordered me to go with him.

"The darkies are fond of you, O'Neill," he said as we hid in the rocks by the sea. "They'll listen to you."

I sat quietly, watching fear envelop him.

"We did what we could for the darkies," he said. "This nonsense will come to nothing."

My desire to kill him was more acute when I recognised our shared behaviour. My clawing at money and land was his behaviour. I had not killed him because I was not finished feasting on him yet. As long as he lived I would make my money. There were times I used the slaves to work on my own small holding of land. When the thought occurred to me that I was content to allow the slaves to work for me, the lines between him and me blurred. He paid me sixty pounds a year to oversee his plantation, flog and hang the rebellious slaves. For the last four years I had skimmed off the surface to make more money. I too had benefited from the slavery system.

THERE WERE TIMES I REBUKED MYSELF FOR NOT KILLING HIM sooner. I could have killed him by the crocodile pond and made it appear like an accident – and there were other opportunities. But each time I didn't kill him because, loath as I was to admit it, I knew I would benefit from his survival. I also kept him alive for the simple pleasure of enjoying his unhappiness. For most of my life, my hatred had become my old friend – it was like a companion I could not live without.

"We both know that slavery can't continue," I said.

"It has to continue," he whispered loudly.

"Their freedom is as sure as the planters' end," I replied.

In the distance we could hear the shots. The only other sounds were the ocean and his breathing.

I continued. "Eventually the ruling classes from places like Lugdale Estate will bend to meet the men from Knocknagashel, Knockbrack and Mein," I said, referring to his local terrain in Ireland. "All over the world the ruling classes will be hunted as they are here."

On recognising the place names his head tilted slightly. I wouldn't tell him my story. He would not remember my father, but he was as familiar with the hanging trees of Mein as he was of his estate of birth.

I didn't say anything else. Under the light from the moon I watched him grow more uncomfortable. For long periods I stared at him, willing my hatred to kill him. It was more pleasurable to hear his shallow breathing as he stared up at the Big House where his family hid in the hiding place beneath the floors of the study.

WE RETURNED TO THE HOUSE THE NEXT DAY AND FOUND THE HOUSE untouched and the family safe. Then, on the 1st January 1832, one of the slaves woke me to tell me about a riot on the neighbouring plantation. Cautiously I investigated it from the safety of the woods. A passing group of rebel militia had set fire to the house. Clearly some of the slaves had got caught up in the excitement, some believing the lighting of fires signified their freedom. They killed the estate hogs and took the rum from the sugar mill. The chaos was one of the most jubilant slave atmospheres I'd ever seen. One of the slaves passed me by as he galloped around the lawns on the owner's horse wearing the owner's hat. When he passed the flame I noticed his expression of unyielding triumph. It was as if 200 years of oppression was acknowledged and he and his ancestors were finally free.

A short time later three rebels arrived onto Mangrove Plantation. The leader rode with intent, carrying his machete high. It was Burdan. Like me he was afflicted with a hatred that would never quench until he saw the Colonel's blood drip. I ran across the lawn to the house, torn between fear of being denied the pleasure of finally killing the Colonel, and fear that my main antagonist would be taken from me. Who could I then hate? Was it a fear of change that prompted me to run faster? Or had I become the slave who learned to love his punitive master? Was this conflict to be my new eternal companion?

In the library three men including Burdan surrounded the Colonel. I grappled with Burdan and protested, using the argument that he would be hunted like an animal if he committed such a murder. The two men held me back while Burdan hacked at the Colonel, his hated father. He removed his head, as the Colonel had done to so many, and galloped from the estate holding it high.

The rebellion lasted ten days with a few whites slain and a great deal of damage to the properties. In the aftermath there were hundreds of slaves hanged and beheaded, some for minor offences like killing the estates' hogs. The courts made no attempt to assess the degree of guilt – the whites were on a rampage of vengeance. The Colonel's un-intact remains were buried quickly.

Immediately after her husband's burial, Mistress prepared to depart with the children. She expressed her gratitude that I had served her husband's plantation. She praised my efforts to save him on the night of his death.

"The children and I heard you trying to tackle the rebels. You did all you could. Your courage and your loyalty to my husband for the past twenty years is admirable."

She spoke quietly. Initially, I was confused and then realised she thought my shouting on the night of his killing was an attempt to save his life rather than preserve it to enjoy killing him myself.

"Edward was so very fond of you, Art," she said. "I know he would wish me to reward you."

In the presence of her attorney from Savanna la Mar and her sons, Blair and Ernest, she had a document drafted and signed by each of the men. I would manage the estate for the next ten years at which stage they would review it each year until Blair was old enough to ascertain his wishes. I would be paid 100 pounds a year and 15 acres of land would be mine. As a token of her gratitude, for each decade of service I would receive one gold coin valued at fifty pounds. Whenever I wished to cease working for the Stratford-Rices, I would receive my gold. In the presence of her attorney and her sons, she showed me a pouch with my name on the front and two gold coins. I held one of the yellow coins and felt the smooth texture. There was a picture of a warrior on a horse holding his sword and on the other side England's new queen, Victoria.

Within two weeks of her husband's death, Mistress left the country. The morning of her departure I travelled with her to the port.

"This is no country for white people. One needs to be born to this climate and people. There is little I will miss," she said beneath the shade of her parasol, inclining her head away from the sun. "The world is changing." She looked out towards the sea. "I dread to think what changes will take place."

I stood with her for a few moments before she boarded the ship, which was called *Eternal*.

She held out her hand. "I don't expect we'll meet again. There is nothing to bring me back to these shores."

I shook her hand and wished her a safe journey. I walked away from the pier and watched the ship depart from a distance. After twenty years I too had the choice to return. I had enough money to leave, to return home and fulfil my boyish dreams of telling my old friends about the sea voyage and this strange country. Just then I couldn't recall what I initially found peculiar about Jamaica.

CHAPTER EIGHTEEN

On Mangrove Plantation the Big House was closed, the domestic slaves and gardeners sent to the fields. They were not distraught at the loss of their esteemed positions – they knew their days of freedom were approaching. The slaves were infected with the air of optimism, but a minority feared their approaching freedom.

"Who gonna look after us? Wat we gonna do wid no masta?"

"Thems dat look after us for all our lives didn't do a good job."

Myrtle bore me a son and called him Chinwe, her father's name.

"It mean 'God Owns'," she told me. "Our Chinwe won't have no master ownin' him, only God."

At least my mulatto children would never have the conflict of life with a master and the insecurity without a master. They would only know independence. I found it hard to adore Chinwe as I adored Arry. My thoughts became consumed again with Arry and Seán. If reports were accurate, they too would be free to return to me if they were in the country. Occasionally I'd go to Black River with the sole purpose of meeting the slave traders. They couldn't tell me anything. "Nothing new since we last met," they said.

Some laughed at my enquiries.

My fear was that they had been sold to Cuba and America where slavery showed no sign of ending.

I went through a period of consulting the Obeah man. He told me Arry was still alive and possibly in Jamaica. He could not see my son Seán.

In 1833, the Emancipation Act was passed. Slavery would be phased out over the coming four years. The slaves were to work as apprentices, then become full-time employees if they wished in 1838. The energy of planters was now to be directed towards converting a former slave-labour force into a permanent plantation labour force. There was anger and frustration that the structure of a slave society remained unchanged. The slaves felt conned. Although they'd been chattels for over 200 years, four years seemed an eternity when they thought freedom was within their grasp. Nothing had changed from the slave's perspective – only their uncertainty about emancipation increased.

Our lives on the plantation kept to the same routine without the Colonel and the Big House.

During those years I continued working. For the first few months I'd cast my eye on the Big House, briefly forgetting I'd nobody to hate any longer.

"You miss hating the old man," Ned said to me.

Strange as it seemed, I did.

I had never told anyone, not even Ned, the details of how my father died and by whose hand. My instinct was to keep that secret hurt deep in my own heart. Yet there were times, like now, when Ned seemed to know. Uneasily I wondered if I might have let something escape as I raved in my rum delirium.

NED AND I BOUGHT LAND AT CHEAP PRICES FROM PEOPLE ON OTHER estates who were eager to leave. We bought clusters of five and ten acres. Some of the land was poor. It was on higher ground and rough terrain to reclaim, but it was ours.

Time passed. Then late in June 1834 as the harvest ended, I was returning to my cabin at nightfall when I heard a horse's hooves approaching. I saw a man riding a horse across the lawn towards me. I closed my eyes and opened them, thinking I was hallucinating from exhaustion. The man on the horse continued to trot steadily towards my cabin. Although there was a sense of gaiety in the country, white men were vigilant of final retributions from disgruntled slaves – and I was white. Slowly I unfurled my whip without taking my eyes from the man until he was in front of my veranda.

It was Burdan. I held the butt-end of the whip, wishing for Sexton's accuracy. As always I didn't know how far the tentacles of Burdan's anger reached.

He stopped in front of me. Without speaking or removing his eyes from mine, he stretched his hand behind him and helped down a passenger.

It was a child, about six years old.

"Papa!"

I dropped the whip. "Arry?"

She ran to me.

"Arry!" I held her face, doubting my eyes, and then scooped her up in my arms.

I looked at Burdan who returned my gaze with his black impassive eyes. Slowly he turned his horse and trotted back to wherever he came from, the only sound the hooves of the horse on the grass.

OVER THE FOLLOWING DAYS ARRY TOLD ME HOW SHE WAS SOLD at Savanna la Mar auction and taken to a plantation a few days away. She had no idea what happened to Seán. In her new home she recognised Bennie, one of the troublesome slaves from Mangrove Plantation who'd been previously sold. When she asked him to take her home, he told her they were in Florence Hall, and it would take two days to get to Black River. He left during the slave revolt and she thought she'd lost her last link to home. But he returned to burn their plantation with Burdan during the revolt.

"Last night Burdan took me in di night. We ride all day to get here."

Arry didn't stop speaking. I could not respond, only stare disbelieving at her face and listen to the octaves of her voice rising and falling.

I showed her the pearls I'd saved for her. Arry held them in the palm of her hand as she did as a small child. Only then did a dreamy quietness descend as she looked at them closely.

"Yuh kept me treasure," she smiled.

I wanted to tell her she was my treasure but couldn't say the words.

As the years passed she grew into a long thin child with spindly legs. Her face grew into a heart shape with a high forehead and wide hazel eyes. She had an independent streak like any child who was forced to forage for herself. With emancipation in our grasp I didn't feel the need to hide her. I built a bigger cabin, and Myrtle and my son lived with us.

There were nights when I opened my eyes to find Arry at the foot of my bed.

"Am checkin yuh still here," she'd say before returning to her bed.

Alone we sat on the porch when she couldn't sleep. She asked about my life as a boy. I told her about Mein, the smell of the burning turf, the wet climate, the rabbits and the fish we poached. I dwelled on the romantic side of life. I didn't tell her about the hanging tree or how misery stalked me until she was returned to me.

We ended the night with a song. I'd sing her the songs I learned as a boy. She'd fall asleep on my lap and every night I'd thank Burdan and God that they had returned her to me.

For four years the apprenticeship system was tested and failed. On August 1, 1838, the British Parliament ended the apprenticeship programme, which had become an enormous administrative burden, and granted full emancipation to more than 300,000 slaves in Jamaica. A great amount of land was sold but the Stratford-Rices clung to theirs. Former slaves found new ways to make a living. Ex-slaves and their children made great strides. Many of them formed villages and communities of their own and worked the land.

Tariq left the plantation which surprised me. Initially he was one of the slaves filled with trepidation at the idea of freedom.

"I neva did know a hungry day," he lamented. "George be good to me, and de Colonel. Is all gone now."

He moved further down the coast with his wife, their two children and members of his wife's family. Tariq hunted and fished with her brothers and sold their produce. I saw him rarely and when I did it was a pleasure. A reminder of how much had changed.

Life was not easy for most but with ambition and pride came success. They grew ginger, bananas and sugar cane, and sold them at the market. The plantation owners hated the free villages that were springing up. They were a glaring sight of independence.

A small number of the slaves left Mangrove. They put their money together and bought small pieces of land – five and ten acres. They moved into the mountains to nurture their new property. They were not interested in economy – their freedom from the whip was enough to make them content. Those years were happy expectant days.

Within two years the land that Ned and I bought prior to emancipation had trebled in price but I had no plans to sell mine. Occasionally Ned and I talked about selling it and returning to Ireland. The wind took our romantic empty words and spun them back to us in our dreams. We'd never return, yet we could never entirely release the dream.

We met the newly arrived Irish and their tale was not a happy one.

"Anything is better than Ireland," they said as they gaped wildly at the scenery and the coloured men and women.

The old slave cabins were rented to the new indentured servants. During those times I'd watch the Irishmen's bewilderment at their new surroundings and strange food. "'Tis a long time since we saw decent potatoes or dollops of cream," one of the men confessed. "For the last few months it was grass and boiled nettles."

Ned and I always went to great lengths to make the transition as easy as possible. I took great delight in showing them the lagoons and fishing spots that Tariq had shown me.

After a few days one man asked when it would rain.

"November," I replied and watched his uncomprehending eyes look towards the sky to find a cloud.

On his fingers he counted the months.

"Then it rains for four months," I told him. "Heavy rain like nothing you've ever seen in Ireland."

They wanted to know everything about their new country. Where was the local sheebeen? Where was the local dance? When would it snow? The times of Mass? When they learned there was no priest, or snow, they shook their heads in amazement but were quick to grasp that their new country could give them a life that had been denied in Limerick and Tipperary and Carlow.

They stared at the coloured women, gripped by their luscious exotic beauty. "Them women would get a snowman excited."

Each decade the Irish brought dreadful reports about diseases, famines and continual oppression. I heard further accounts of how they ate grass and walked for weeks to get the boat away from Ireland's shores. I heard old Ireland was exhausted and tired after failed rebellions and famine. With all of these reports, I could never understand my peculiar longing to return to such a conflicted country. At night they'd eat the fruit and comment on its brilliant colours. They'd sing sad songs, the Irish melancholy rising to the top like the cream they hadn't seen for so long.

CHAPTER NINETEEN

By 1850, I had four sons and two daughters with Myrtle. My sons were men who worked our land in the hills. My daughters, Josephine and Oluchi, were only six and four years old. My daughter Arry lived close by in one of the free villages with her man. On the surface she appeared like her contemporaries. She moved out of our cabin to live with her man at an age when girls moved on. She worked at the market as did some of the women, her clothes and appearance were similar to her friends. But there was an intensity in Arry that occasionally could not be contained. She was strong, fiery, generous and sometimes volatile. Although she was my daughter and closest kin, sometimes she was unknown to me. She was a striking girl with chocolate skin, black hair and the same hazel eyes as her mother. Her effusive spirit was reminiscent of her mother's but, in a time of freedom, her temperament was an asset.

Each Saturday she attended the market to sell produce from our land and a few neighbouring farms, earning some money on her sales. She also sold trinkets she crafted using beads, pearls, glass, and stones. She made bracelets and necklaces. She had a great talent for matching the colours to make her bracelets sought after. Arry had a reputation for selling most of her stock.

Occasionally I joined her at the market and watched, mesmerised at how she used an array of voices and behaviour to suit each customer.

"Dis time of de year de ground perfect." Arry held a melon aloft as a woman paused to examine her fruit. "Pick from de ground dis mornin'."

The woman hesitated.

Arry scrunched up her nose as if she was biting into the yellow watery melon balancing on the palm of her hand. "Delicious!"

The woman nodded and bought it.

Arry would then change her "speak" to suit another buyer. "Good mornin', lovey! Yuh lookin' for somethin' nice for a lady friend?" she'd ask the men and hold up a beaded necklace. "She'll love dis one – feel de weight. Real pearl from de sea. Look!" Arry would hold her wrist high as if surprised to see she was wearing the same bracelet. "I'm wearin' it meself!"

They'd buy.

"Yuh need somethin' to keep yuh goin' on a day like dis!" She'd fan her face and hold up the oranges as if she too needed them to overcome the heat.

The men were helpless. More money changed hands.

"Have a good day!" she'd call after them sweetly before assuming a different persona for the next comer.

Arry could be as acidic as she was sweet. When an army officer asked how much she cost, she raised her proud Igbo eyebrows and sized him up condescendingly. "Yuh money couldn't buy me. Small man like yuh is no good to me." She shook her head distastefully.

The soldier shuffled along feeling as if he was the one who had been violated.

I was proud and occasionally disturbed by her behaviour, her capabilities a reminder of how much she had to endure to survive when she was a child-slave. If her mother Flora had freedom she would have thrived like Arry. Man nor God could not hold down women like her.

Arry lived with a man called Freddie. He was handsome and charming. Once Arry set her sights on him, I was not surprised when she promptly set up home with him. They chose to live in one of the free villages. It was Arry who said she would not pay rent to any master.

"Dey own us long enough," she said.

She had one daughter who she'd intended on sending to the missionaries to be educated.

"I'm too late to learn bout nothin' excep' buyin' and sellin'. The missionaries can learn my Eleanor how to read and write."

Arry and Freddie's arrangement turned out to be violent. On one occasion I saw her with a mark on her face. Despite Myrtle warning me to stay out of Arry's affairs, I went to the cabin to confront Freddie. When I saw a cut running across Freddie's cheek and a swollen eye, Arry's bruise paled into insignificance.

"Arry nearly kill me," he moaned. "She de one need to be scolded. Look at me! I lucky to be alive."

Proudly I told Myrtle how Freddie hobbled around his cabin, filled with sympathy for himself.

"My Arry," I said, "she's the best woman to take care of herself."

Not long after that Arry told me when I visited the market that Freddie was gone.

"I kick him out," she said as she prepared her stall. "Him is useless and good-for-nothin'. Foolin' around with Poppy. That will teach him. Freddie thought I should go, I say neva! I bring in de money. For what? For him to lie in bed. Lazy lying man!"

She told me how Freddie's mother pleaded with her to take him back.

"I say neva! If him stay my daughter would learn to be lazy like him and find a man lazy like him when she is a woman," she said with anger, then she smiled as a woman approached her stall, holding a little girl's hand. "Oh, dat is a lovely little girl!"

Arry smiled at the small child and wrinkled her nose in affection. "So beautiful. How old she?"

"Six," the woman replied.

"She needs fruit at dat age." Arry held up a pear.

"Looks good," the woman said.

"Best time of de year wen the ground is dry." Arry continued talking to the woman about children and the best food for a girl that age. She told her pears would keep her hair fresh and her skin pretty. "Is de wet fruit dat make dem healthy and strong, better dan meat or fish. Fruit make de hair strong and de mind clever." Arry tilted her head sideways and smiled lovingly at the child, as if regarding her with great fondness.

The woman agreed. She also loved the fruit and appeared to agree with Arry's opinions.

"All my life I eat it and I neva did know a sick day," Arry added while the woman nodded in agreement.

When the sale was finished and the woman wandered away, laden with bags of pears and apples, Arry sat beside me.

"Some women is terrible stupid," she sighed.

CHAPTER TWENTY

In 1850 Blair, now aged twenty-seven, returned to a very different Jamaica than he had left eighteen years previously. The Big House was re-opened and painted. It was as if Mistress had returned from Ireland. There were carts of paint and paper wheeled to every entrance of the house. A fire blazed for days outside with the old furniture and curtains his mother had spent such time deliberating over. When the house was ready Blair took up residence and summoned me.

As I sat in front of him in the old study, I wanted to keep an unbiased open mind about him. My life for the last few years had been free of hate. Initially I longed to see the Colonel alive, if only to sense my old familiar feelings of hatred again. As time passed I became acquainted with contentment. It would be more difficult to shrug off the well-worn happiness than reunite with that old sense of loathing.

Blair had added a painting of his father to the montage of formidable portraits of the Stratford-Rice and Beaufort men that adorned the walls of the house. Colonel Stratford-Rice appeared bigger in size, dressed in the red coat of the British Army.

"O'Neill, I'm grateful you're still with us," Blair said.

He was small and fair like his father, with light blue eyes and a more rounded face like his mother.

"It's been a long time with a great many changes," he said.

I listened to what he had to say. I reminded myself that Blair was no longer the master but the employer. Slavery was no more.

We talked about our lives in the intervening years. His mother was alive and well and living in Ireland.

"More at ease with the climate and culture there."

He told me he'd just finished a stint in the British army. He'd been to India and returned to England but found he couldn't ignore his longing to return to the Caribbean.

"Like my father," he said, "I've always been drawn to Jamaica. Despite everything that has happened, it's my home."

He asked me about my family, how many sons and daughters I had. Was I happy to continue working for him?

"Yes," I said. "It's my home now."

He counted out three gold coins valued at fifty pounds apiece. "As agreed by my mother we'll add another coin each decade."

I looked at the coins. Each coin had Queen Victoria on one side but the images on the back varied. The original coin with the man on horseback holding his sword was there.

Maybe he was different, I thought. Young men like Blair from the governing classes knew they had to accept the great changes.

"We will produce more than sugar cane," he told me. "The sugar yield has dropped. There is too much competition from Cuba and Haiti. We need to explore other avenues. I'm interested in rum." He patted a bottle of the dark liquid on his desk. "I'll brew the finest rum for my friends in England and every sailor on the seas. I want my rum to be as good as Mount Gay rum." He was referring to the most popular Jamaican rum.

Immediately he hired indentured servants. Most were newly arrived workers from India and China – a few came from Ireland, Wales and Scotland. The new servants lived in the old slave cabins. Blair established the brewery where the old sugar mill stood. He also rented some of his lands to the ex-slaves. Each week part of my job was to collect the rents.

"The soil is exhausted from sugar cane," he explained. "The new tenants will plant crops or graze cattle and give it new life."

Like his father he sat at his desk with the map of the world behind him. Blair unfurled great drawings of the distillery. He had logbooks with calculations and pricing. The price of labour and yield per man. He was animated and excited by his new ideas.

Within a few months the tea parties and weekend parties resumed. Each Friday night he hosted dinner for the overseers and any passing visitors. His friends were men who talked about a different Jamaica, the good days when money was money, the sugar business boomed and the blacks knew their place. Some were sons and grandsons of previous guests. Lady Hedley's son, Marcus, was a regular. There were some military men, sea merchants and men with titles. They talked at length about money, how to make it and how to keep it.

"The roulette tables are the best way to fluctuate." Marcus Hedley wagged his finger at Blair.

"Every man needs one vice," he countered.

Over time I watched his porcelain exterior crack and was in some perverse way relieved I had not trusted or liked him. His greatest enemy was the roulette tables. I watched Blair rise and fall like the tides with his winnings and losings. He was boyish when he won – unable to hide his joy he'd whistle aloud, the clear bounce in his step obvious at a distance. The disgruntled man angry with his loss was as glaring. I learned from his demeanour how he had fared at the roulette tables from the way he drove his carriage in the gates of the plantation. Those who worked for him also learned how to gauge if he'd won or lost. Gradually he lost the confidence of his workers, his behaviour a reminder of what they'd gained with emancipation. Some valued workers left. Those who remained had been born in the cabins where they lived. They were the most susceptible to Blair's abuse. He treated them like slaves, they in turn found comfort in domination. It was all they knew.

He had a constant stream of passing employees – none lasted

very long. The consistent problems in the brewery were a result of inexperienced workers. Replacing the valued workers was more difficult than losing them. Eventually he stayed away from the brewery, allowing Ned Doyle and me to oversee it.

By the late 1850's half of the plantations in Jamaica had folded up. Many of the plantations were partly or wholly abandoned and the price of the property plummeted. During those years, Ned Doyle and I bought pockets of land.

"We won't be going home in the next few months," I said to Ned as we inspected our new fields.

Returning to Ireland had become an ongoing joke between us.

"We'll do a day's work first and then we might enquire about the tickets," Ned said as we stood on at the top of the hill, looking at the five-acre wilderness.

We were holding our billhooks, about to do our first day's work on our new purchases and giddy with excitement at our lot. We knew how much the tickets to Ireland cost and we knew we'd never leave Jamaica.

BLAIR WAS NOT COMFORTABLE WITH ROUTINE OR STRUCTURE. ONCE the plantation was running reasonably well, he became restless and found something new to explore. One such venture sprang from the way indentured servants arrived on his dwindling plantation. He invested in a ship.

"The world is shifting," he told one of his friends. "We can transport people around the world in less than three weeks. The great citizens of England, Ireland, Germany, Italy – they have come to realise that America is the land of opportunity. We can transport these people from England to their new home in America in sixteen days. My good friend, Sir James Berkinshire, made his fortune transporting the Irish and English to America. In ten years he could afford a fine stately home."

Unlike his father, Blair talked about money and often referred to 'losing his shirt' or 'making a killing.' Some ventures did not work out as he wished. One of his friends talked about the profit in beef production. Blair reneged on his lease with some of the old slaves who rented his lands. He invested in livestock. Disgruntled ex-slaves who spent years harvesting crops on the land killed his livestock. When Blair asked me about his dead cattle, he could not see how any fault lay with him. He tried his hand at other businesses, always keeping the brewery and banana business going.

He tried his hand at coffee but the ex-slaves sold him inferior coffee plants. He tried to default on his contracts with the Irish. They'd been told their indenture lasted fourteen years, then he increased the number of years to twenty-one.

"The Irish won't take it," I said.

"They must take it." He was unable to see fault in altering verbal agreements. "You didn't do too badly. Influence them. You're a man who talks their language – tell them about the great fruits of your labour."

I knew from his words that he too would die a death roaring like his father. I began to realise he was as hateful. The old loathing returned to me, like a diseased dog it lurked at my feet and I happily patted it.

CHAPTER TWENTY-ONE

Three years after his return to Jamaica, Blair went on a holiday to England for two months. He returned with news of his mother's death and a new bride, Mistress Catherine. Initially he lavished her with attention. He'd walk around the garden in the evenings with his arm protectively resting on her waist. Occasionally he'd sit in the shade reading to her as his own parents had done. For the first month of their married life, it appeared that the gambling tables were a thing of the past. His wife was his new obsession. She was fair and pretty, like an immaculate doll. It was her pale skin that was most discussed.

"Where him find such a white wife? She come from country wid no sun?" Phoebe asked.

When the Big House was reopened, I had reinstated Phoebe to her old position. She continued to relay all of the goings-on to me.

She thought the new mistress might have a disease. "White face, white hands, white teeth and white hair," she said. "She sick?"

I gathered from titbits of gossip that Blair did not marry her for her pallor.

According the new Lord Hedley, she was untitled. "But an heiress to a great fortune." Blair had landed on his feet.

During her ten months in Jamaica I only laid eyes on her a handful of times. On one occasion she was sitting in the cool library with her eyes closed. She was so still and white I thought she was dead. She found the heat suffocating. As time passed Blair's interest in her dwindled. He stopped walking around the gardens with his new bride, and spent a few nights each week in Black River. Twice during his ten-month marriage he asked me to source Red Grass for a disease from lying with infected women. Like so many newly arrived foreigners, Blair's wife dried up and wilted beneath the Jamaican skies. Ten months after her arrival she was found dead by the redundant chessboard.

Within a few weeks Blair seemed more relieved with her passing than grief-stricken. A short period after her death Blair made a few trips to America to invest his money in shipping companies in the up-and-coming country.

Blair found a second wife in 1857. Mistress Bernadette was a big strong white Jamaican-English wife. They made a peculiar sight as they linked arms and walked around the gardens. She towered over him and appeared twice his size with her wide hips and statuesque frame. On Friday night she'd join us at dinner with an appetite as great as McCovey's.

When I congratulated him on his wedding, he looked up at the painting of his father. "We've been here for two hundred years – I hope to have sons to fill my shoes."

Mistress Bernadette was with child within a year. Unlike the other wilting lilies, that did not stop her striding around the gardens or walking to the lagoon to swim each evening without the need for a housemaid to hold an umbrella over her head. Blair's humour was upbeat in anticipation of the arrival of his son. There was no doubt in his mind that Mistress Bernadette was expecting a boy.

Phoebe came to my cabin late in September. "She have girl."

Blair said the following day, "It's early days. My wife is young and strong."

In 1859 she delivered another girl, followed by a third girl the following year.

Each year I chuckled at the news and took a moment to admire my five strong sons and three daughters. Although I never said it aloud, Arry was my strongest and most clever child.

Blair returned to his old ways. He'd go to Black River for a few nights, and sometimes he went further afield to larger towns. His losses were heavy. There were times I saw him in the library, unclean and despondent. He was often angry and sought arguments with the workers.

He tried to insist that the employees sign contracts. "At least we can lock them into an agreement. Then they won't find it so easy to abandon their jobs."

I tried to tell him the workers would abandon any employer who was reminiscent of the slave era. I took the contracts to the employees and advised them not to sign.

When some of his workers left his employment but continued to rent the cabins on the plantation he increased the rents.

Each week I collected the rents and when the tenants hadn't the money to pay, I told Blair he could put them out and have no tenants or leave the rent as it stood and have tenants. He chose to evict them and recruited new workers. Thus began a rotating cycle of staff, using Blair's plantation as a first step into Jamaica before moving on to a more amenable employer.

"His mama didn't beat him hard enough," Phoebe would say to me and shake her head in exasperation at his torrents of abuse and anger.

When Blair won he was his old playful and entertaining self.

One Friday night I watched him open a bottle of rum. The dinner table was packed with white workers and visitors. Theatrically he poured it into a glass and held it to the light.

Blair began to sing an Irish ballad called "The Sporting Hero".

"In rum, gin and brandy, I would spend all my store! And when that was all done I would boldly rob for more, Mush a ring a ding a da, ri too ra la, Ri too ral laddy O, There's whiskey in the bar! "

The table erupted into laughter. That night he told anecdotes and imitated his friends like Lord Hedley by scratching his beard and speaking in an exaggerated British accent with a lisp.

The only reason I remember that night in particular was that it coincided with Mistress Bernadette's death. Later that night she died while giving birth to her fourth daughter.

FOR YEARS MY LIFE MEANDERED ALONG, THE PASSING YEARS ONLY evident when I'd see an old friend and notice their aged faces and stooped bodies. I had little to complain about. My sons were hard workers. My second oldest son with Myrtle, Taigh, worked on the whaling ships and travelled the world. Every year he reappeared, laden with money and stories. He told us how the Americans were at war with each other: one side wanted freedom for the slave and other didn't. The fact that white men were fighting for the coloured man's liberty made us see Americans in a new light. Taigh paid for a small fishing boat for my son Emmet who caught fish which Arry sold at the market. I was proud of all of my children. They worked hard and most spent their earnings wisely.

My life was not without concern. Occasionally my sons drank too much and behaved badly but only one of my sons inherited my weakness. Kevin's love for grog outweighed all of his desires. He chased grog during every waking moment of his day. There were times when he allowed his wife to do his job while he lay stupefied in his bed. When I was tired and ashamed of seeing his wife and children doing his work, I dragged him from his bed and ordered him to work. That day I remained close by, I watched him empty his stomach and noticed his shaking hands, unable to lift the water to his mouth. He told me the grog was no more. I pretended to believe him and praised his resolve but knew he occasionally fell into the cauldron. I allowed him to make his mistakes and hoped with time he would learn to live without the grog forever.

MUCH OF MY TIME WAS DIVIDED BETWEEN MY OWN ACRES OF LAND and working for Blair. Each year I reminded Blair about my gold coin for every ten years of service. Once after a lucky streak Blair promised me ten gold coins a year. I told him I didn't want his ten gold coins, I wanted my promised one gold coin for every decade. I doubted I'd ever see the gold. I had already received payment from what I took from the plantation for my own land. It was one of the reasons I took such liberties – a master's promise was rarely fulfilled in my country. Yet I had to remind him. If I didn't I would appear like the fearful slave, content with only half of a bargain.

ONE DAY I WAS WALKING AMONG THE PINEAPPLE PLANTS AT THE BACK of the old slave quarters where I had five acres of land to use as I pleased. Every three years I rotated the crop: ginger, coffee, banana, peppers. It was important I did not allow the soil to tire from the same crop. Kevin and I examined the leaf and stems of my pineapple crop, picking up specks of stray dirt and examining anything suspicious. I turned back to admire my harvest and the strong healthy leaves.

Kevin smiled. "Yuh is smilin' at de plants like dey is a beautiful woman."

I hadn't realised I was smiling.

"Worth pullin' dem weeds every day," Kevin said, looking at his coarse hands.

It was a good period of his life when he stayed away from the grog. Each day he worked and seemed to grow with the crop. At last he appeared as healthy as my pineapples.

"A job well done," I said and clapped him on the back. "You've done well."

As we stood admiring the crop I watched Arry saunter through the old slave quarters. Blair was walking towards her.

They stopped to speak. I was too far away to hear what was said. Every moment I expected her continue walking, I assumed she was going to my cabin, but instead she remained. Then I saw Blair place his hand on her back. Arry didn't step away from him, but continued talking as if she was comfortable in his company, at ease with his touch.

Kevin was looking from me and back to Arry. When I saw the fearful expression on his face, I knew his guilt. He knew what Arry had been doing.

The sight of Arry and Blair was like a plague blighting everything I owned.

Later I went to her cabin to confront her. She was sitting on her porch making trinkets with beads to sell at the market.

"What de fuss?" she shrugged.

In anger I toppled her table, knocking hundreds of beads to the floor. They bounced between us as we stared at each other.

"*He's using you!* " I shouted, in disbelief that Arry could allow it to happen.

Arry ignored my anger. "Who gonna pick up dem beads?" she said, looking at the sight of her stock on the floor. Then, with anger similar to her mother Flora's, she leaned towards me. "*How yuh know I'm not usin' him?*"

Arry was not afraid of me as my other children were. They would have cowered away from my anger. Not Arry, she matched it. I looked at her wide hazel eyes and heart-shaped face. It was the most perfect face I'd ever seen. She could have any man on the island, yet she allowed the most despicable kind to use her.

FOR ONE WEEK I STAYED AWAY FROM ARRY. I GRAPPLED WITH ANGER and disbelief. Finally, when the rage abated and I had no other choice but to accept it, I called to her again. I hated fighting with her. I tried to tell her how the white man used slaves but I knew she was not listening. She seemed indifferent to my concern. Finally we drank coffee and talked about other matters yet I couldn't concentrate on anything without having visions of his clawing hands on my Arry. She, my most clever and able child, was inviting the same behaviour that the slaves fought against for centuries.

When I left Arry that day, I went to Blair. I sat in his study and demanded I see my coins. I was approaching my fifth decade working for the Stratford-Rices.

Blair told me the coins were locked in the safe. "In the same pouch where my mother placed the first two coins in 1832."

That day I insisted I see the coins.

"Don't you trust me?" he asked, reddening at the cheeks.

I didn't answer him.

Much to my surprise he left the study and returned almost immediately holding the same pouch his mother had shown me thirty years before. Blair upended the pouch and five gold coins rolled out. I saw Queen Victoria with various headdresses on the coins.

"You'll be the richest man in Jamaica," Blair said.

Matching Blair's theatrics, I picked up the five coins. "Gold is not that important to me." I allowed the coins to drop through my fingers onto his mahogany desk. "If my daughter is harmed I will gladly spend the gold executing my rage on her wrongdoer."

He looked at me under his eyebrows.

WHEN I LEARNED THAT ARRY WAS EXPECTING HIS CHILD, INITIALLY I was devastated.

"Maybe it be a boy," Myrtle said, knowing how Blair wanted a son.

"It makes no difference what it is," I said. "Blair won't be interested. He will tire of Arry and the child."

In the height of the summer, when the sun was at its hottest, Arry delivered a baby boy. They gave him an Igbo name, Okeke.

Okeke had lighter skin than even my offspring had. But instead of Blair's light-blue eyes, his were Irish green.

I refused to sit with Arry and Stratford-Rice's child. I recoiled from my grandson with the same level of revulsion I felt towards Blair and all belonging to him.

In the evenings I'd see Blair take his carriage out of the plantation and head in the direction of Arry's cabin.

"Try not to worry," Myrtle would say when she'd see my angry gaze follow Blair.

I didn't trust any of Arry's capabilities anymore. Maybe I had adored her too much, I thought with regret.

Blair appeared to give his son a great deal of attention and lavished him with presents.

I saw expensive toys in Arry's cabin, unlike the crude items my children and grandchildren played with. There was a rocking-horse made of wood and items too big for the green-eyed boy to use.

"Maybe Okeke will be Blair's only son," Myrtle said.

The same thought had occurred to me. My old obsession of watching the Big House returned.

Phoebe reported to me daily. Blair's four daughters were tutored at home each day by an English teacher. Their days were structured. When Blair was not in the house he was on the plantation. The old hatred coiled its way around my neck and peace eluded me.

CHAPTER TWENTY-TWO

When Okeke was four he began to be educated in the Big House by the English tutor with his half-sisters. They addressed him with an English name. Though this was a sign of Blair's acceptance of him, it angered me so much I never once let it pass my lips. They gave him a biased education. They told him how the abolitionists destroyed the very nation that spawned them: No slave, no plantation, no money.

"We took the slaves from the jungle and gave them a life where they would flourish," I heard Okeke tell Arry when she asked about his day with the tutor.

I told him how the black man was enslaved.

"We gotta forget de past," Arry said.

Okeke grew up to be clever. With his fair skin and green eyes, he was more white than black. On Saturdays Arry insisted he accompany her to the market to sell our produce. Although Okeke spoke perfectly good English learned from his tutor in the Big House, he could lapse into "Jamaican speak" to sell. He was quick to read people, those who had more money and those who couldn't differentiate between overripe vegetables and under-ripe.

"Okeke will have de best of two worlds," Arry said. "The teacher will show him how to read and write and teach him how to be polite. I will show him how to survive."

She told me this early one Saturday morning when I joined her and Okeke as they set up the stall. There was an on-going problem with one of the sellers at the market. I had heard about it and went to the market to see if I could help to solve the disagreement.

"It's a sweet thing for yuh to come but I be fine," she said before returning to the conversation about Okeke's education. "Me boy will know more dan most," she said, adjusting her table and arranging the fruit on her stand. She affixed a narrow beam across the top where she hung her jewellery.

She then stood back to admire it and eyed Peter, the man responsible for the recent quarrel. He had broken their code of conduct by selling rancid produce and insinuating that some of the fruitsellers had diseased produce. It was bad for business for everyone.

"Me want no trouble from yuh today!" Arry shouted down to him. "We all got to make a livin' but not de way yuh do!"

He shrugged and ignored her.

Arry pointed at him aggressively. "No more, Peter!"

Then she returned to our conversation.

"Already Okeke know weh de other countries is. Him showed me a picture book wid yuh country in it," she told me. "He show me a map and him say, 'Dat is Ireland, Art's country'."

I conceded that maybe Arry was not that foolish after all. Whatever grasp she had over Blair, he was educating Okeke and doing more than any of her previous ancestors did for their offspring. I looked at the little fellow. He was now seven with watchful eyes. Although an attractive child, I found it difficult to warm to him and scolded myself for spoiling what could have been a happy relationship.

"But words and knowin' countries is not good enough for me boy," Arry admitted. "Him need to know how to work."

A customer interrupted her flow.

She smiled sweetly at the man who was admiring her necklaces.

"Every girl on dis island want two or three of dem. Look!" She held out the different colours. "Colour for mornin' wear so da woman feel fresh, and day for strength and evenin' dis colour help her relaaax." Arry made the word 'relax' sound provocative. "It help a woman mood all day and night long," she continued in the same sultry tone.

The gentleman smiled appreciatively at her. She leaned forward and made her sale. When he ambled away she poured a coffee and continued.

"Yeah, de work and learning to be strong and clever and know to be tough is the most ..." She stopped what she was doing and stared.

Maye in the next stall shouted at Peter, *"Yuh done it again, yuh cur!"*

Arry marched across to Peter's stand. "I saw it too. Saw it wid me own eyes. Yuh shaked yuh head to tell dat woman not to buy from Maye stall. Now she gone and didn't buy nothin' from any of us."

Peter denied it then muttered some profanity to her. Arry threw her coffee at him. With that he pulled a knife and pointed it at her. At a furious rate she began to pick up apples from his stall and throw them at him. She swept away most of the fruit from his stand and then upended it. The other women gathered round to intimidate him further.

As Peter retreated and began to pack up his goods, he continued to shout abuse at the women.

Arry returned to us breathless. "Stupid man," she muttered quietly. "Das wat I'm talkin' about – me boy needs to see dat idiot and how he get wat comin' to him." She exhaled loudly, as if exasperated with the interruptions. Then she suddenly looked at Okeke as if she only noticed him then. Holding her fingers wide apart, she pushed her hand through his hair. "Me special son – yuh see wat happen' to dat man?"

The special son said nothing. He looked from his mother to

Peter who continued to swear over his shoulder as he moved away
with his stock.

"Me special son have de best of everything. He have me, and me
Igbo blood, me Irish blood and him's English blood. Him have
everything."

Only then did the chosen child return her smile. In Ireland,
there's an expression for a child who says little but sees and knows
everything. "He was here before," they say. Okeke was that child.
Did he believe her nonsense or was my own vision of the child
clouded with my hatred for the Stratford-Rices? Was he as ordinary
as my other grandchildren or could I just not see the adorable and
gifted qualities his mother saw? I looked at the boy's curly hair. I had
no desire to push my fingers through his hair or playfully tickle him.
He was as remote to me as the rest of the Stratford-Rice offspring.
His distant knowing eyes were unsmiling when he looked at me.

"ARRY KNOWS WHAT SHE BE DOING," MYRTLE SAID.

I was looking at Okeke as he played with the Stratford-Rice children and friends on the lawn of the Big House.

"Dis de first time I seen any white masta teach his coloured child
and allowed him play so freely wid him own children," Myrtle
continued. "It's true, Okeke is a quiet boy around us, but den none
of your children make bold wid yuh except Arry." My wife nodded
her head adamantly as if she wholeheartedly agreed with her own
statement. "Arry sure knows how to make bold wid you." Then she
corrected herself. "Arry makes bold wid everyone." Her head shook
as if surprised at Arry's antics.

I watched Okeke bounce around the lawn with Blair's girls. He
would never be as pale as the Stratford-Rice children with their
white hair and blue eyes and milky-white skin. Okeke threw his
head back and laughed as Elizabeth chased him. I watched the tutor
come to the door and beckon the children to return to the classroom
to continue their lessons.

Maybe I envied Okeke. He had opportunity, youth, education,
the presence of a mother and, although he was not Blair's legitimate

child, Blair was an added presence in his life. If he was wise he could have a wonderful life. I was getting old.

My good friend Ned Doyle died. He got spots on his body that grew with each passing week. His spots began to ooze. The Obeah man prayed over him but couldn't say if he'd get better. For the last month of his life he lay in his cabin with his wife tending to his sores and pain.

A few months later my wife Myrtle died. She died in her sleep.

My old hatred for the Big House swelled the gap of loneliness. It made me sick and angry. Looking back, I should have taken Ned's advice and moved away from Mangrove Plantation then. I could have bought more land with my gold coins and found contentment far removed from my persecutor. I had learned to live with the hate. It was so raw and vile I believed it was the catalyst that kept me young and more able than any man of my age.

CHAPTER TWENTY-THREE

A group of visitors arrived from Europe in 1876. They were English and Anglo-Irish. One tall fair Anglo-Irish woman was much talked about. Not only because she wore a wide-brimmed straw hat and fashionable clothes. She brought with her a black box which she stood on three legs. When she'd spot a flower or a setting sun, she'd go through the ordeal of setting up her black box, cover her head with a black cloth and peer into the box. We thought it was hilarious until she showed us the magic her box created. It made pictures of us. She took hundreds of them. Miss Lydia was her name. She was a pensive girl who saw beauty in the most surprising places.

She talked about the scenery, how the wildlife was "utterly different from Ireland". She loved the greenery and used many ways to describe it, "luscious green", "sea green", "soft green". She was not frightened of Hapi, the house snake who'd been replaced several times to keep the house rodent-free. Miss Lydia examined Hapi with genuine interest and didn't balk when it slithered up her arm.

"There is something strangely endearing about it except its

purpose," she said and then asked if I'd sit for a photograph with Hapi.

After a four-week holiday, the group of friends left.

Miss Lydia remained to become Blair's third wife.

When I heard the news I knew Blair was still trying for a legitimate son. Suddenly I saw his contemplative wife in a different light. I watched her for signs of ill health and speculated whether she'd survive to bear him a son. When I caught myself wishing signs of sickness on this young innocent woman who had not wronged me, I realised that I was as depraved as Blair.

"No title," Lord Hedley said as he gossiped among his friends about his host. "A distant cousin of his mother's from Ireland. He's wants an heir."

Lord Hedley's wife noted the age difference. "She's far too young."

"Too young for this country," another said.

"One wonders why she'd marry him?"

"He's adorable," Lady Hedley said. "Charming and irresistible."

As they spoke Blair was walking Mistress Lydia around the gardens.

A wedding gift arrived from Ireland. It was a large painting of Lugdale House. It was hung in the white room.

"It's my home in North Kerry," Mistress Lydia said when she saw me looking at it.

I interrupted her. "That's Mein on the upper left," I said. "Ballintobeenig is a little higher."

Mistress Lydia looked at me in surprise.

I hastened to explain to her how Cian Donnell had taught me so much about Ireland, especially Lugdale.

She was so young and happy then. Jamaica was new and she was new to Blair.

After a year there was no child from Mistress Lydia which was a talking point among the community.

"She too thin," Phoebe said.

Okeke would remain the only son.

Blair continued to educate the boy. Each day Okeke arrived at the Big House early in the morning for his day's lessons. By the age of ten he spoke with their accent, and knew other languages. He could read and write as well as any learned man. Arry was proud yet clever enough to continue teaching her son the value of hard work.

During harvesting season Okeke would join my sons and me as we worked together on our land in the hills. At night we'd gather in my cabin and talk about work and politics, and tell stories which included a great many stories from Ireland. At that stage I began to talk about Mein, the hanging tree and the ghosts that were said to haunt the hills. The new Irish brought songs from home. Okeke sat through those nights like a bystander. He didn't laugh at the anecdotes or waver at the sad stories. His expression was unreadable.

During one of my visits to Arry's cabin, Okeke asked me to address him by his English name.

"You will always be Okeke to me," I said. "Don't forget your Irish and African origins are as important as your English origins, Okeke."

He looked at me out of the corner of his eye without smiling.

WITHIN TWO YEARS OF MARRIAGE, MISTRESS LYDIA WAS AS discontented as any redundant white wife in Jamaica. The days of her open smile and curiosity faded. She complained about the guests and the bookkeeper's filthy fingernails.

"Last night I placed you sitting beside me because I could not have eaten had I to look at his filthy hands," she whispered to me as if I should be pleased with the seating arrangement.

It was like watching the Colonel's wife again. Mistress Lydia was confined in a marriage with a man who designated more time to his cane fields, the roulette tables and other women than to her. There were no more evenings spent together in the garden watching the sun set. By the time she realised she was stuck in a man's country with little room for the sensitivities of a white woman, it was too late. She had no role apart from playing his wife when their guests arrived.

"I love your accent," she said during one of her more disillusioned moments. "If only there were a few drops of rain, I'd feel as though I was truly in Lugdale."

I looked from the clear blue sky to her blue eyes and felt it was only a matter of time before she too would wilt beneath the skies.

CHAPTER TWENTY-FOUR

I t's the surprises in life that kept my spirits alive. Ngozi was a woman who lived with her parents in the old slave quarters. A few months after Myrtle's death, when I was overworked and morose, she called to my cabin with ackee and salt fish. The following week she called again with another dish and cleaned my cabin. She called again and again and gradually she spoke to me and provided a little respite. She didn't harass me as my daughters did about the state my health nor was she afraid of my sadness and didn't slink away from me as so many did.

Ngozi came one Sunday night and stayed for good. I had known many of Ngozi's family. Her father was Irish – Kirwan from Galway. He lived briefly in Jamaica before moving to America. The father of Ngozi's children was a rebel, vicious in the battlefield and their home. Eventually he was executed in Morant.

Ngozi was a large abrupt strong woman. She was generous and could also be angry and dismissive. She believed food was the best nourishment for every ailment and unhappiness. For grief, sickness, tiredness and drunkenness she insisted on feeding the afflicted. When we went to the hills to work she prepared the best fish and rice dishes. I would watch her hum as she sprinkled our meal with spices.

"Yuh talk foolish," she said to my grandson Jerome whose wife had put him out for drunkenness.

Jerome claimed his wife was at fault. "She visit anotha man."

"No, she just sick of yuh and the grog yuh pourin' into yuh body. Make yuh crazy," Ngozi said, pointing at her head. "Yuh sit der and eat," she scolded him as she handed him food to sober him.

When he objected she pushed him roughly onto the seat.

"Sit and eat first, den yuh can fight. Yuh gone so thin from de hooch and ganja yuh look like man wid the Blue Death," she said, referring to the dreaded cholera.

As the end of the 1870s approached, things took a turn for the worse for Mangrove Plantation. Blair's crop spoiled for two years in succession. He was forced to close the brewery and lease most of his lands. Few were willing to rent it, afraid he'd renege and take it back after they had sown their crops. Eventually he leased it at a reduced price.

He stopped his Friday-night dinners. The opulence of the Big House began to fade. Most of the slaves moved away from his plantation and joined the free villages. The empty slave village and fields sectioned into small holdings was a clear sign of the dwindling empire.

My jobs were light. I collected the rents and looked after the livestock Blair kept. He talked about buying cattle and exporting the meat, other times he talked about returning to planting cotton trees. In those days he talked a lot but did little.

"Why yuh hate Blair?" Arry boldly said when she saw me watching Blair pass on the main road in his carriage. "Him makes money like yuh do, him livin' wid woman who could be his grand-daughter like you do! You just like him!"

We were sitting on the rocks by the sea. Okeke was diving for oysters, hoping to find pearls.

"With all of Blair's land and wealth he is useless," I said.

"Blair will think of something," Arry said. "Him is clever."

Okeke came out of the river with an oyster.

"Me boy wants to make me a necklace of de best pearls in de sea," Arry said. She took the oyster from Okeke and inserted her knife into the opening. Much to my surprise it contained several perfectly formed circular ivory pearls.

When Arry saw them she gaped disbelievingly and then planted a loving kiss on his wet head.

NGOZI BORE ME A CHILD IN MY SIXTY-NINTH YEAR. A SON TO WHOM I gave my uncle's name, Leon. I noticed this boy like I noticed Arry when she was an infant. I was interested in everything he did, from the gurgling sounds he made to his unfocused eyes passing over mine.

"Why yuh look so surprised?" Ngozi asked when I marvelled at him.

"I thought I was too old," I confessed.

She laughed. "Some things a man will always be able to do."

I asked to hold him. Ngozi put him onto my lap. Each day I held him. With childish wonderment I watched his small hand hold my finger and felt a lump rise in my throat as his grip tightened.

"Yuh have time now," Ngozi summed it up for me simply. "Yuh work too hard and not see yuh otha children. Dat is why children have special place for dem grandpapas."

"Maybe," I replied.

I watched him grow. I noticed him lying on his back and putting his toes into his mouth, then crawling and then standing.

Ngozi explained the different stages. "Little children needs to put everythin' in dem mouths and touch everythin'. It is their way of knowin' de world."

Ngozi and I went to the springs to bathe in the water. I thought of Arry as a baby. How I'd bathe her in the springs with her mother Flora who was so wild she could never be tamed.

It was a great time of my life. A time when my day's work on the plantation was light, my sons worked our own land and my troubles were next to nothing. At night my daughter Josephine, her husband and their new son, Akeem, would sit with us. Our porch was always full of voices. Leon would roll on the floor with Akeem.

On one such night Cristof, the Obeah man, called.

"What can you see in my Leon?" I asked, sounding foolishly prideful to my own ears.

Cristof indulged me. "Him will live long and have many children."

"Will Leon be like his papa?" Ngozi teased. "Able to make babies wen him is old man?"

"No," the Obeah man was firm, "no man in the world is like old Art who can be a papa at his age."

We laughed and the women joked about my virility.

"You see anythin' else?" Ngozi asked. "Will him have many more brothers or sisters?"

The laughter reached a higher pitch.

We talked about the plantation and the ongoing struggles for the old slaves. Although slavery was abolished, the ex-slaves were discriminated against, and lived in abject poverty. And there were ongoing epidemics of cholera and smallpox.

Cristof said, "At least we getting' betta – no more slavery."

He told me he was twenty years of age when he was freed. His mother had trouble adjusting without a master.

"Beatin' slavery was only de beginning of our war," he said.

As Cristof and I spoke, I picked Leon up and rested my hand on his back. I wanted to stave off the child's struggles, to banish the sicknesses that took so many infants and protect him from the many wars he must wage.

CHAPTER TWENTY-FIVE

And suddenly the stillness in my life gave way to the Blue Death. The cholera. First I noticed my daughter Josephine's sunken eyes and blue complexion. She and her husband died, leaving their little boy, Akeem, who was the same age as Leon. Immediately I took Leon to the hills to my son Chinwe's family until the Blue Death passed.

On my return, I saw the same blue hue on my Arry's face. She was sitting lifeless in her cabin. Her burial was hurried, fear of the spreading disease keeping most away. It broke my heart. Cristof, the Obeah man, prayed over her remains, but those who came to pay their respects did so quickly. A few sang and danced by her body, preferring to respect the dead despite the risk of contamination.

Okeke sat on the side watching with arched eyebrows as if our simple burial was beneath him.

I buried my Arry beside Myrtle in the little cemetery where the lemon trees thrive. During the burial I looked at the rotting lemons on the tree. The idea they would re-ripen did not renew my spirits as it once did.

. . .

THE DARK RUM HAD NOT PASSED MY LIPS IN DECADES YET I THOUGHT incessantly about the burning liquid hitting the back of my throat and imagined the heated sensation as it sailed down my gullet and relieved the pain of loss.

My grandson Jerome was only a young man and his eyes were yellowed from the rum houses. I knew he too would not see thirty – the awful affliction that cursed so many who shared my blood would kill him too. I watched him in his cabin lifting a bottle of rum to his mouth with trembling hands. I knew how he felt, the urgency to guzzle as much as possible as quickly as he could to drag him from the dungeons of that inhumane labyrinth of fear. I knew only one mouthful of rum would bring me to his terror, yet I envied him. I envied the release he felt when the bottle was drained.

He stepped back and rested against the wall behind him. He closed his eyes and remained still for few minutes to allow the rum to do its job and lubricate his senses. He didn't see me watching him. Slowly he opened his eyes and held up his trembling hands.

The shaking would subside in a little while, the rum would set him at ease so that he could sail through his day without the grief that assailed me.

Each day I bathed in the sea and wished the waves would take away my sorrow at losing Arry and my daughter Josephine. Within a few weeks I took Leon home again. Josephine's son, Akeem, had survived. Ngozi brought him to live with us. I loved her for it. Her simple suggestion was that they, Leon and Akeem, would be good for one another.

"Maybe dey be good for yuh sad heart too," she said, rocking in her chair on the porch. "Dey be good for all our sadness."

MISTRESS LYDIA WAS NOWHERE TO BE SEEN. I IMAGINED HER BODY would be vulnerable to attack. When I saw a new nurse arrive, I believed Lydia was also infected with cholera.

When Blair sympathised with me over Arry's death, I scrutinised his expression but was only met with the same despair as my own.

When Mistress Lydia had not appeared for two weeks I asked how she was.

"Resting, thank you," he replied.

Was he trying to cure her from the Blue Death? It was possible – some people survived. His short response made it clear he did not wish to discuss it. The secrecy added to the rumours of her illness. Or was it her nerves? Had the climate of this country finally forced her behind the closed door of her bedroom to die a miserable and lonely death far removed from her beloved Ireland? Phoebe could tell us nothing, only that Mistress was to remain undisturbed. Three times a week Phoebe was to scrub Mistress's room when she was in the bath where Nurse washed her. The doctor called a few times a week. I saw his carriage arrive and roll up to the main door. I watched Blair so closely it was a sickness in itself. A man fixated on another's happiness cannot be happy. I scrutinised his expression: I wanted to see a flicker of unhappiness. I was revolted by him and everything he represented. In my own sordid way I hoped she was dying. Yet I knew he didn't value her.

Finally Phoebe came to me with news of Lydia.

"She is big wid a baby in her belly," she gasped. "I walk into her room dis mornin' cuz I thought she was in de room with de bath. She was not in bed but sittin' in a chair. Nurse was walkin' across de room to put a blanket on her when I seed her belly."

"Why does she need to stay in bed?" I asked.

"De doctor say she could die with de baby if she walk." Phoebe paused before admitting to listening at the door. "Wen I walk in, Nurse Nancy scream at me to get out. A few minutes later de doctor came to see her and I stay outside listenin'. Doctor say she special and no walkin'."

We both stood in silence, considering it.

I nodded.

"White mistresses be strange," Phoebe said quietly. "Wat kind of child will be born wen a mother does not get out of bed?"

I admitted I didn't know.

"A lazy child, dat's what," Phoebe said.

. . .

ALTHOUGH THE PRACTICE OF OBEAH WAS CRIMINALISED, CARRYING A prison sentence if found with Obeah objects, Blair wanted Cristof to pray over his wife that she'd deliver a son. In the past he'd ridiculed the use of Obeah as a "hocus-pocus affair for superstitious uneducated Africans", yet now he wanted to use it on his wife.

"Pray that she has a son," Blair ordered Cristof.

Cristof explained, "Is not right to force de hand of de gods. De gods decide if yuh have a boy or girl."

Blair threatened to turn him over to the law if he didn't comply.

Cristof told me how Blair then took him to his wife's chamber and ordered him to pray over her.

"It's bad to tamper like dat." Cristof was upset after it. "Only brings evil to force de hands of gods."

I asked how Mistress Lydia reacted.

"She want a son too."

TWO WEEKS LATER MISTRESS GAVE BIRTH TO A BOY.

Blair and two of his friends spent the day drinking.

Phoebe relayed the events to me that night.

"Dey call de new baby four names …" She hesitated. "Henry and some more names. I can't remember de othas. Masta kept saying de names of his new baby and Mr. Rednapp and Mr. Masterson told him how happy him was over and over again. Then Masta and Mr. Rednapp start marchin' up and down de house singing 'God Save the Queen'. Nurse came down to tell dem to hush up but Mr. Rednapp runned after her and caught her on de stairs. Him ripped her dress before she escaped and runned up to de bedroom weh de baby was with Mistress. The doctor stopped Mr. Rednapp and told him find anotha woman. Nurse Nancy was needed wid Mistress."

"Who did Rednapp find?" I asked cautiously, hoping Phoebe had not been the poor wretch they used.

"I don't know. I sneaked away."

"Where are they now?"

"Masta getting' sick in his room. Rednapp is gone off on him's horse and I don't know 'bout Mr. Masterson."

OKEKE WAS ELEVEN YEARS OF AGE WHEN HENRY WAS BORN. HE remained living in Arry's cabin most of the time. Other times he drifted from cabin to cabin. Some nights he would stay at my son's, other times Ngozi asked him to stay with us. She prepared a bed and made a fuss of him.

"Only stay at night," she suggested when she saw his reluctance. She thought he would be more open to the idea if she was not forceful. "Come and eat and den come back and sleep."

I agreed with Ngozi and told him we were his family. "Don't be a stupid boy staying alone in Arry's cabin, missing Arry every time you put your head down at night. We are family. Live with us or Emmet in Black River," I suggested, referring to my fisherman son.

Emmet's children were the same age as Okeke. "Or Eleanor would be delighted to see you." Eleanor, his sister, was living with her flock of children further down the coast.

Okeke indicated the Big House. "They are my family," he said assertively. "I should live there."

"Yuh be waitin' a long time," Ngozi said. "Das not gonna happen."

"Why not?" he asked in the accent of the Stratford-Rices'.

Ngozi shook her head over the fact that Okeke regarded himself as a son with entitlements, "Because men like Blair don't do dat. Dey only do dat for dem own white folks."

Okeke mentioned a renowned case in Gordon Town where the planter moved his African woman into the Big House with her offspring.

Ngozi held up her finger. "One white masta did dat in all of Jamaica. Blair not like dat man in Gordon Town."

Okeke was not listening to Ngozi. He was looking towards the Big House.

"You're too young to understand now," I said. "In time you'll be happier that there is more African and Irish blood in you than the blood of the Stratford-Rices." I wanted him to see the great attributes from his African and Irish family. "You know that men came from all over to buy your grandmother's flutes?" I told him once again how Flora's mother could make the best flutes from the bamboo shoots. "You come from strong intelligent hardworking stock."

"I am more like my father's people. My grandmother Flora was crazy and you are Irish," he said as if my nationality soiled his pedigree.

That day I thought he did not realise how offensive his comment was. Later I realised offending us was irrelevant to Okeke.

WHEN I FIRST SAW BLAIR'S SON HE WAS SIX MONTHS OLD. HE WAS IN his pushchair in the gazebo, flanked by the nurse and Mistress Lydia. So afraid of the sun and illnesses, Mistress Lydia and her son were confined in the nursery by Nurse who had become a permanent fixture.

"How are you, Mistress Lydia?" I asked.

"Art, it's so lovely to see you," she said, smiling and sounding genuinely pleased.

She told me with wide startled eyes how she was confined to her bedroom and the nursery for the last six months. "I used to sit by the window and see you pass. Nurse and Doctor Manuel forbade me to leave. Blair and I were so fearful I did exactly as I was told. They were ever so kind but naturally it was difficult to endure such a lengthy confinement."

She spoke quietly as if recalling a barbaric period of her life.

"I'd see you pass and wish to hear your lovely Irish accent that makes me feel I'm in Lugdale House during the hottest day of the year," she said, looking at me kindly.

"A lovely little boy," I said. He looked just like every other small newborn.

"Doctor Manuel says it's a fine time of the day for a child to get fresh air," Mistress Lydia said.

I agreed.

Nurse nodded politely. There was nothing more to be said. They had their heir.

LIFE RESUMED AS IT ALWAYS DID. OUR LIVES CURVED TO accommodate the many changing streams and gullies that branched off it. My daily jobs for the Stratford-Rices were at a minimum. Each week I collected rents for the lease of the land and the remaining families who lived in the slave cabins. Once a week I rode the horse around the lands. The weeds crawled up the redundant mill, engulfing it, the dilapidated site a reminder of the changes. With every passing month the structure of the mill grew smaller – at night the old labourers who built it took the stone to build their own new structures. Once a day I walked around the lawns to see that the gardener was doing his job. I counted the fowl and ensured the livestock and stables were secure at night. The jobs were so simple I could have sent Leon, my little boy, out to do my day's work.

At that stage I had worked for the Stratford-Rices for sixty-six years. In five years' time at the age of eight-one, I would receive my seven gold coins for each decade I had worked on this crumbling plantation.

IN THE AFTERNOONS, LEON AND AKEEM RETURNED FROM THEIR lessons. They were both attending school with the missionaries. When they returned they'd come with me while I did my afternoon errands. They'd give me an account of their day. At five years of age everything is new and alive. They never sat still for long. As we checked our traps and walked from field to field, they ran beside me and jostled each other. Occasionally one tripped the other, their winded laughter rising to meet my ears. I kept walking, knowing they'd catch up with me. For a few hours each day they'd go to Emmet's cabin close to the seafront. Leon and Akeem would swim in the sea with the other children. Sometimes I joined them for the simple pleasure of watching them.

Like me, they enjoyed looking at the ships and sailors. There was a sense of purpose on the pier, an excitement at the unknown, the camaraderie among the crews evident as they loaded and unloaded their cargo. Akeem and Leon loved to look at the ships – every movement and feature was remarked upon. They talked about a ship's size, how many men would weigh as heavy as the ship. They asked about the cargo and the logwood tree trunks that had been sent down the rivers and loaded onto the ships for exportation. Why do they want our logwood? Where will the logwood go? Do other countries not have logwood or cattle skins? They contemplated the ships and sailors, the notion of strange lands spiralling in their imaginations.

After examining and commenting on each ship we'd walk to the smaller pier. They had learned quickly how to swim and dive from the pier. With age I worried for their safety and couldn't watch for long. Ngozi would tell me not to fuss and would remind me how I used to jump off the same pier. Together we'd watch them run and jump high, holding their legs close to their chests, their bodies rigid with determination.

Leon would call to one of Emmet's dogs who'd sit beside Ngozi and me on pier.

"*Puppy!* "

The dog was as much part of the family as Ngozi and me.

"*Puppy!* " he'd call again. "*Look at me!* "

The dog would look, his eyes following the sound of his voice.

Leon would run and jump high, spin in the air and dive deep under the water. He'd resurface elated and ask, "Yuh see dat, Puppy?"

I'd put my hand on the dog's head and push it up and down as if the dog was nodding.

Satisfied his dive had been witnessed, Leon would flip over on his back and float on the water.

Akeem would race towards the pier. "*I will go higher!* "

Their exuberance was as new to me as life was new to them. I was grateful for the small mercies, the fact that they were healthy and spirited, boisterous and able. Even their small kind gestures pleased me.

．　．　．

Blair's son was not so fortunate.

Within two years I heard the first rumours about his difficulties. He had trouble sitting up, then he had trouble walking. There were doctors from Kingston, America and England, with varying diagnoses. One of the many doctors who came from London affixed boards to his legs.

"Him look like dere are no bones in his legs," Phoebe told me. Demonstrating, she walked unsteadily across the room.

Henry could walk short distances but mostly he got about in a chair with wheels. One of the staff had to push him. Each year there was a new theory and a new doctor. I had enormous sympathy for the boy. Not only did he not have the freedom to run and play as every child had, but the examinations must have been torturous and humiliating.

CHAPTER TWENTY-SIX

There were guests who came and went from the Big House but one man stayed longer – Mr. Nicolas Ffrench. When Blair renovated McCovey's cabin for his guest, there was cause for great speculation. He was not white nor English. Some deduced he was a Frenchman from his surname, Mr. Ffrench.

"Him a prince from France. He gonna marry Miss Jane," Ngozi said, referring to one of Blair's daughters.

The name, the French Prince, stuck to him. He didn't have a solid routine. He remained for weeks, then left for two weeks and returned again. Some said he was an officer in the French Army, another theory was that he was a scholar studying the Jamaican wildlife. He'd spend hours sketching the crocodiles at the river – he could be seen sitting on a tree trunk watching them. Others thought he was another doctor for Blair's son.

"Maybe a doctor for Mistress Lydia," one of the domestic servants said.

Mistress Lydia grew older and thinner as time passed. She was like a woman suspended in no-man's-land, always pining for the country she had left behind. Strangely, I understood it. Ireland has a way of never letting you go – the land, the storytellers, the voices, the beautiful island on the edge of the world. Mistress Lydia was a woman whose exile brought little happiness, making Ireland's grip stronger and more romantic. Her conversations were dominated by Ireland. Each year she struggled with the heat, her head inclined away from the glare of the sun. Each year she recalled the same memories.

In September she said, "I expect my brothers and their children are grooming their horses for the hunt in Lugdale."

Other times she would long for frost. "The fires will be lighting in every room in Lugdale. It's a wonderful house for Christmas."

She often reminded me of the Irish who died shortly after their arrival to these shores. They were too consumed with memory to find pleasure in the ordinary beautiful sight of their new home.

"If she go any whiter or thinner we not gonna be able to see her one des days," Phoebe said. "She be like a Duppy and fly away."

The French Prince was not a doctor for Mistress Lydia or Henry. Blair had several doctors to deal with Henry. Blair spoke to one doctor who told him it was Henry's heart, a new condition that made him gain weight and made his muscles lazy. Dissatisfied with the explanation, Blair spoke to a different doctor who told him the problem with his son's legs was a disease of muscle. Unless exercised, the muscles in his body would waste until eventually he would not be able to use his arms or the muscles in his face to eat.

Blair insisted the boy begin with short walks around the garden. When Blair helped the boy from his chair, his legs would not hold his weight. He collapsed and lay exhausted on the ground at his father's feet. Blair took the chair, insisting that Henry crawl. On that occasion, I came upon him crying alone on the lawn. I pitied the boy but, to my shame, did nothing to help him. All I could do was offer some encouraging words and watch as he dragged himself painfully across the lawn and Blair at last came out of the house to pick him up.

BLAIR KEPT HIS OTHER SON, OKEKE, CLOSE BY. WHEN HE WAS thirteen Blair told him he didn't need any further education but instead would work for him. Each day Okeke went to the Big House – some days he worked in the gardens, other times he ran errands for the bookkeeper or took the carriage to Black River. He was no longer able to pass the time between classes playing with his half-sisters or the visitors who came from other Big Houses. When Mistress Lydia's niece and nephew visited from Ireland, Okeke was not invited to join them. I caught him at the side of my cabin spying on them as they played cricket.

Okeke was displaced with his mother's death and his father's disinterest in him. He was suddenly invisible to the very people he adored.

"You'll drive yourself mad," I said to him and tried to console him. "At least you learned how to read and write. You have more knowledge than any son of a slave or any other mulatto boy."

"I'm not just any other boy," he retorted angrily.

Arry had been foolish to adore him as she did and fill his head with nonsense. She told him often that he was better than the Stratford-Rice children – he was a boy. She led him to believe his maleness set him above Blair's daughters.

"I am better than his own son," Okeke said, referring to Henry.

I knew he resented Henry. I'd seen him treating the crippled boy with the same contempt as Blair did.

I tried to keep Okeke close to our family, to allow him to build a bond with his uncles and aunts, and find his role among his cousins. I hoped his resistance to his mother's family would soften. I wanted him to find strength in our unity. I told him how we were climbing from the sewers of slavery to find our own dignity. I wanted Okeke to sense the solidarity in those evenings among our people. I watched him look indifferently as the older boys played with Leon and Akeem. I watched his face closely to see a flicker of delight at the sight of the two young boys picking at the clay earth, copying the adults at work. Their small endeavours would make the sightless grin yet Okeke couldn't muster a faint smile.

One day while Okeke was working with my son and me as we planted jicama seeds, Mr. Ffrench sent one of the servants to fetch him. Eager to please, Okeke dropped his tool, dusted off his clothes and went immediately to him. A few moments later Okeke was seen leaving the plantation with a parcel. It was several hours later when he returned.

"What did Mr. Ffrench want with you?" I asked as he sat down.

He shrugged and cast me a sideways glance. "A little business in Black River."

"What kind of business does Mr. Ffrench do?"

He appeared annoyed with my question. "What? Why do you ask? It's my father's business."

"Because I'm worried, only looking out for you," I said.

"Mr. Ffrench would never harm me," he said.

"How do you know?"

"Mr. Ffrench likes me – he told me I remind him of his son. His only son's boat went missing last year. Every time he sees me, he says I'm like his son. Mr. Ffrench would never harm my kind."

"Your kind?" I repeated.

He looked at the clay on his hands. After our day in the fields the soil was imbedded in his nails.

"They know I'm smart," he said. "My father and Mr. Ffrench know I could work at something so much better than planting yam bean."

He didn't add anything further, only rested his chin on his hand.

I leaned across the table and slapped his hand away from his face. He looked back at me, stunned.

"Never be any man's master. Blair is your father but that is all. You will never be one of their people."

I was too forceful. I wanted him to see with the wisdom of an old man. I wanted him to sense the allegiance within our community and family, cousins and uncles and aunts who would make great sacrifices for him as they would for any of their family. In the end it was pointless. He rejected us and only sensed shame from his darker colour.

Eventually I left him alone and finally he stopped coming to my home, then he stopped speaking to me. Occasionally we'd meet in the Big House, but he stopped acknowledging me and in turn I ignored him. The last time I stood in close proximity to him was in

Blair's study. He was leaving as I was entering. I didn't feel anything for him. I had come to accept he was more like the Stratford-Rices than us. There was nothing else I could do.

Eventually I found his absence an ease. The sadness of Arry's death was lessened when Okeke was removed from my sight.

CHAPTER TWENTY-SEVEN

For years we remained a happy unit with our growing families and our work. At night after we ate supper, Leon and Akeem told me the numbers and letters they were learning at school. When one was uncertain over a letter the other would know it. They wrote the initials of their names, then asked for the first initial of my name and wrote A in the sand. "What does it mean? Art?" they asked. "Where is Ireland?" They were soaking everything into their growing minds – the language, my language, strange accents, the wings of an insect, the claws of an eagle, the shell of a tortoise. They noticed it all, even that which was not spoken but felt. They had compassion. At that stage of my life I welcomed that attribute. I'd see them help Henry when his father took the wheelchair and made him crawl. Occasionally they suggested we take Henry swimming. For those few hours Henry had the pleasure of feeling that the useless legs which could not carry his body were lighter beneath the water.

Akeem and Leon also worked with my sons on our land and were mostly happy boys. But they sensed the fear over a missing boy in the vicinity. He had vanished. Some said he was fishing and drowned, others said they saw him walking on the road. The Duppy was blamed. Then another boy a few miles in the other direction also vanished and another from the Crawford area. Leon and Akeem joined us in the search for one of the missing boys. We combed the fields near his homes, the rivers where he swam, and looked for traces of him around the crocodile pond. His mother asked the Obeah man who looked into her frantic face with a new blankness.

"I cannot tell, I do not know."

Some saw his vagueness as confirmation that something terrible had happened.

"Christof won't tell very bad news," Ngozi said. "Das why him pretend he don't know."

Leon and Akeem's game changed. They chased about the cabin after each other. *"I am the Duppy who will make yuh vanish!"*

Only at night when they slept was there some semblance of quietness in our cabin, their endless running and playing ceasing for a few hours. Their hot bodies smelled of salt. When I saw them sleep, a calmness descended on me. I knew they would be there when I awoke – the Duppy or whoever took the other boys would not enter at night. In the morning they would bounce around the cabin, renewed for another day.

When they were sleeping I'd sit on my porch and invite anyone who passed to join me. There are old friends but none as old as I am.

OCCASIONALLY OKEKE REAPPEARED, A BOY DRESSED AS A MAN. I'D heard from Emmet that he was a sailor on a ship that went to Africa. He'd earned money and dressed in the rich clothes of moneyed men. Eventually he stopped calling to my son's house. When he returned from his trips at sea, he stayed in Arry's old cabin.

One day I was sitting on the porch when I saw him arrive. He was in a carriage with Mr. Ffrench. I saw the carriage stop at the front door of the Big House. Blair came out the front door and raised his arm jubilantly as if delighted to see his son. He walked down the steps and shook their hands.

Just then I recalled Okeke's ability to use different voices and accents while selling goods at the market with his mother. Like Arry he was good – he could present himself as a different person at will.

Okeke was clearly very comfortable not only using the accent but playing the role of the elite white man.

Ngozi shook her head with bewilderment as she sat down beside me.

"Who dems men?" Akeem asked me.

It had been so many years since Okeke visited that Leon and Akeem had forgotten him.

Ngozi and I remained silent while we watched the men disappear inside the Big House.

"Who he, Papa?" Leon asked.

When one was curious, they were both curious. But they fell quiet, watching us monitoring the movements of the men.

"He's a boy I used to know," I said with acceptance.

"Come, Papa, we feed de pigs," Leon said.

Leon took one of my hands and Akeem the other.

At that age it took me longer to stand up. The boys believed it was their strength that got me to my feet.

They began to count. "One," I rocked back and forth in the chair, "two," they pulled, "three," I was standing.

Akeem handed me my cane. They ran ahead to the piggery.

"Okeke is probably happy doin' wat he doing," Ngozi said, "and we is happy wid wat we doin'."

As I passed her I caught her hand. Although unaccustomed to such sentimental gestures she did not look surprised.

"Yes," I said, looking into her solid brown eyes, "we are more than happy with what we have."

She acknowledged what I'd said with a nod of acceptance. I released her hand and followed the boys to do our evening chores.

· · ·

I AGED SLOWLY AND LEARNED TO READ FASTER. I BOUGHT LOOKING-glasses in Black River and it lent a new quality to my days. For an hour each day Akeem and Leon sat at either side of me, listening to the stories that began to flow freer as the words became more familiar. There were books about castaways on desert islands, adventures at sea, and pirates. The boys listened wide-eyed.

IN 1889, I KNEW THINGS WERE SOURING BETWEEN BLAIR, OKEKE and the French Prince. It began with their shipment of cargo on Black River's pier. His goods had spoiled, I heard. I asked what products Blair was shipping abroad but nobody knew. Blair did not employ local labour or invite anyone onto the ships. There was talk that it was rum destined for France. His ship was docked a few miles out at sea. I heard at night they dumped the spoiled produce. The French Prince and Okeke were seen taking a small boat late at night to investigate the cargo. They spent the night working under lanterns, and one of the fishermen saw them dumping the cargo under the cover of darkness. Nothing happens on the pier without someone seeing it. A fisherman was close enough to hear the splashes. The fact that none of the local stevedores were hired to clear the ship caused further suspicion. They whispered about all kinds of stock that was on the boat.

"Crocodiles to bring to de Queen of England for her to taste."

We laughed at the suggestion.

"Is Arry's boy, Okeke, he de boss," the fisherman told me, as if I were a simpleton. "He know wat happen, ask him."

It took me a few hours to do my chores and then I went back to Black River. I sold one of my old books and bought another. Each time I finished a chore I returned to the seafront to look at the ship. They had brought it further out to sea, but by evening it returned to the dock at the far end of the marina. I rode the pony as close as I could and watched the ship rock unsteadily with the gathering winds. I dismounted and went closer. There was no gangway, only strong chains anchoring it to the pier. The hatches were firmly locked down, there was no sign of life, not even a broken bottle of rum or snoring crocodile. I stepped away from the pier. Unlike my sons who loved the great ships and seafaring lives, it brought me no lust, only an old sense of trepidation.

THE FOLLOWING MORNING I NOTICED THAT OKEKE HAD RETURNED in a carriage with Mr. Ffrench. A grown man of nineteen years of age, older than his years, with his top hat and silk shirt. It was around midday when the sun was at its hottest. I was standing beside the main entrance to the plantation. Their horse stalled. Okeke's eyes met mine. That day he did not look away but stared at me. He appeared like the young tired men who spent their lives at the sea, lonely, rootless and hard. I allowed my eyes encounter his hate-filled gaze.

Later Phoebe told me that Blair and Okeke had fought.

"Everybody in de big house is scared." she said. "Masta say him will kill Okeke and Okeke say him will kill Masta."

None of it surprised me. Nature would take its course with every man and Okeke and Blair were no different.

Strangely, that day I recalled the Widow McAuliffe's curse. Would life ever bring Okeke to that cornered juncture where he would turn on his own for survival? Would he turn on the very man whose attention and gratitude he craved?

Okeke spent a few hours in the French Prince's cabin before leaving with some men. I didn't watch him leave. I sat with Akeem and Leon as we read from a collection of stories.

I finished reading a rather mournful story to the boys and thought about my lost grandson, Okeke. I examined my conscience and found it was not clear. My bias towards that eternal hatred for the Stratford-Rices in Okeke's case discoloured any natural feelings for him.

"Dem stories is makin' yuh go mad," Ngozi cautioned behind me. "No man gonna get happy wid dem sad words."

I didn't answer her. I watched Akeem and Leon skip down the hill and scamper onto the back of a passing pony and trap to go to my son Emmet's house. They were happy to do an hour's work in return for an evening swimming in the sea with my son's children. I imagined their laughter, louder than the crash of the frothy waves.

I quelled a strange urgency to call after them to come home. The sight of Okeke's large rocking ship had left me with an equally unsteady sense of foreboding.

THAT EVENING I WAS RESTLESS. I TOOK MY PONY THROUGH THE fields and checked my traps. Empty-handed, I took the long road home and rode the pony down to Arry's old cabin. One of his neighbours told me that a few strange men had stayed the night with Okeke.

He told me he thought Okeke was a big man now.

"Me ask Okeke for work for me son on his ship," he told me. "Okeke say no." He imitated Okeke's English accent and touched his nose with his forefinger, an insinuation that Okeke felt above his neighbour. "Him say, only special men work on his ship."

I nodded sympathetically without condemning the grandson who had left me so conflicted.

Inside Arry's old cabin, it was almost empty. The smell of fresh food hung in the air. The floor was swept, the cleaned pot hung on the hook. The mattress was pushed against the wall. When I saw the secret hiding place exposed I knew Okeke was not coming back. In the corner of the cabin was Arry's old hiding place where she hid her money. After Arry died Okeke hid his belongings in the same place. Unknown to Okeke I used to come into the cabin and peek at the boy's most coveted possessions. As time passed his secrets within the box reflected his growth. He kept a little money, Arry's pearl necklace and bracelet, there were maps and letters he stole from the Big House. Sometimes there were letters from Ireland addressed to Mistress Lydia. I can only assume that Okeke took the letters for a while before replacing them and taking a different letter. It left me sad. Saddened that he was so taken with the Stratford-Rices that he read Mistress Lydia's letters to get a bigger glimpse into their lives.

That day in March 1889, the set of pearls was gone, and there were no letters or maps – only an upturned wooden box that once kept his sparse coins and stolen letters.

I rode back the way I had come along the seafront. Old memories of Okeke returned, deepening my sense of failing him. I thought of him as a boy learning to speak with Anglo syllables. As he grew he became more and more like the enemy. I was conflicted at his departure, pleased I would never need to see Blair Stratford-Rice looking back at me from my grandson's face. There was shame and relief in my admittance, shame I could wish my eyes would never fall on one of my own kin and relief that I had admitted the truth.

They were my thoughts as I arrived at the foot of the hill on which my cabin sat. I saw a group of people close to the water's edge. They were standing on the rocks, looking into the water that lapped at their feet. Christof was among them.

I dismounted and walked towards them.

"Yuh see wat de sea threw up?" my neighbour said.

There was a woman wailing as she ran towards the gathering.

"*Is it me son?* " she pleaded.

She was the mother of the boy who'd disappeared a few weeks previously.

"No," the men said.

I joined them and looked into the shallow water.

There was a boy, aged about eight or nine. He was roughly the size of Leon and Akeem but darker-skinned. He was floating between the rocks with his eyes closed and arms by his sides.

Around his waist was a rope. I stepped into the water and pulled him out and laid him on the rocks.

"He have disease, Art," one of the men said.

The gathering moved away back.

"Anotha boy came up in Hunt Bay," Christof said, referring to a beach a few miles away. "Him was alive for a while and diseased."

I examined the rope around the child's waist. There was a noose on the end of it, as if it were wrapped around a weight and freed itself.

Okeke's spoiled cargo was not crocodiles or rum, rotten bananas or cattle. It was slave children destined for another country that still enslaved the black man. I thought of the locked-down ship on the pier and wondered how many slaves died. Sea merchants had to replace damaged or lost cargo. It was pointless to sail for weeks without a ship full of stock. The easiest pickings for slave traders were on the seafront. Boys cascading in on the waves, their youthful eyes eager to see the inside of a ship. It was an easy way to replenish the lost consignment. The crowd around me moved away.

My son Emmet was making his way towards me. When I looked up to see his distressed expression, I knew. I knew only Okeke could commit such a vile act against one of his own.

"Akeem is missin'." Emmet's voice was barely audible. Helplessly he pointed out to sea, aware it was futile.

On the horizon was Okeke's ship as it embarked on its voyage. I stumbled into the sea and roared as loud as my voice would carry, the truth of Okeke's malevolence cascading down upon me. Wishing my voice would carry to the ship-compartment in which Akeem was chained.

"*Akeeeem!* " *I called out his name.* "*Akeeeem, I will find you!*" My voice died with the ebbing ship. "*I will find you!*" I said, collapsing into the waves.

CHAPTER TWENTY-EIGHT

There are only so many times a man can lift his head from the claws of despair. In the weeks after Akeem's abduction, I stumbled about in a rage that gave way to a haze of despair. The day of his disappearance we went immediately to Black River Pier where we learned that Okeke's ship had come from Cuba and was going to Morocco. Three years previously, Cuba had freed its slaves. It was one of the last European colonies to abolish slavery. Okeke was taking freed slaves from Cuba, luring children, young men and seasoned slaves onto his ships and selling them to countries as far away as Morocco where slavery continued.

Frantic, I went to the the Big House with a group of locals. Blair was not there, I was told. I checked all of the rooms.

In the study Mistress Lydia and Henry were frozen with fear when they saw us arrive. I checked the hiding place underneath the floor which was empty. The map of the world caught my eye.

"Show me Morocco," I demanded.

Henry's small undeveloped white finger pointed across the sea. "Only that part is Morocco. The continent is Africa. Morocco is here," he said, circling the north-west corner.

Before leaving I climbed the stairs of the Big House as if it were my home. Blair's bed was made, his room cleaned awaiting his return. The room for his bath was also empty.

A few hours later we returned to find Ffrench sleeping in his bed. We pulled him from his slumber and pierced his belly with a knife. We began to kick and strike him. When he sat dazed I ordered him to stand and asked him where Okeke had taken Akeem.

He tried to threaten us as he held his hand over his wound. "You'll hang for this."

We loaded him onto the back of a cart and took him to the crocodile pond. At the pond we tied a rope to his feet and threatened to use him as bait if he did not help us. He told us he didn't know our children had been taken. He admitted the children on the beach were taken for Morocco by Okeke. He swore on his dead son's life that he would get our children back. We learned he was not French nor a prince but a man from Cuba who owned ships and sold slaves. He mentioned the name Dockworth and Ignatius Duffy – Irish Ignatius, still in business, with his sons who continued in the same profession. They were every bit as ruthless as their father and continued to feed slaves to destinations where slavery still thrived.

"Mr. Dockworth is the slave trader in Morocco," Ffrench told us.

While dangling above the crocodile pond he swore again to travel to Morocco and buy our children at the slave auction.

At the utterance of the words slave auction and the prospect of our children being forced to return to servitude, we teased the crocodiles by tossing his body into the water and pulling him out several times. When he was pulled out the last time it was I who stuck the knife in his neck repeatedly. We threw him to the waiting float of crocodiles who were infected with our bloodthirsty frenzy. When our rage had been satisfied we sat in a stupefied exhausted haze as if the crocodiles had feasted on us too.

There were three children taken from the shores of Black River. We learned from one of the other children how Okeke had asked the boys if they'd like to see the ship. Not all of the children were brave or adventurous enough to go.

I learned that Leon was swimming at the time. When he noticed

Akeem's absence he assumed he was in my son Emmet's house. Sometime later he saw one of the mother's calling her son's name. Another man came to the shore for his son. Their unconcern turned to unease when their calls were not answered and they established that three boys were missing. A short time later they noticed Okeke's ship pull away from the pier. Even then they did not realise that my grandson had taken their children, to be sold for a few coins of gold and a vague acknowledgement from his father Blair.

EACH DAY MY NEIGHBOURS AND I WENT TO THE SAILORS FROM THE newly docked ships and asked if they were going to Morocco. In the weeks after, none of the ships seemed destined for that cursed place.

We went to find my old acquaintance Ignatius Duffy, the slave trader. He was an old man then. His son and namesake, who carried on the foul trade, claimed he knew nothing about Akeem and had no dealings with Okeke. Later, there were times that I went alone and asked Ignatius if he'd seen Okeke on his travels. He always denied it.

At night my neighbours and I sat together, each family swearing retribution on my grandson. Some were kind enough to say it was Stratford-Rice blood that destroyed him and disassociated him from my family.

ONE WEEK AFTER THE INCIDENT I SAW THE LIGHT FROM Blair's study. I knew he had not gone anywhere previously. Phoebe had told me he just galloped away on his horse when he saw us approaching.

Blair was our only hope of finding the children. The men who took them were his kind, wealthy men who clawed at the dregs of slavery to maintain their lifestyle. The night I saw the light in his study I went to him, using the servants' entrance.

He nervously jumped to his feet. "You have no right! Who is with you?"

"Where is my boy?" I asked.

"I don't know what you're talking about," he said, stumbling backwards.

I struck him in the mouth with the handle of my cane. His tooth dislodged – he spat it from his mouth and looked at it in his hand.

"I heard about it," he admitted, "but I don't know anything about it. I have been as anguished as you."

"You will write letters to your friends in Morocco, slave traders, plantation owners and Okeke. You tell Okeke I will kill him with my own hands. I will not rest until -," I had to stop speaking. I was choked with rage and the need to simply curl up and cry. I couldn't allow Blair see the broken man I had become. "I will not rest," I continued in a low contained voice, "until Okeke is dead and the children are found."

"I had nothing to do with it," he repeated quietly.

I didn't believe him yet he was my only hope.

CHAPTER TWENTY-NINE

In the weeks after Akeem's capture I thought of snow, large flakes of white snow dropping down from the sky. As I lay in my bed I imagined the cold soft snow covering my cabin, the plantation and the island. I longed for the silence that early-morning falling snow brings, flakes lodging and mounting, smothering me beneath its weight until I was no more and all belonging to me was gone, melted away like the snowman with the stones in its eyes and twigs as arms. I was sorrowful and strangely longing for Ireland, for sounds and long-forgotten memories.

"Papa," Leon was pulling my finger, "read to me some of de story."

I looked at the book in his hand and roused myself.

"Do yuh scary voice," he said.

I had learned to be theatrical when I read, raising my voice and lowering it to a whisper. Sometimes Akeem and Leon used to look at my changing face rather than the words in the book.

I held the book and felt the hard cover. I put the book on the floor and instead put my arm around his shoulders. "I will tell you a different story," I said.

He looked at me with wide expectant eyes.

"I was born in a parish called Mein – it means a grassy patch on the slope of a hill. My cottage is high in the mountains overlooking the wild Atlantic Ocean," and so I began telling Leon the whole story. The plagued Irish, the constant war, the old Irish that returned to me. I bought paper and a quill, and I took him back back to the beginning.

TWICE A WEEK I WENT TO BLAIR WITH THE RENTS FOR THE LAND. Our mutual detestation, like a faithful old yapping dog, kept us company. We were comfortable in the familiar ugliness of hatred. Like miserable men find miserable men good company, or the dignified are comfortable with gracious comrades, hate-filled men need hate-filled men.

"Any word from Morocco?" I asked each week.

"I send regular letters but never hear."

"What about Okeke?" I asked.

He'd shake his head.

There were times I believed it was pointless. During one of the days I told him a story. I sat in front of him like the most carefree man in Jamaica about to regale an old friend in a tavern over a glass of rum.

I told him about a woman in Ireland whose reputation stretched around the world. "She does magic, she kills animals and curses families and men." I told him about my seeing the Widow McAuliffe preparing her bloody curse.

As I told the story I reminded myself of Okeke taunting Henry.

"On a wet street in Ireland she hurled the bloodied innards of the animal at a certain couple. She cursed each generation of the family."

Blair didn't ask anything. He remained staring at me as I spoke.

I continued. "She screamed out her curse, saying that in each generation the offspring would kill their father."

His head moved back slightly when I said that.

"Burdan was the last man to enact the curse," I said casually.

I waited for him to lunge at me. He didn't.

Quietly I left.

IN THE LAST FEW DAYS OF 1890 I TOLD BLAIR I WANTED MY GOLD coins and would stop working for him. At the mention of the gold coins he hesitated.

"I've served my time," I said.

Blair sighed and unlocked one of the drawers behind him. He took out a logbook.

"You arrived in my great-uncle's time, Major George Beaufort's, in the year 1821. Yes," he tapped his finger under my entry, "you were approximately eleven. Didn't the English do you a great service?"

"I want my coins," I said.

"I can't give them to you today," Blair said, matching my even tone. "In ten days' time you will have seventy years' service completed. Legally the coins will be yours then."

I believed if we travelled to opposite ends of the earth, we'd find each other. Our hatred was so strong it was like a magnet. To survive we needed to inflict suffering on the other. We thrived on it. As a grown man aware of my all-consuming hatred, I should have left years before, but couldn't see through the haze. Hatred was my lifelong companion. It kept me strong, it was that force that propelled me to rise and fight each day, to fight for my sons so they would not look at a master and find comfort in the most violent thoughts. I told Leon about the hatred, what a waste it had been.

Blair and I looked across the desk, each gauging the other. He knew I would kill him and I was aware he would do the same to me, both of us slowly strangling the other.

"You've outlived all of your contemporaries," he sighed. "You've lived a long and good life. You have sons and grandsons. You worked hard and earned a great life here."

"You sound as if I'm about to die," I said.

"We never know what tomorrow brings."

"Possibly your own death," I responded.

He laughed nervously.

CHAPTER THIRTY

The days pass. My life is in order. My sons have enough land to allow them be their own masters. Their children are learning to read and write. There are grandchildren and great-grandchildren who are hale and hearty. There are hard times and good times, times when the sun brings days we remember.

On this day, 2nd January, the year of the Lord in 1891, I go to the Big House for one last time. I will meet the remaining member of the family who caused me to be taken from one green sloping hill to another green hill. I do not believe Blair will give me the coins. He will kill me first.

I watch Leon examine bird pepper seeds. He has a mixture of orange and yellow seeds in the palm of his hand. At his feet is a pot of clay. He roots his hands deep into the clay and inserts the seeds. Like me, Leon has a passion for plants and experiments with seeds. His hands are neat, he works cautiously. For a moment I contemplate not collecting the seven gold coins. I know I've already made enough money from the Stratford-Rices.

Leon suddenly asks, "Are yuh sorry you killed de man yuh hated?"

I have told Leon everything. I told him about the man I killed, Mr. Ffrench.

"I'm sorry the way I killed him," I admit. "Even in death men deserve a little dignity."

He looks across the table at me. "I will mind yuh today, Papa."

For the last few days he has sensed the trouble between Blair and me. He knows something will happen.

My sons have said Blair will not part with the coins. They say he will kill me first. They too have asked to accompany me to the Big House. I declined. For seventy years I've sat in the study of the Big House. I will not bring any man with me on my last trip. I scold myself for thinking too deeply about it.

Leon packs the clay on top of his seeds and levels it with the palm of his hand. Satisfied, he sets the pot aside and contemplates it.

"Papa, last night I dreamed I was in Di Kingdom." He refers to my home country in Ireland. Leon imitates me by pronouncing The Kingdom with my guttural Irish accent.

I've told Leon about the bog, the smell of wet gorse, the bluebells where the fairies play, the eggs or fowl that carry evil spirits, the whitethorn in the dung-heap to ward away evil spirits, the yellow thatch. The smell of my country, my island.

"I dreamed yuh were wid me," Leon says. He smiles at me.

I wonder will he poke fun at me. Like Arry, Leon makes bold with me.

"I dreamed we were walkin' together in Mein, de soft soil and de smell of de heather. We were saying," he grins, he's about to tease me, "*Ár n-Athair atá ar neamh, Go naofar d'ainim, Go dtagfadh do ríocht …*" He recites the prayer *as Gaeilge.*

There are tears in my eyes. I blink them away. My son must not know that I am afraid.

He stretches across the small table that separates us and taps my hand lightly. "Don't go to Blair. Come fishin' wid me."

I think for a moment and shake my head.

He nods, he understands.

I close this book with my simple story and slide it across the table to him.

"Mind that and don't follow me," I say.

PART II

CHAPTER THIRTY-ONE

January 14th, 1991 - Ireland

Yseult woke irritated on the morning of her eighty-first birthday. It had been a rare restless night's sleep. She lay still and exhaled loudly before rolling over to look at the time. It was almost nine o'clock. Normally she'd be up two hours ago.

"What has this damn day brought me?" she whispered.

Slowly and laboriously she pulled the bedclothes back and stood up. "This damn house," she continued, muttering to herself in the same laconic tone. She walked across the room in the semi-darkness. "At my age. Madness."

As she opened the curtains she thought of their old housekeeper Nellie Brown saying, "Four pounds for the velvet material and three weeks to make them". Nellie was so impressed with the curtains, she'd regularly hover by the window and delay for a moment to feel the smooth texture of the velvet between her fingers.

Yseult shivered in the early-morning coldness. "What good are velvet curtains when the house is a nightmare to heat?" she muttered.

The house was over 300 years old and had been passed down several generations.

"What did I keep it for?" She shook her head as if in disbelief that the house belonged to her. "A vegetarian daughter who writes prissy articles about food and nutrition?"

It wasn't only her daughter's vegetarianism or the cold that irked Yseult this morning. It was that damn skeleton found beneath a tree. The only indication of his identity was a single gold coin dated 1870.

WHEN YSEULT RECALLED THE EVENTS FROM THE PREVIOUS NIGHT that sense of apprehension returned. She thought of her farm manager Brendan arriving with a member of the Gardaí. The Garda seemed more taken with her drawing room than delivering news of the discovery in the locality.

"A body?" Yseult had exclaimed when she initially heard it.

"No, a skeleton." The Garda dragged his eyes away from a portrait and back to her.

"A what?" Yseult had said incredulously.

"Speak louder," Brendan quietly said to the Garda. "She's a bit hard of hearing."

Yseult had heard perfectly but she allowed the Garda to repeat what he'd said, which gave her time to think and regain her composure.

The Garda added that they needed to use one of her lanes to access the skeleton.

"We'll need to seal off the lane leading into the bog. You'll probably see a bit of coming and going over the next few days."

"Seal off the area?" Yseult interrupted him in a low angry voice. "This is one of the busiest times of the year."

In fact, it was one of the quietest times of the year. A time when the farming community had little to do during the sparse few hours of daylight except stare at the empty fields and make plans for the spring when nature came to life again. Sealing off the lane was not inconvenient – however, she couldn't have the Gardaí thinking they could saunter through their procedures, infringing on her land.

"It'll only take a few days," the Garda said.

"Who found the skeleton?" Yseult's annoyance was clear in her sharp tone.

The Garda explained that a local petty criminal had been apprehended while trying to sell a gold coin they had reason to believe was valuable. That night he confessed that he'd found the coin in Mein. It was close to a skeleton beneath a tree on Lugdale Estate.

"The coin was minted in 1870," he said.

Slowly she turned her back to them and looked out the window into the dark night.

The Garda continued talking. He mentioned the storm and the tree but Yseult had stopped listening. She didn't ask him to elaborate on the details of the coin. She was aware of a strange shift within her, a sweeping coldness that rendered her breathless and unable to ask about it. It quelled her rage and took the night in a different direction. Yseult only asked where the tree was situated.

He admitted he didn't know the exact location.

When there was nothing to add Yseult remained silent, staring out into the darkness, until she saw the men's reflections leave the room.

YSEULT KNEW WHAT THE LOCALS THOUGHT OF HER. AS THE YOUNG people said she couldn't give a fiddler's. She had run the farm for the last fifty years without a man. From the beginning, she had to make a point that she was not one to be taken advantage of. Like every person in the farming community, she knew the price of cattle, sheep, pigs and tillage. Initially there were a few men who had used an imbecilic way of talking to her. Indeed, some behaved as if she were a simpleton. In the early days she had manners – she was restrained as she declined their bids. As the years passed her manners faded and the niceties became irrelevant. With age so much seemed immaterial.

This morning she was tired before the day began. She delayed by the window looking at the lawn and the avenue leading up to the house. The great oak trees that were planted many lifetimes ago had lost their leaves for the winter. Although stark, they remained imposing. There was a lone blackbird perched on an oak's branch.

Yseult admired the January landscape. The surrounding hills that rose on both sides of her house were green and then brown. In the distance she could see the Atlantic Ocean, with the little inlets that the blue sea filled. Yseult loved the expectation that each season brought. The dark evenings of winter gave her time to recoup. Not only did the creatures and plants of the habitat lie low, she too found it a valuable time to plan and take stock. For the last seventy-one years Yseult had woken up in this creaking old house. Ordinarily she loved it. She loved its great size and its location nestling between the mountains, the lodge at the entrance and its formidable piers. She loved its seclusion with the forest behind it. She loved the longevity and history of the house.

Every decision Yseult made revolved around her house and estate, and there had been great decisions. Not only when she chose holidays or invited guests but great decisions like her choice of husband. In the end it was the love of her estate that kept her in seclusion. There were times when she saw the estate as her first and only and true love. Lugdale Estate was her life. She gave out about it, complained about the heating and the costly renovations, yet the estate contained her soul. Like a lover whom she regularly fought with but could never live without. Lugdale was the catalyst that kept her heart beating. She had sacrificed everything for it, possibly even the salvation of her own soul. She could justify her actions. Lugdale would never have survived in anyone else's hands.

Yseult dressed quickly and retrieved her binoculars from the wardrobe. On this morning, the day when word would travel around the hills about the discovery of a skeleton, she could not resist. Initially she had used the binoculars to keep an eye on Brendan and the farmhands. She also checked the land for poachers and cattle rustlers. Other times she liked to admire the landscape, or she'd watch the birds in their nests. Dusk was her favourite time. It brought a stillness over her as she observed nature retreat for the night.

There was a time when she always ended up taking a look at the land of her neighbour, Mary O'Neill, then around her house. A memory of her father scolding her for spying often returned when she did so. But Yseult's habit of spying had served her well.

Yseult used to see Mary O'Neill feeding her hens each evening. Mary moved in a sprightly fashion as she doled out the feed. She'd watch her walking her greyhounds towards the slips with her son. She had cordoned off a slip of land at the edge of one field where her greyhounds raced. It was not like Mary to waste land. She watched her hold the dogs as her son ran to the top of the field. He had a mechanical contraption that appeared in the distance like a small animal running up the hill – it was a ruse for the greyhounds. When Mary's son got to the top of the hill, Mary released the dogs. Yseult would watch them gallop up the field. Then Mary's son would walk back to her with the dogs. They would discuss the dogs, walk a few paces then stop to talk again. They'd point at the slips, then pat the dogs.

Other times she'd watch Mary teaching her grandchildren how to ride their pony. Mary would move the height on the jumps, then she'd run across the paddock and applaud her grandchild's efforts.

Yseult felt sly and strangely lonely watching Mary O'Neill galloping her greyhounds and teaching her grandchildren to ride. After that she hadn't used the binoculars to spy on Mary. Instead she took in a walk each day and rode her own hunter around the estate until she felt as fit as Mary O'Neill appeared. They were the same age after all.

"Childish but necessary," Yseult said aloud now as she recalled it all.

This morning she pointed the binoculars at the lane. The lane separated her land from the O'Neills'. In recent years it was only used at the end of the summer to bring turf from the west bank of the bog. In bygone times it had led to a few cottages that belonged to the estate.

Yseult wanted to establish where exactly the skeleton was located. She knew every tree and landmark on her estate. There were 627 acres in total. It was a mixture of good land, bogland and forest with rivers and fishing rights. When she took over the estate there were 533 acres. The reason she could not accumulate as much land as Mary O'Neill was because the Irish in the so-called Kingdom of Kerry remained suspicious of the "Proddy" as they referred to her.

Yseult looked for a sealed-off area. She saw nothing but a lone Garda standing in one of the gateways, looking at her cattle in the rear meadow. He was leaning on the gate, smoking a cigarette, staring at the grazing Angus cows. Yseult moved the binoculars up to Mary O'Neill's higgledy-piggledy house. It was Lugdale's closest neighbour. There had been closer cottages but over time they were vacated and some fell brick by brick. The derelict cottages were now used as shelter for the cattle. Although Mary had married, her farm was still identified as "the O'Neills'" and she was still known by her maiden name. Similarly, Yseult was also known by her maiden name. In her case, her marriage was so brief that nobody could recall her husband.

Yseult watched the creamery truck arrive at Mary O'Neill's. She thought of a rhyme an old neighbour used to sing to tease Mary:

Mary O'Neill, where are you from?
Some say The Kingdom
Some say the seas
Nobody knows, nobody cares.

In fact, people in this small insular community used to care where Mary O'Neill's father and mother came from. They were not local. It wasn't only the Proddy who was viewed with suspicion. But, at this stage, it was irrelevant where they originated. They had accumulated enough land to make their mark in this corner of the world.

CHAPTER THIRTY-TWO

Yseult returned to her bedroom and carefully picked her hearing aids from their holder. All these months later she was still fascinated by their small size and the new strength they loaned her. Those minute little clear spidery objects changed so much. Like the binoculars, her hearing aids kept her informed. They were her new secret toy. Last night Brendan talked loudly as if she was still the deaf difficult old lady. Yseult admitted she remained difficult and old but no longer deaf. Thanks to a man in Limerick city she had the hearing of a youthful woman. After the initial period of getting used to them, Yseult was surprised and delighted to hear sounds she hadn't heard for years. The tyres on the gravel, the birds singing, and one day she stood still to listen to the wind howl. It lifted her spirits tremendously. Nobody knew about her new hearing aids. Her daughter did but thought Yseult had discarded them, not having the patience to get used to them.

Yseult descended the two flights of stairs to the kitchen, thinking over the plans she had made for the day. Today she had intended to check the fencing in the lawn field and high wood, prepare the sheds for the cows about to calf. This afternoon she'd go to town to settle a few bills. As she approached the kitchen she could hear voices –

Brendan the farm manager and two workmen. They normally ate their breakfast at nine. That was a valuable lesson she had learned from her days when she frequented Mary O'Neill's house. Well-fed men worked harder – not only did it keep up their energy levels, it brought out a sense of loyalty. It was nature, as Mary said all those years ago: "The dog remains fondest of his feeder."

Yseult hesitated at the door. She could hear Martha, the new housekeeper, say, "It beggars belief."

"Fucking creepy," one of the farmhands said.

Yseult shook her head in exasperation. More and more people used foul language – it rolled unconsciously off their tongues as if it were part of the local dialect. Not only farmhands or coarse men but women too, and from every class of society. Her own daughter was fond of the "fucking" word. Disgusting, she thought.

Suddenly there was silence. Yseult heard a low whine from the other side of the door. The dog had given her away. She smiled at the thought of her eight-year-old sheepdog, Laddie, thrashing his tail wildly, waiting at the other side of the door. Slowly she entered and then bent to pat the dog. All remained quiet.

Then Brendan spoke. "There are graveyards all over Ireland," he said.

"Good morning," Yseult said as she moved to the sink to fill the kettle.

"Morning, Mrs. Ffrench," Brendan said while the others murmured a response. He continued talking. "It makes sense – we could be sitting on dead bodies right now."

The others shyly muttered replies.

"Maybe."

"True."

Yseult was accustomed to the silence when she walked in on their conversations. They were not afraid of her – however, they were not comfortable with her either.

Obviously they'd been talking about the skeleton found beneath the tree.

Brendan continued, "A few years ago they found a fella in the bog in Kildare, and he was over 2,000 years old. He was fully intact with a fine head of red hair. The scientists said he was a nobleman because he was dressed in a woman's cape and had his nails painted."

"No way?" one of the farmhands said.

"True as I'm sitting here," Brendan continued. "He'd have been a kinda crossdresser."

Yseult was surprised by the silence that followed. She had her back to them. In the kitchen window she could see Martha's reflection – she had her hand held over her mouth. Then she saw the farmhands' shoulders shake. They were trying to hold in the laughing.

Silently Brendan shrugged.

Yseult herself found the idea hilarious – she was smiling as she waited for the kettle to boil.

This is why she loved Brendan. He was an eejit – a thundering eejit. Albeit an eejit who was one of the best farm managers in the county. He was one of her longest employees. He had managed the farm for ten years and did the best job since the first manager Butch Slattery in the 1920s. Brendan knew everything about farming. He could diagnose sick animals, knew when to sell stock, and often knew from a cow's gait what was wrong. He was better than a vet and saved her a mint on bills. When he discussed farming, his voice was low and confident and his opinion was valued. But, apart from farming, he had no sense and moved his love-life from one doomed relationship to another. Recently she noticed Brendan directed most of his conversation to Martha, their new housekeeper. Brendan was falling in love with a separated mother of two children. Poor Brendan would always be a martyr. When he wasn't in love or some woman wasn't running circles around him, he often talked about going to America. He'd like to see the Kentucky Derby. Yseult knew Brendan was going nowhere. He'd be in that gate-lodge until he died – or stole from her, and then he'd be out on his ear like the rest.

The clock in the hall chimed. It was half past nine. The men stood up, their chairs scraping on the floor, their morning break over. She could hear them walk outside and then their sudden burst of laughter was so loud it reached her hearing-aided ears.

"Fuck me," said one of the farmhands, "what a fucking conversation!"

Brendan returned to the kitchen almost immediately.

"Mrs. Ffrench, I moved the bull from the paddock this morning. Thought it would be best while there's traffic in the lane."

"Yes, good thinking," Yseult said. She remained standing with her back to him and Martha. "Tell me, did the men know about the discovery before they came to work?"

"Yes, it was on the *Nine O'Clock News* last night and this morning it was on the radio again."

Yseult turned to face him, alarmed. "Lugdale was on the news?"

"No, Lugdale wasn't mentioned – only Mein and the fact that human remains were found."

Yseult turned back to the sink. "Where exactly is it?"

"We don't know yet. I drove down this morning but the Gardaí blocked me. I think it's at this side of the forest, around O'Neills' Hill."

Yseult nodded. She heard Brendan close the door behind him.

The skeleton was more than likely an IRA boyo. But, whether it was an IRA chap or a murdered woman, the last thing Yseult wanted was a load of people trespassing all over her land.

"My land or Mary O'Neill's?"

"What's that, Mrs. Ffrench?" said Martha.

"Nothing." Yseult realised she had talked out loud again. It was one thing doing it alone and another thing speaking to herself when in company.

Yseult couldn't wait any longer. She took the keys to the jeep and left with Laddie following her. She had to establish where this skeleton was.

YSEULT ACCESSED THE LANE FROM THE GRAZING LAWN. THE JEEP bounced easily in and out of the potholes. Within a few minutes of driving her mood improved. Laddie was perched on the passenger seat. She rolled down the window and allowed the winter air and the sound of the countryside into the jeep. There was something utterly soothing about the morning smells and sounds. Normally it was her best time of the day – during those few hours she thought clearly.

She noted the thick overhanging hedging – another job to be done. They'd trim that during the week. She passed one of the crumbling cottages – the Nolans were the last to live there. In the next the Brodericks used to live with their six strong sons, all of whom went to America. For most of her life she knew each cottage, the occupants, who were good tenants and farmers and who were poor farmers. The hard workers and good farmers were the owners of the cottages that remained the longest – they had held their ground. The Carneys had moved further into the hills – they were great workers. Now they owned their own fine farm in Knock.

The O'Neills remained, their waiting hands ready to snatch any bit of land that bordered their accumulating fields.

Yseult noted the O'Neills had trimmed their hedging. It was a neat job. Like Yseult, Mary O'Neill left nothing to waste. Even after the age of central heating their children and grandchildren picked kindling for the fire.

"No wastage," Mary O'Neill was known to say, slicing the air with her hand.

Yseult couldn't see their house from her jeep. It was at the top of the hill, opposite the gate that led into her rear meadow. Every night for many years she'd walk through the meadow, cross the lane and ascend the steps that brought her up to O'Neills' garden.

Yseult stopped the jeep. She could now see the old crude steps leading up to Mary's home. She recalled her first time in the O'Neill house.

SHE WAS ELEVEN AND HAD MOVED TO IRELAND FROM ENGLAND WITH her family. It was an aimless lost and lonely time for her and her sister, twelve-year-old Portia. They spent their days rambling around the gardens or accompanying the farmhand Butch Slattery on his chores. There was a sense of doom among the British and Anglo-

Irish living in Ireland at the time. During Ireland's conflicts in the 20s the Anglo-Irish became the hunted rather than the hunter.

On her first day in Mary O'Neill's, she was surprised at the sight of their garden. It was filled with the brightest pink and lavender, blue and orange flowers. The garden seemed out of place in their peasant dwelling.

It had been decades since Yseult set foot in the O'Neills' house yet she always remembered her first visit. It was one of those memories that remained as vivid as the startlingly colourful shrubs that surrounded their oddly shaped extended cottage. She and Portia accompanied her father's farmhand, Butch Slattery, to see a hunting stallion that was talked about the length and breadth of the country. In the yard at the back of the strange house she remembered the sight of the stallion and the owner's daughter. The horse was beautiful – he was seventeen hands, chestnut with a white star on his forehead.

In England Yseult had outgrown her pony which was twelve hands. She'd been learning to jump, each week raising the bar higher. On Sundays her father took part in the hunt. Her dream was to have a horse the size of her father's gelding which was over seventeen hands. She'd like to jump the dykes and ditches he effortlessly scaled. But until that afternoon in the O'Neills' yard she'd never seen anything as majestic as the O'Neills' hunting stallion.

It wasn't only the horse that grabbed her imagination. She marvelled at the girl leading him out. The youngest daughter of the house, Mary O'Neill, had paraded the animal around the yard with a confidence that Yseult admired. Dwarfed by the stallion's size, Mary walked him back and forth. The men watched the horse. Butch Slattery wiped his chin with his hand and shook his head in awed silence while the owner, Mr. O'Neill, stood with his hands in his pockets.

"I bought him at the fair in Killorglin," Mr. O'Neill explained. "He was only a colt – I never thought he'd grow to be that size."

"Is he for sale?" Butch asked.

Mr. O'Neill shook his head.

Butch grew quiet. Yseult waited for Butch to ask how much it would cost to service a mare.

Yseult watched Mary O'Neill closely. She held her hand close to the bit. She stroked his nose and loosened the reins when the horse flexed his head. When he grew restless she gently shushed and rubbed his shoulder. She managed the horse as if she were a man, not intimidated by its size and strength. Yseult guessed that Mary O'Neill was the same age as she was.

Later, while Butch discussed the horse with Mary O'Neill's father, Yseult and Portia had lemonade and cake with Mary by the warm range. Silently Yseult and Mary ate their cake, each surveying the other.

AT THE SOUND OF A CAR HORN BEHIND HER YSEULT SNAPPED OUT OF her recollections. In the rear-view mirror she saw a squad car. She remained where she was, they beeped again and still she didn't move until the driver got out and came to her car window.

"Good morning, Mrs. Ffrench."

Laddie stood on all fours and began to bark.

"Quiet, Laddie," Yseult said to the dog. "Sit!"

He whimpered before obeying.

The Garda nodded tolerantly as he eyed the dog on the passenger seat. Yseult waited until there was silence before speaking to him.

"Where is the skeleton?" she asked.

"It's around the bend but you won't be able to see it."

"I've no interest in gaping at a crushed skeleton," Yseult snapped. "I want to see where the tree is."

"You can go on another bit but it will be difficult to turn. The area is sealed off. You'd be better off parking."

Yseult didn't need to hear any more from him. She drove on. A stranger on her land telling her where she'd be able to drive on her own estate. "Outrageous."

But she was amused that the Garda would think she wanted to view the remains. What class of macabre nutcase did he think she was? She imagined herself with the Gardaí and their forensics standing around the tree examining the disjointed skeleton and passing comments. "Well, at least he had a fine set of dentures."

With any bit of luck every bone from his body and his remaining teeth would be on Mary O'Neill's land. It was possibly one of Mary's sons' ex-girlfriends – maybe a lover's tiff that went too far. Or possibly a woman Mary O'Neill disapproved of. Maybe she felt threatened if her son was making the wrong decision about a girlfriend and Mary had killed her rather than running the risk of him marrying a freeloader.

Would Mary O'Neill kill someone rather than allow one of her sons to marry a local girl who'd take half the land? Of course she wouldn't. However, Yseult allowed herself to indulge in a little fantasy. Mary had whacked the girl over the head with a shovel when she feigned pregnancy in the hope of marrying into the farm and having security for the rest of her days. She imagined Mary loading the body on the back of the pickup truck and herself and the son burying her. Yseult even imagined Mary giving the orders with her bad grammar and guttural mountainy Kerry accent. "Now, Patrick, stick her in the hole like I told ya!" Then she imagined Mary's face reddening when she heard the woman she murdered had been unearthed. "We dunno nothin' about that," would be Mary's fervent denial.

She rounded the bend and slammed on the brakes. "Christ!" she gasped.

The skeleton was not on Mary O'Neill's land but on the borders of her bog. There was a white tent-like structure covering the base of the tree. Protruding from the tent and lying flat across one of the dykes was a tree.

Only then did Yseult see Mary O'Neill. She was talking to the local Garda who was resting against a car that blocked the lane. He was drinking a cup of tea and eating a sandwich. Mary O'Neill stood beside him holding a plate. They stopped talking and looked in Yseult's direction. Mary O'Neill shielded her eyes from the morning sun.

Yseult uttered a word that had never before left her lips. "Cunt," she said aloud, then repeated it. The obscenity was aimed at everything: Mary O'Neill, the skeleton on her land, her life, her estate, her entrapment, her daughter, her brief marriage, her sister Portia, her Aunt Lydia, her crude father, and the fact that she couldn't drive forward or reverse with the other squad car behind her. Yseult hesitated a moment before slowly turning the steering wheel right, then she stuck her foot to the accelerator. She broke through the bushes lining the lane and the electric fence. Laddie was up on all fours again barking. Yseult felt the briars sting her face through the open window. Despite the electric fence strewn across her windscreen as the jeep bounced over the rough terrain, Yseult did not take her foot off the accelerator until she was at the back entrance to her house.

CHAPTER THIRTY-THREE

The back door was sticking. Yseult pushed the top and then kicked the bottom part. The door burst open with the metal handle rapping loudly off the wall behind it.

The housekeeper had been washing the floor.

On seeing it was Yseult, she appeared relieved. "It's only you," she said, holding her chest and laughing.

"Quickly, out of my way, Magda," Yseult said. Her name wasn't Magda – it was one of those Bible names – Yseult didn't have time for that now. "I need to get into that press!" She indicated the press where the woman stood. Martha – that was the name.

Yseult grabbed a set of keys from the press, and then walked hurriedly through the kitchen towards the back staircase and began climbing.

Breathless, she arrived at the steps to the attic door. She climbed up, unlocked the door and stepped inside. It had been years since anyone had ventured into the dark space that kept the old relics from the last 300 hundred years. Rachel had entered it as a girl but left as quickly at the sight of the cobwebs. Her daughter was terrified of spiders. She was terrified of mice, of cross dogs, and bulls. Her daughter's litany of fears sickened

Yseult. She hadn't time to think about Rachel's fussy preferences now.

The attic had been reorganised sometime in 1920s by Portia and Nellie the then housekeeper. They made it their little project during the summer holidays. Yseult remembered Portia taking her to the attic to see the completed project. The old paintings were organised together, all of the trunks placed in a separate area. There was furniture, boxes of silverware. They'd got one of the men to build shelves onto which they put the old photograph albums. Since then more rubbish had accumulated − boxes of Rachel's toys, clothes, more paintings, and God knows what else. Another job to do before spring, Yseult noted.

She shone the torch on one of the travelling trunks and noticed the steam-liner tag still attached. *Mrs. Lydia Stratford-Rice − January 1891* − Kingston, Jamaica, bound for Ireland.

"Rubbish," she sighed, thinking how idiotic it was to hoard a trunk belonging to her grand-aunt who had returned to Ireland one hundred years ago. "All for the quarry," she muttered, pushing bags and boxes out of her way.

She found the shelves that contained Aunt Lydia's old photo albums at the back of the attic.

Their Aunt Lydia was one of the first people to use a domestic camera. She had returned from Jamaica in 1891 with her son and a trunk of photographs. She spent her remaining years in Lugdale taking pictures of anything and everything. Portia and Nellie had arranged the albums by year, country, and what each album contained. Just then Yseult remembered Portia labouring over the photographs, her large blue eyes scanning the pictures, humming happily as she worked. That was the type of trivial chore Portia relished. Yseult had little interest in that type of thing − it was a menial task for a vague girl like Portia − whereas Yseult had spent her first few months in Ireland pestering the men on the estate to take her fishing and envying Mary O'Neill whom she saw on the road with her dogs or on the fringes of the estate with her fishing rod.

Yseult wiped the dust from the spine of one of the albums.

"*Jamaica 1880–1890.* " She wanted the Irish albums. She knew the tree where the corpse lay was not planted in the last fifty years. She had no reason to plant a tree specifically on that spot. For a moment she doubted her own recollection. Could she recall every tree she planted in the last fifty years? In her father's time they planted larch trees for roofing sheds, windows or rafters. Other trees were planted for firewood. Trees remained where they stood until nature and the wind decided otherwise. Yseult pulled out one of the albums titled *Men at Work by Lydia Stratford-Rice 1891–1900,* filed by *Portia Ffrench and Nellie Brown.*

Yseult flicked through the album. There were photos of men saving hay, men outside the cow house, a young boy holding two buckets at the back door. He looked out from under his cap, ill-at-ease with the scrutiny of the foreign camera. There was Nellie the housekeeper, a younger slimmer version without her thick milk-bottle glasses. There were pictures of the bog, of plants, of lone trees, of rocks.

"Bin, bin, bin," Yseult said with irritation. "Such foolishness."

She tossed the album at her feet and took an album from 1910 – 1920.

Impatiently she flicked through the pictures. When she found a photograph of the bog, she slowly scanned the background to see if it held a clue. Finally she found a picture of the bog where the tree should have been. Yseult removed the picture from the album and looked at the background scenery. *Butch Slattery, Eamon and Angus, footing turf, July 1913.*

"Planted after 1913," Yseult said aloud. "How long after 1913?" She looked at the shelves of photo albums.

Feeling she was none the wiser and reluctant to spend her day poring over every single photo taken since 1913 in the dimly lit dusty attic, Yseult clenched her teeth and inhaled with annoyance. There was little else she could do now. But she knew she would not be able to sit still until she established the facts. She picked out the albums she felt contained the key and began to fire the heavy dusty folders through the opened door of the attic onto the landing beneath. She'd look through them in the comfort of her study.

When Yseult came out of the attic she found Martha on the landing below, staring at the albums at her feet. She gaped up at Yseult as she climbed down the stairs.

"I came when I heard banging − I thought you'd fallen," she stammered.

"No, but it is a damn death trap." Yseult gestured to the narrow steep stairs leading up to the attic. "Help me take these albums down to the study and please bring me a pot of coffee." She picked up three of them.

Martha hesitated. "Yes, Mrs. Ffrench," she said after a moment and began to gather up the remaining albums.

Only when Yseult was passing the mirror over the fireplace in the study did she realise why Martha had hesitated. Her hair was covered in cobwebs and she was bleeding from scratches across her cheek acquired when she had driven through the briars. There was stickyweed in her hair and jumper. She peeled off the plant and quietly chuckled when she thought of Martha's horrified expression at the sight of her appearing through the attic door dripping with cobwebs, stickyweed and blood.

Yseult got settled in the armchair under the lamp. Each time she found a photo from the area of the bog where the tree was found, she set it aside, noting the tree had not been planted. She paused at a photo of one young labourer. He was a cheeky lad, his mouth set in a straight defiant line. Yseult had been fond of him. She couldn't think of his name just then. She smiled at the picture, finding it hard to believe how terrified she had been of the Irish when she first arrived in 1921 as an eleven-year-old girl.

YSEULT NO LONGER REMEMBERED VERY MUCH ABOUT THEIR LIVES IN England. The most memorable facts were that she had shared a bedroom with Portia and there was a Yorkshire housekeeper who made scones and spat on the iron to test it. She remembered the hissing sound when the saliva bubbled off the surface.

But she remembered the night they were told by their father that they were going to live in Ireland.

"Next month we are moving to live in Lugdale Estate."

"Are we going to stay with Uncle Cyril and Aunt Sarah?" Portia asked.

Lugdale Estate was their mother's home. Her mother's brother, Cyril, had inherited the estate but spent most of his time in England with his wife and two daughters.

"No, Uncle Cyril and Aunt Sarah are going to live in London. We are going to live in Lugdale Estate." Tobias spoke as if it were a simple exchange.

The girls stared at him, unable to take it in. All they knew was in England.

"New schools, new country, new beginnings," he said with finality. "We will make a new life on Lugdale Estate."

"Can we come to England for holidays?" Yseult asked, thinking of the lovely summers in the country and her winter outings in London to the pantomimes and visiting her cousins and friends.

"Your life will be in Ireland," her father said.

Yseult looked at her mother who remained silent.

"Can I take Tucker?" she asked.

"You've become a little big for Tucker. I'll buy you a new pony in Ireland."

"Will we have jumps and a paddock?" Yseult asked.

"Yes," her father smiled, "and dogs and plenty of fields to roam, our own land and estate and privacy far removed from prying eyes, gossip and," he paused and pointedly looking towards the end of the table at his wife, "temptation."

Portia was horrified at the idea of moving to Ireland but not for the same reasons as Yseult. That night she told Yseult that their move to Ireland signified the end of their world.

"Father wants us all to die – that's why he's moving us to bloody Ireland."

Yseult smiled when her sister swore – she was normally so poised and ladylike. It was Yseult who was forever being corrected for poor language and slouching shoulders.

"Ireland is at war with England," Portia said. "They're killing anybody who is not Irish, burning down their houses, throwing them into streams – *or setting them alight!* " Portia's voice reached a crescendo and she began to sob.

"It might not be that bad?" Yseult said, feeling helpless.

Portia had heard about the carnage in Ireland. She knew one girl in her school who'd left Ireland because her father was shot by the Irish.

"He was a soldier, not a girl like us – nobody is too troubled with little girls?" Yseult said hopefully.

Portia wiped her eyes. "You know Tilly who wore the red dress and red ribbons? The girl who sat throughout Margaret's party without speaking?"

Yseult nodded.

"The reason Tilly doesn't speak is because of what the Irish did to her."

Yseult was almost afraid to ask any more yet she felt the need to know. "What did they do?"

Portia sat up in bed. "Tilly lived in Ireland. She was very happy. She had a dog and a pony." Portia had a way of telling a story, her voice rising and falling to match each scene. "One night Tilly went to bed with her dog. In the middle of the night," her voice grew grimmer as she continued, "she was woken from her sleep by a man wearing a scarf over his face so that Tilly wouldn't recognise him. He held a gun to her head and dragged her downstairs by the hair and stood on her bare feet." Under the candlelight, Portia's eyes were fixed on Yseult's. "Tilly and her family were made to walk outside into the rain, still wearing their nightgowns. The man wearing the mask and holding the gun made her watch as others set their house alight."

"What happened to her dog?" Yseult asked, more concerned about the welfare of the terrified animal than Tilly's safety.

Portia hadn't thought about the dog. "I suspect the Irish broke its neck and threw it into the flames. I didn't ask." Portia had forgotten about her frightening voice and staring eyes. "The Irish are murderers and vagabonds. Poor Tilly and her family will end up in the mental asylum after what the Irish did to them. Aunt Sarah said that." Portia sighed loudly in her wise-old-woman way.

Yseult noticed how many of their mother's gestures she mimicked, including fanning her face with her hand when their bedroom was not that hot.

"Father wouldn't move us to a country where we're going to be murdered!" Yseult pointed out.

"*Nonsense!*" Portia almost shouted. "He hates us! He hates Mummy and me! You are the only one he likes!"

Yseult couldn't argue with that. The rare times she saw Father he was far nicer to her than to Portia. Father spent most of his time away at sea or on business in London. He owned a shipping company, his boats travelled all over the world including America and Africa. Each time he returned he brought back a small present for Portia and a bigger present for Yseult. There were matching gold bracelets from Morocco: Yseult's had three diamonds, and Portia's had none. Yseult's was presented to her with slight emotion. "I saw this in the bazaar in Morocco – I thought it would look lovely on my little Yseult's wrist." Almost as an afterthought he gave Portia hers. "For you too." Sometimes there was no gift for Portia – when alone with Yseult he'd present her with a ribbon, "For my daughter's wild black hair."

"You look like him," Portia said. "That's why he's nicer to you."

Yseult didn't think that made sense. True, she and her father looked alike, both sallow-skinned with dark hair, while Portia looked like their mother with her fair silky hair, so blonde it was almost white, and her light-blue eyes. Portia was the envy of all their friends. She was so lovely and petite. At eleven Yseult was taller than her and sometimes she felt like bending her knees to make herself seem smaller. But, for all of her ungainly size and common appearance, Father did prefer her, she conceded. But surely not just because she looked like him?

YSEULT EXHALED LOUDLY. SHE HATED RECALLING THOSE EVENTS.

"Old childish nonsense," she sighed.

Eventually she found the picture that confirmed the year the tree was planted. Sometime after 1923, two years after their arrival in Ireland. Lydia had written on the back, *Butch accompanies the Dawn Chorus, March 1923.* Butch was in the centre of the photo with his right arm extended and his eyes closed as if he were singing. The workman beside him was laughing. On Butch's right was a sapling tree, planted a few months prior to when the picture was taken. It appeared to be a birch tree but Yseult wasn't certain.

Yseult's hand shook as she held the photo. The skeleton was indeed on her land, beneath one of her trees which was planted during her father's time.

"Damn it," she seethed. "Damn it to hell."

Yseult ripped the photograph once, then twice, and a third time. When she couldn't rip it any more she made a tight ball of it in her fist.

CHAPTER THIRTY-FOUR

Yseult slumped in the chair close to the stove. The door of the Aga was open. Page by page she ripped up Aunt Lydia's old photo albums and fed the old black-and-white photos to the flames. She watched the last of the pictures curl at the corners until each smiling Jamaica face and every Irish freckle were swallowed with orange flames. She wished it was as easy to burn away the old memories that had come to the fore at the sight of the photographs.

Laddie put her head on her lap.

"If only it were that simple," she said, stroking his head.

WHEN YSEULT FIRST HEARD OF HER FATHER'S PLANS TO BRING THEM to Ireland, she went to her mother to ask if it was true. "Is Father taking us to the savages in Ireland? Will we be shot and burned in our beds?"

Instead of consoling her, her mother admitted she didn't know. "I don't know anything anymore, darling. Go along and don't make a nuisance of yourself."

Instinctively she knew not to ask her father. Instead she listened to what the adults discussed over the following days. There was a constant stream of visitors and most concurred with Portia.

"Dear God, has Tobias lost his mind? I fear he has spent one too many days on the open sea," their mother's friend said. "Constance Olivier's husband was blown up. They said Ireland is as dangerous for any non-Catholic as the trenches of the Great War"

It was at that time that Yseult began her lifelong habit of eaves-dropping. She would hide behind doors and curtains or outside windows.

Their Aunt Sarah was the only person who felt the move to Ireland was a good idea. However, Aunt Sarah spoke about a different reason for moving.

"Emilia, it was never going to be easy," she said to Yseult's mother.

The women sat in silence while Yseult held her breath, keeping her shoes sideways so that they would not be seen beneath the curtains.

"You can only bear with it. It is of course a consequence of ..." Sarah's voice trailed off.

"A consequence of my foolishness," Yseult's mother finished her aunt's sentence.

Aunt Sarah didn't respond.

"Must I suffer for the rest of my life?" Her mother's voice shook.

Yseult knew her mother was trying not to cry.

"Darling Emilia, it might be best. It may not be forever – perhaps just a temporary arrangement until people here forget."

"People will never forget. I cannot forget despite the penalties. When I saw Jonathan again, I knew I would never forget."

"You must forget him," Sarah said gently.

They fell silent and then her mother continued.

"It was I who sought out his company again – I ought to be ashamed," she said remorsefully.

"Go to Ireland and allow time to pass," Sarah said. "Jonathan is making plans that do not involve you."

"You are the only one who knows the truth," her mother said.

"And it will remain so," Sarah reassured her. "However, you must push forward like a gallant soldier, as Jonathan has done."

Their voices were reduced to a barely audible whisper.

Yseult listened. She could hear movement and then the curtain was pulled back, exposing her. She knew she had been caught doing something very bad. It was wrong to spy.

The alarm in her mother's eyes changed to anger, her lips forming a long thin angry line. Roughly she pulled Yseult out from behind the curtain.

"How dare you!" she said.

Yseult still remembered the shock at being pulled so roughly. Nobody had ever manhandled her like that. She was even more confounded when her mother's hand rose and slapped her across the face. There wasn't much time to recover as she then struck her again. There was blood on her mother's hand. Yseult's nose was bleeding.

"Just like him, conniving and devious!" her mother wailed.

When she was about to hit her again, Aunt Sarah intervened.

Yseult ran away to the sound of her mother finally breaking and crying.

"What have I done?" she sobbed.

Once Yseult recovered from the shock, she deliberated over her mother's secret. Within a few days she began to hide and listen again. Like the jewellery box from Portugal that her father had gifted her which had a secret compartment where she could hide little keepsakes, Yseult felt eavesdropping was another means of gathering and storing private conversations. Although she couldn't articulate it at the time, the information she accrued lessened the worry. It was easier to deal with the upcoming changes when there was a reason.

According to her mother, the reason Yseult's father wanted to live in Ireland was because he was filled with false pride.

"Tobias fancies himself as an Irish landlord," she scoffed to Sarah. "Everybody is laughing at him!"

Yseult noticed that when her mother spoke to women other than Sarah, she pretended she was pleased with the move to Ireland.

"Tobias is so kind to return to Ireland with me. Lugdale is my home. I'm so looking forward to returning!" Then when she was alone again with Aunt Sarah, she reverted to her normal tone. "Tobias is a pig, I only married him because Jonathan abandoned me."

Aunt Sarah reminded Emilia that Jonathan abandoned her in many ways.

They were quiet for a while before Emilia called Tobias a pig again and said he married her to improve his social standing. Aunt Sarah agreed.

At one point, she heard her mother suggest that the move to Ireland would be good for her.

"By now Yseult should have outgrown preferring to fish with the cook's son."

Yseult learned that her father bought Lugdale from Uncle Cyril – for a fair price, according to Uncle Cyril. He encouraged the move although he himself would not dare live in Ireland in the current situation.

Cyril said, "It's my home – however, Sarah is a London girl and prefers the sights and sounds of a busy city. We both prefer London."

His argument for moving sounded forced.

"Lugdale needs new life and you're the man to do the job," he encouraged Tobias. "You're the best man to keep the tradition of Lugdale alive. Aunt Lydia is the only soul in that great house. She'll be delighted with the company. If you play your cards right, you'll have a wonderful life in Ireland. You'll have the prestigious house, the lands, hundreds of acres. You can live like a king."

"Any words of advice?" Tobias asked.

Cyril paused. "Things will go well if you treat the locals with respect. They're coarse and rough, the English can't govern them. They're a thorn in the side of the establishment but, if you can get along with them, you and your family will have a privileged life."

"I've dealt with the Irish, I know how to treat them," her father said.

"Let them know that you are not a Stratford-Rice. My ancestors' relationship with the Irish has been turbulent."

"Go on," Tobias said.

"A great many men from the locality were hanged on the say-so of men like my ancestor Colonel Edward Stratford-Rice," Cyril explained. "Those who remained are all too aware of the history. The stories have been passed down like a sacred chalice. They will never forget how their menfolk were whipped and hung, and some deported. Certain Anglo-Irish families have a good relationship with the locals but not the Stratford-Rices."

"So why has Lugdale not been burned to the ground like most of the other Anglo-Irish Big Houses?" her father asked.

"Maybe they like to look at it!" Cyril said lightly. "It's a fine house.

"There's a story I heard many years ago about Lugdale," her father said. "A story that the heirs to the house were jinxed."

"That's all nonsense if you ask me."

"Humour me," her father said

"There was some damn foolish old woman who cursed every heir of the Stratford-Rices. The story is so old, I've almost forgotten."

"What was the curse?" Tobias asked.

"She claimed each heir would die at the hands of one of their offspring. The locals like to think she was right."

"Was she right?" Tobias asked.

"Admittedly there were a few tragedies," Cyril acknowledged. "However, the only cursed object in beautiful Ireland are the natives. I think Lugdale has been left alone because those insane locals get more pleasure from what they perceive is Lugdale's curse." He laughed. "Like all uneducated nations, the Irish are a superstitious lot."

It wasn't only her parents whom Yseult eavesdropped on. Behind the evergreen hedging, she distinctly heard Uncle Cyril say to Aunt Sarah, "They're definitely going and not a moment too soon."

Aunt Sarah agreed. "Emilia's a disgrace."

Uncle Cyril referred to Tobias as an imposter.

Yseult had to look up *imposter* in the dictionary.

. . .

YSEULT WAS SITTING BY THE STOVE LOST IN THOUGHT WHEN THE dog raised his head suddenly.

Brendan arrived, accompanied by a member of the Gardaí. Yseult was grateful she had the last of the album pages in the stove. With the exception of one photograph of Nellie Brown that she had kept for some peculiar maudlin reason, the rest of the photographs were turned to ashes. The smell of the plastic from the covers of the album cast out a caustic odour.

"This is Garda Tim Riordan – he just wants to ask you about the estate," Brendan explained. "They're trying to establish a few facts about the skeleton."

The Garda was in his forties, a more distinguished-looking chap than the Garda from the previous night.

Yseult remained seated as she shook his proffered hand.

He removed a notebook from his pocket. "Do you mind?" He indicated one of the chairs.

Yseult gave him a curt nod.

"Forensics will tell us a great deal about the skeleton," he said, "but we'd like to establish all we can in the meantime."

Yseult nodded.

"Mrs. Ffrench, have you any idea when the tree was planted?"

"I have no idea," Yseult said, taking a cup of tea from Brendan. "I can't account for every single tree on my estate."

"Were you born on Lugdale Estate?" the Garda asked.

"No, I came as a young girl." Yseult could have told him the year and regaled him with stories about arriving in the thick of the War of Independence as an eleven-year-old girl.

"How young?"

"Maybe fifteen or sixteen," Yseult said. "Possibly a little older."

The expression on Brendan's face didn't change. He knew she was lying and being difficult.

"It's a beautiful place," the Garda said. "I've never been here before."

"And hopefully it will be the last time," Yseult said. "Nobody likes to see the Gardaí in their home."

He laughed politely.

Yes, the house looked impressive, she thought. From the outside it looked like a house for the privileged elite. In truth, behind the opulent bricks of Lugdale they too had to learn to survive.

"What year was it built?"

Yseult exhaled loudly. "About 300 years ago. Do you think the human remains date back to the late 16th century?"

"I don't know, nor will we know until the forensics get to work on our skeleton. The house belonged to your father?"

"Yes." Yseult wasn't going to enlighten him.

"Your daughter lives with you?"

"That's correct."

"OK," the Garda said slowly. He paused for a moment to look at Yseult. Then, as if changing tactics, he asked about the bog. "Do you rent the bog – lease it to a company or individuals?"

"I lease it to individuals." Yseult watched him make a note of it.

"You took over the farm thirty or forty years ago?"

"Yes, that's about right, maybe thirty-five years ago," she lied.

"Prior to that?"

"There was a farm manager, Butch Slattery." It was best to keep her father out of the scene.

"Do you know if your father leased the bog each year? Or did he cut and sell the turf?"

"I've no idea. I was at school or abroad for a number of years." Yseult sat back in the chair and crossed her legs. She found the scene disconcerting. In the fire, the ashes from the albums were grey. She recalled vividly her father leasing parts of the bog to men like Red Murphy, the O'Sullivans, the O'Gradys. She could pinpoint the plots they took every year. They'd arrive each spring with their wives and children and grandparents to begin the back-breaking process with an air of unity and joviality. Part of the payment for the lease was a trap of their dried turf sent up to Lugdale each year.

It was strange to have this Garda sitting at her table, diplomatically trying to get her to name the many faces she suddenly recalled.

"Can you give me a list of those who worked for you during your time of managing the estate?"

"Brendan will give that to you," Yseult said. "At my age I'm no good with names."

"Did you keep any of the paperwork? P60s from your staff, tax receipts?"

At the mention of tax and P60 certs she felt like sticking her hand into the hot ashes and pulling out the picture that identified the year the tree was planted.

"I don't deal with all that. Maybe Brendan can find something."

"Well, it's possible recent paperwork may turn out to be irrelevant. Do you have the paperwork from your father's period? It would help if we knew who rented the bog then or if he worked it himself, or who worked for him."

"What are you going back to my father's era for? That's a lifetime ago," Yseult said, alarmed.

"Your neighbour, Mary O'Neill, thinks the tree has been there for the last sixty or seventy years," the Garda said. "Documents or old rent books would help."

"A few years ago I cleaned out the house." Yseult flicked her hand impatiently. "There were logbooks and documents about the estate for hundreds of years clogging every drawer. I threw everything out." She raised her voice. "The lot, into the fire!"

Yseult got up and began flexing her knee. She wanted this business over and done with.

"Is your daughter home?" he asked.

"No, she's in Dublin on business."

"When is she due home?"

Yseult hesitated. She was getting furious with his intrusive questions.

"She runs the estate with you?" the Garda asked. "Rachel, isn't it?"

Rachel would do anything except what was expected of her. She loved doing courses. Was it an inquiring mind or was she so averse to working she'd rather study? There was an agricultural course when she finished her schooling, then a course in nutrition, then something to do with oils and herbs, then something to do with cheesemaking. They all sounded nice and highfalutin with science attached to the title. Last year Rachel did the most idiotic course Yseult had ever heard of.

"Massage," Yseult said aloud in disbelief that her own daughter would be interested in paying money to learn how to put her hands on another person's body. Women who did that in her day were called prostitutes. Rachel tried to tell Yseult they used oils and there was a science to it. "Another science." At one point Rachel suggested turning Lugdale into a health farm for women and men. They'd give them organic food from the farm and massages. Not only was Rachel wasting her life on her courses, she was a vegetarian who wrote prissy articles advising what people should eat. Yseult was not able to listen to a girl who was about to fall into a 300-year-old estate who wouldn't eat meat yet dictated to the masses about good food. Yseult had listened to enough ridiculous nonsense to last a lifetime.

The Garda was waiting for her to answer. "Rachel? Is she the estate manager?"

"My daughter is studying cheesemaking in Dublin at the moment," Yseult said, thinking it was a silly course befitting an idle girl like her daughter.

"So she doesn't manage the estate?" the Garda pressed her.

Rachel did not manage the estate nor would she until she learned the value of Lugdale, instead of suggesting turning it into an upmarket brothel with homemade cheese served to its exhausted punters.

"Rachel is …" Yseult felt the need to give Rachel some role, "furthering her studies in organic food production." She had no idea where she got that line. "Brendan manages it for the moment."

The Garda stood up and gave her a card with his name on it. "Ring me at any stage. We'll be great friends by the time this is finished."

He winked at her.

The cheek of him, Yseult thought.

Yseult remained in the kitchen as they passed the back window. She listened.

"How the fuck do you put up with that old nag?" the Garda said to Brendan.

"She's not the worst of them," Yseult could hear Brendan say before their voices drifted off.

Yseult returned immediately to the study and began pulling out drawers and rooting in presses that had not been touched in decades. *Mary O'Neill thinks the tree is there for the last sixty or seventy years.* There was a time when Mary O'Neill wouldn't talk to the Gardaí, a time when the O'Neills hid the rebels from the authorities and Mary O'Neill's mother brought the men on the run breakfast to the barn. Yseult saw the men more than once. Old Mrs. O'Neill gave them scones and sandwiches as they left, scurrying along the hedges with their guns and murderous intentions to their next safe house. There was a time, not too long ago, when all poor decent folk were suspicious of those in authority, a time when people sorted out their own disputes and disposed of dead bodies on their land.

As Yseult tugged at the drawers she couldn't help thinking how people changed when they got a bit of money and land and suddenly thought they had status. Why didn't he talk longer to Mary O'Neill instead of barging into her home with talk of tax certs and P60s? Yseult pulled at the drawers to her archives. The first was stuffed with yellowing papers. Most of the archives were locked. She rattled the handles. She checked for the key. Rachel used the study – where did the girl leave it?

"Rachel, bloody Rachel!" she said as one of the handles came off in her hand.

CHAPTER THIRTY-FIVE
DUBLIN

Rachel began, "The O'Neills of Mein came from nowhere. There were no brothers or sisters, or aunts or uncles, there wasn't as much as a long-lost cousin belonging to the O'Neills in the vicinity or surrounding counties. His accent was not local nor from any of the surrounding counties. There wasn't a job or civil service position to bring him to Kerry. Nothing, only rolling hills of bad land and a view that opened into the mouth of the ocean. His name and the names of his children were Irish, he claimed to be Irish, yet he came from nowhere. His wife Eileen was a small dark woman with grey translucent eyes and peculiarly high cheekbones. Her origins were as unknown as her husband's, her accent unidentifiable. She claimed she came from a place at the opposite end of the country but no-one there had heard of her. They were rootless, without origin or beginnings."

Marshall had an amused expression. "Rachel, you tell a great story," he said in his Southern American drawl, "but we all come from somewhere."

"You don't understand," Rachel continued in the same mock-sinister voice. "In Ireland everybody comes from somewhere. Everybody knows everybody. If they don't know you, they'll know someone who knows someone belonging to you."

"Maybe the O'Neills moved to the location for the view," Marshall suggested.

"People in Ireland didn't do that ninety years ago. They stayed put, married locally or went to the bigger cities. Most emigrated."

This morning Rachel felt reckless and playful. It was seven thirty and she and Marshall were the last remaining duo from an all-weekend party. They were in an "early house", having a final drink. Last night she had heard about the human remains found in Mein.

She explained to Marshall that there were only two large farms in Mein, her mother's and the O'Neills'. "And," she said, raising her index finger and narrowing her eyes, "the O'Neills sure as hell didn't move to Mein for the view or the rich land."

"Were they the only family with the O'Neill surname in the jurisdiction?" Marshall sounded genuinely interested.

"We didn't call them jurisdictions," she corrected him. "They were called parishes or townlands. No, there were other O'Neills living in Mein and Knock and Kilflynn – some were related to each other but none to Mary O'Neill and her parents."

Marshall lifted his wine to his lips as he considered it. He was the stereotypical all-American man. He was enormous – at six feet, four inches with great big shovel-like hands and glowing white teeth. In the snug of the early-house, his teeth looked even whiter and frame even bigger squeezed into the small wooden seat as he held a delicate wineglass.

Rachel continued in the same vein, although she knew it was pointless trying to explain rural Ireland to a man like Marshall Lewis from Atlanta in the US, one of the most densely populated states in America. He would never truly comprehend Ireland – the distrusting villages and the continuity of families and shared histories, how some could trace their roots back hundreds of years in the same parish. Somebody local always knew something of somebody's history.

Marshall said, "With all those men staying local and marrying the local girls, were they not afraid of marrying one of their cousins?"

"Of course it happened – cousins married cousins – and not by accident. Years ago marriage was a convenience – it was more important to marry lands than to marry people."

Marshall asked, "What part of the country was Eileen O'Neill supposedly from?"

Rachel was happy to return to her playful antics and exaggerated Irish lilt – her mother often told her she'd have been better off onstage. "Eileen O'Neill claimed she was from Malin in Donegal, the most distant northern point of the country, yet nobody in that town had ever heard of her. We think she only made that up."

Marshall began to laugh loudly. "You think she made it up!" he repeated. The more he thought about it the more he laughed.

Realising how idiotic it sounded, Rachel also began to laugh into her drink.

"Oh, that's so funny," he sighed when he'd finished his guffawing. "Maybe the O'Neills were ghosts," he went on, doing a bad imitation of the accent, "or spirits from the other world. *Oooohhhhh!*" he opened his eyes wide. "Or Eileen O'Neill was a bun-shee!"

Whether it was the drink or his mispronunciation or his incomprehension of the little island she inhabited, Rachel didn't know, but laughed even more.

Their laughter was so loud that the group at the bar turned their heads and looked at them inquisitively.

"Well, Rachel, I sure as hell feel as if a bun-shee has haunted me since I came to Ireland," Marshall continued. "I've never drunk as much in three days as I have in the last six months."

"What the fuck does that mean?" Rachel was laughing uproariously again and just when she thought she'd choke from it, the barman appeared in front of them.

"Right, I want the two of you out of here now."

Rachel was happy to leave. She was afraid if she remained in any place for too long her surreal morning would crash into smithereens. On mornings like this she knew she could collapse and sink at any stage.

Linking arms, they walked in the early-morning mist down the quays, over the Ha'penny Bridge and through the cobbled streets of Temple Bar. Little remembrances from her weekend returned to Rachel. She remembered the taxi ride to a party in Rathgar last night – it was then she heard about the human remains in Mein. At some stage during the night she had sat on the bathroom floor with her friend and helped her clean up after her nose bled. Then she recalled the cascading blues and reds in the fireworks display from the party two nights ago, and she thought of the song "Nights in White Satin" and began to sing it. Marshall joined in.

In Camden Street, they found a small dingy eatery and ordered breakfast. The radio was on in the background and playing a song that Rachel could have danced to.

"Are you going to write an article on how to cure a hangover?" Marshall asked.

He thought it was hilarious that she wrote about nutrition for a health magazine.

"No, that's too obvious. I'll probably write about how to detox after a weekend with a Yankee called Marshall Lewis."

It was all harmless fun, Rachel conceded. She was lucky. A lot of her old friends were at the age of raising children and sitting in on a Saturday night.

"Seriously, what will you write about in your next article?"

Rachel thought. "Something typical. At this time of the year people's resolve to keep their New Year's resolutions begins to wilt. I'll suggest varying their healthy lunches and dinners."

He had an amused expression as he listened. Rachel wasn't offended. Whenever she met Marshall or her Dublin friends, it always appeared as if she partied from sunrise to sunset. The truth was a lot different. Her friends didn't see her on Friday at a cheese-making workshop or the many other courses she did. They didn't know about the great plans she had. Marshall was a celebrated architect. He was part of her plan although he didn't know it yet.

Her serious side was best kept quiet until it was time to act. Lugdale would eventually be hers and she had plans.

Backbreaking farm work did not factor in any of them.

Rachel ordered toast, beans and a bottle of wine. She needed weekends like this, a few days away from Lugdale to release the pent-up tensions of the farm. While she waited to inherit the farm she had no real role in Lugdale. Several times she had suggested venturing into different areas like cheesemaking, or renovating the old cottages on the estate and renting them as holiday homes. Her mother almost had a fit at the notion.

"Tourists on my land?" Her face had puckered in horror.

Rachel had pointed out that Ireland was on the cusp of great changes. They were one of the fastest-developing countries in the world. It was 1991, and time to act.

Yseult had cut her off. "You'd want to come into the real world."

Rachel was thirty-eight years old and, as her mother quite often pointed out, she was the most well-educated woman in the country. When she was twenty-two, she had finished her degree in Agricultural Science, a mandatory course to inherit a farm in Ireland. Reluctant to return to Lugdale to work with her mother and manage the estate, she went to Israel to work in a kibbutz. Then she went to America and did a course in nutrition. She returned to Dublin and did a journalism course and began writing articles in a women's health magazine. It wasn't as if Lugdale was going anywhere, and her mother showed no signs of slowing down. On Rachel's 35th birthday she was considering going to England. Her mother put an end to that notion over the phone: "Home. Not another damn penny. Time to start working."

When Rachel initially moved home her mother wanted to teach her all about the estate. Rachel accompanied her around the farm and to all of the farm-related meetings. Yseult was equally cute and suspicious inside the home and outside it.

Rachel accompanied Yseult to the accountant for her annual visit, but she stopped Rachel at the door.

"She was like a Garda at a checkpoint," Rachel told Marshall, holding her hand in front of his face, imitating Yseult. "You just sit there and wait while I have a private word with him first."

Marshall laughed at Rachel's performance.

"We could do so much with Lugdale," Rachel said informatively, "but my mother is only interested in the agricultural end of it."

Any initiative Rachel showed was met were fervent denials by her mother. The estate was perfect for cheesemaking – they had all of the raw materials – but Yseult wouldn't budge. Her mother said that Lugdale Estate had been farmed for 300 years and that would not stop now. Rachel explained that Lugdale would make a perfect venue for a boutique hotel, a perfect spa retreat, a perfect location for holiday cottages. All her suggestions were shot down dead before she could show her mother the plans she had drawn up. Apart from doing the wages each week and running small errands, Rachel had nothing to do.

Rachel imagined her mother in Lugdale spitting fire over the corpse, the interruption of her working day, making life difficult for the Gardaí, cursing the land and the cost of the upkeep of the house and pushing anything or anybody out of her way.

Marshall finished eating and paid the bill. They took the bottle of wine and stole two wineglasses.

They began to walk up Camden Street.

"Have you a boyfriend in Lugdale?" Marshall asked.

"Yes, you could say I have a boyfriend in Lugdale."

Rachel's engagement to Laurence, according to her mother, was the only decent thing she had done since returning to Lugdale.

CHAPTER THIRTY-SIX

A
ll afternoon Yseult had back pain. She took a double dose of her painkillers. Once the tablets took effect she returned to the attic with her torch and sat on one of the old travelling trunks. She shone the torch the length of the attic. She had made up her mind to do a big clear-out, not only of the attic but the entire house, months before the skeleton was found.

When Rachel got engaged to Laurence six months ago, Yseult had sighed with relief, toasted their future and silently thought of all that needed to be done. The house would eventually be theirs to do what they wanted with it. However, she was not comfortable with the idea of Laurence rummaging through their old forgotten mementos. She was not going to fool herself and say they had nothing to hide. Every family had something to hide … especially theirs.

The best way to clean Lugdale was from the top down. Yseult would need a skip, several skips. She didn't know exactly where to start. She walked to the other end of the attic. She looked closely at the trunks with their copper fasteners and leather straps. They opened into tidy wardrobes. Yseult knocked on one strong container and felt the texture of the leather exterior. There were several trunks, made so solidly they had stood the test of time.

Yseult looked for the old travelling trunk she had brought from England when they first arrived in Lugdale.

Yseult remembered how all of their belongings were dispatched to Ireland in 1921. A few days later Yseult, Portia and their parents travelled together. During the trip their mother was subdued and their father overjoyed while Portia felt she was going to be murdered.

In the carriage, Portia said to Yseult, "This is where most of our boys were killed." She nodded towards a narrow bridge. "The Irish blow up bridges for sport in their country." Then she asked the family to join in and sing "The Hearse Song." According to Portia, the English soldiers sang it when facing death in the battlefields of Europe.

Portia began to sing:

"Don't you ever laugh as the hearse goes by, For you may be the next one to die. They wrap you up in big white sheets, And cover you from head to feet."

"That's enough, darling," their mother said. "The Irish are not going to kill us today."

"Not today?" Portia retorted. "What does that mean? Tomorrow is a more suitable day?"

Yseult remembered the landscape. There were narrow roads, small cottages and green hills that would be great to explore on her new pony. She remembered the pleasant smell of freshness and saw a girl walking with her dogs. She began to feel a little hopeful. From eavesdropping she had learned that, if they survived, Ireland was an idyllic place for fishing and hunting.

Apart from Portia singing "The Hearse Song," Yseult remembered her first sight of Lugdale and her father's reaction. They passed through the pillars with resting lions on the top, then the carriage took them along the S-shaped tree-lined avenue.

Her father sat sideways in his carriage seat, staring expectantly out the window.

When they rounded the bend and got their first sight of Lugdale House, they could hear him gasp at the sight.

Yseult noticed its great size and the steps, baluster railings and stone urns leading up an imposing front door. At each side of the door were three enormous windows. The storey above that had ten smaller windows and another storey at the top had a row of smaller windows again. On the façade above the front porch was a triangle with an etching of a lion and bull. They were facing each other and as if in mid-dance. Yseult later learned it was the family crest.

Their father shouted, *"Stop the carriage!"*

He got out and stood staring at the house with his hand held to his mouth.

Yseult remembered not knowing if he was overwhelmed or appalled at the sight.

Emilia sighed. "I don't know what the fuss is about. I've seen bigger houses."

"It's much bigger than our house in England," Portia noted.

"Come, Yseult – see your new home!" Tobias said.

Yseult remembered thinking she was the only one, apart from her father, who seemed happy with the new home. She got out and stood beside him.

"Do you see those trees?" he said, pointing to the oak trees on the front lawns where the cattle grazed. "Some of those trees are as old as the house – 300 years old."

"Tobias, we're getting our deaths from cold!" their mother called from the carriage. "Please get in and close the door."

After a minute their father obeyed.

That first evening in Lugdale House, the staff were lined up in the hall to greet them. The butler, footman, cook, maids, cleaners, drivers and gardeners. The butler and footman bowed, the other men removed their hats and bent their heads. The women curtseyed in their starched uniforms.

The only one who appeared clumsy yet friendly was a young Nellie Brown.

"Wisha, 'tis lovely to see your children, Miss Emilia!" Nellie smiled and bent down to inspect Yseult and Portia as if she was the owner of the estate greeting her subjects.

The head cook gave her a rebuking glare.

Nellie Brown was the only member of staff her mother seemed pleased to see. "Nellie, I hoped to find your gay smile greeting me in Lugdale."

Yseult's father acknowledged each of them before stepping aside to examine the portraits of his wife's family that lined the walls. He read the names beneath each portrait, some dating back to the 1750's. He stopped at a painting of Colonel Edward Stratford-Rice and stood back to look up at the portrait. Several nights after that Yseult found him staring at the portraits in the same hypnotised way.

THE NIGHT OF THEIR ARRIVAL WAS THEIR FIRST TIME MEETING AUNT Lydia, her mother's aunt who had returned from Jamaica after the death of her husband. Lydia was very old and all the same colour: white. Her hair and skin were the whitest Yseult had ever seen, her large eyes were a dull blue colour, like a blue dress that had been washed too often and lost its former brightness. Yseult remembered watching her mother and Aunt Lydia embrace in the entrance hall. Aunt Lydia dropped her walking cane but she ignored the clattering sound. Instead she and Emelia held each other tightly, both uncharacteristically demonstrative. When Aunt Lydia stooped to greet Portia and Yseult, she paused and regarded each girl carefully. When Aunt Lydia shook Tobias's hand she was not demonstrative or warm. Throughout dinner she kept looking at him.

That first night their father barely spoke and for the rest of the week he was out of sorts.

Yseult heard Nellie Brown say Aunt Lydia was not herself either.

"I don't know what's wrong with Mistress Lydia. She's right strange since Miss Emilia came back. Maybe 'tis having a man about the house." She nodded towards Tobias. "Himself seems to like the house?"

Yseult thought it amusing that all of the staff referred to her father as "Himself."

After a week, when Tobias found his voice, he had the same strange stillness about him.

One evening he was standing at an old music box. On it there was a painted picture of a lady and gentleman bowing to each other before they danced the minuet. Her father wound it once, then twice and a third time to listen to the same music and stare at the same dancing couple.

"Tobias, if you don't stop winding that music box you will drive me even more insane at the prospect of living in this forgotten backwater!" her mother snapped.

Yseult and Portia were sent to bed but Yseult remained listening outside the door.

Her father sounded emotional when he spoke. "Every sea crossing was worth it, every night of storms, enduring the accusing eyes of men and women. It was worth it all to be the man I was born to be and own Lugdale."

"Yes, Tobias, I imagine Lugdale cost more than a few slaves."

From her tone of voice Yseult knew that her mother was being nasty to her father. But she didn't understand what she said.

For those first few weeks Tobias oscillated between euphoria and melancholy as he admired his new home and lands. At night Yseult could hear her father's shoes on the wooden floors as he walked the house like a man coming to terms with a change in fortune.

CHAPTER THIRTY-SEVEN

Rachel did not arrive on the train as expected. Yseult drove home and immediately began filling in the potholes in the lanes surrounding the estate with Brendan. They were in the south lane at the back of the estate. They had the trailer filled with gravel hitched to the jeep. Yseult drove a few yards with Brendan following on foot. She stopped at each hole to allow him to fill it in.

"These holes are the bane of my life," Yseult said, getting out and standing to watch him. He made the laborious job seem easy as he shovelled mounds of stone and packed them tightly. She marvelled at the younger man's strength and was reminded again how age and back pain brought such restrictions. For the last few months her days were measured in pain. Sometimes it was torturous, other times she felt so well she hoped it was a figment of her imagination.

"Tar is the only remedy," Brendan said.

"Tar!" Yseult scoffed.

He was right. The natural springs below the surface would push the stone out eventually, creating new potholes like mushrooms in autumn. Repairing the lanes was a constant job yet Yseult had no notion of spending money tarring every lane.

She spotted an empty beer can in the hedge. "Tarring my lanes for vagabonds and trespassers to have an easier time making bold on my land!" she said, throwing the empty can into the trailer.

They continued repairing the holes until they were at the end of the lane. Across the field Yseult could see the tent at the scene of the fallen tree. She couldn't see any Gardaí but there was a car parked there. It wasn't a Garda car as far as she could see.

"Those Gardaí would be better off solving crimes from today instead of piecing together a skeleton from ..." she paused, "probably the Viking age."

"Maybe," he said noncommittally.

Yseult would like it if Brendan were the type to complain about the Gardaí. They could have a good moan about their lack of priorities. But Brendan was not the type to complain about the Gardaí, or any sector of society. He was too moderate for that type of thing.

Yseult looked across the field, up the side of the hill. She could see Mary O'Neill's house and the smoke rising from her chimney. She imagined Mary's family sitting around the table eating and talking about their morning's work. They'd plan their afternoon and what they'd work at. One thing was certain: "Their arses won't spread from sitting down," as Nellie Brown would say.

The O'Neills were ferocious workers. When Yseult looked out her window at midnight during the silage season and saw the O'Neills working under the lights of their tractors she was secretly empowered by them. They'd done well for a family who had started off with a few bad acres.

To supplement their income, Mary's father was a rabbit-trapper. Estates hired him from all over Munster to decrease the rabbits that multiplied at a furious rate and ate the grass intended for their cattle. She often saw Mr. O'Neill walking home with a mound of rabbits thrown over his shoulder.

Once when Yseult marvelled at his strength, carrying so many rabbits, he told her that he didn't mind the weight.

"'Tis the fleas from their fur that eat me," he said.

Each week Mary's father would park his donkey and cart in the train station and sell the gutted rabbits. Gradually he added land to his mountainy acres until they had a farm almost the size of Lugdale.

A few weeks after Yseult's first encounter with Mary O'Neill and the talked-about stallion, she saw her on the road with her father. They were walking greyhounds. Another day she saw Mary freewheeling her bicycle without any hands on the road into town. Yseult was impressed with the speed at which she travelled. Another evening she saw Mary and a few of her friends on the outskirts of Lugdale with their dogs. Mary had a big fawn-and-black lurcher. She'd love to have chatted with Mary and ask if they were hunting and if they'd caught anything. Mary and her friends were not allowed into Lugdale's forest or to fish in its rivers. Yseult had made up her mind she wouldn't tell if she saw them making free with her father's estate. She'd have given anything to join them and their dogs.

MARY O'NEILL'S LIFE SEEMED SO CAREFREE COMPARED TO YSEULT'S as she wrestled with new beginnings in Ireland. Tobias insisted on retaining the traditional formality of the English upper class. Each evening they had to dress appropriately for dinner. The servants were given gleaming new uniforms and instructed in the correct manner to serve their courses.

"The first sign of an institution collapsing is when standards are allowed to slip," Tobias repeatedly said each time he felt the girls' table manners were lagging. "And Lugdale is a wonderful institution that has survived for three centuries and will continue with you and your family, Yseult. Just because we live among the crudest people doesn't mean we can allow protocol to slide."

Almost immediately Tobias employed the services of an English governess to tutor Portia and Yseult. As well as enduring her hours of lessons, there was also music and singing lessons. Portia excelled at the piano, but Yseult hadn't a note in her head and she had no interest in piano or violin.

Yseult felt there was no escape from their new life. Each night after they ate dinner, Portia and Yseult had to play the piano.

"Dear God, no!" Tobias would moan during Yseult's recital.

She was hopeless at music. But she was not at all perturbed by the criticism. She hoped Tobias would see how futile the lessons were and stop them.

In those early days there was very little to do in Lugdale. Yseult explored the house and the many rooms. She roamed around the outhouses, the barns and stables. In one of the outhouses she found a trap too big to catch foxes and rabbits. Portia told Yseult it was a man-trap to catch trespassers.

Yseult examined the large teeth that had the strength to sever a human leg.

"It will give me nightmares," Portia said, turning away from it while Yseult examined it for traces of blood and then tried to pull it apart, hoping to hear the snapping sound.

There were three cottages on the grounds of the estate. Only one was used by Butch Slattery. She found rosary beads in one of the vacant cottages, and Catholic statues – one of a crowned child in a cloak puzzled her so she asked Nellie Brown about it. Nellie said it was Jesus as a child and that it was called the Infant of Prague, but she couldn't say why. Yseult didn't think Jesus was ever in Prague.

Portia spent her time helping Nellie Brown with the baking and cleaning. Each day she baked a cake, perfecting her skills. At night they'd sample a slice. Portia also developed a strong bond with Aunt Lydia. She was allowed into the darkroom when Aunt Lydia developed the photographs that she had taken. Only once did Yseult accompany them. She knew Aunt Lydia preferred Portia to her. At dinner she would pull out the chair next to hers, inviting Portia to sit beside her. Regularly she stroked Portia's long smooth silky hair and praised her various accomplishments. Yseult told herself she wasn't bothered by Aunt Lydia's preference. And she had no interest in dying of boredom while watching pictures dry, images of people whose faces she already knew. It seemed as pointless as learning to bake a different cake each night.

On Sunday afternoons the English officers would visit, and they'd play tennis or backgammon. They seemed to favour Portia too.

THE HIGHLIGHT OF YSEULT'S DAY WAS RIDING HER NEW PONY. IT WAS a chestnut Connemara gelding and two hands bigger than her pony in England. Her mother promised that she could take part in the first Lead Rein event in the district. Yseult called her new pony Hazel and adored riding her, but she was not allowed to leave the estate or venture too far into the forest with the threat of the rebels.

When Yseult objected, her father became annoyed. "Are you forgetting there is a war? Leaving the estate is strictly forbidden."

When Yseult tired of her normal route she ventured farther afield with her favourite dog, Ginger, a golden retriever. Each day Yseult, Hazel and Ginger varied their route. On hot days she took the pony and dog into the river and walked into the deep waters, sometimes frightening herself when she felt out of her depth. Sometimes she'd pack lunch and ride Hazel to higher ground. Alone, she'd eat, admire the view and share her sandwiches with Ginger.

DURING THAT TIME IT WAS AN ADDED STRAIN HAVING THEIR FATHER constantly around. In England their father spent most of his time away. On his return and for the duration of his stay, which usually was no longer than one month, there was an atmosphere of tension. Although they weren't sure why this edgy cloud descended, for those few weeks they were on their best behaviour. Since moving to Ireland, not only did Tobias not show any signs of departing for sea, but sometimes for several days he didn't even leave the house. During such days he wandered around the rooms of the house, examining its every detail. He found wine that was over one hundred years old in the cellar. At night after dinner he spent his time reading old letters in the study – letters that had been sent to the Stratford-Rices from distant aunts and uncles and cousins from across the globe. The letters had been kept in a series of drawers in the study. The Stratford-Rices fancied themselves as keepers of the past. Some of the letters dated back to the 1820s. Yseult's father briefly looked at the old letters from his wife's extended family who were serving in Afghan and India, and those living in England. But it was the letters from Jamaica that he mostly pored over. Each night under the lamp he read and reread letters from Edward Stratford-Rice and his wife Victoria who lived on a plantation there. There were also letters from Aunt Lydia during her time in Jamaica when she was married to her cousin, Blair Stratford-Rice.

Yseult's parents made friends with the Hamiltons who had children of Yseult and Portia's age. On Friday nights and Sunday afternoons the two families had dinner parties, played bezique card games and charades. They watched movies on the projector that Tobias had brought from America. When the Irish rain was not tumbling down they went for picnics or went shooting. Occasionally they ran races. The Hamilton children were no competition for Yseult. She could outrun Portia and the Hamilton boys, once even stopping to pretend to yawn during one of their races. She could hear her father delight in her antics, clapping loudly when she won.

"Tone deaf but my Yseult makes up for it in other ways," he said.

Mrs. Hamilton seemed to know everybody, and could give a run-down of their family's ancestry. Her comments varied between "wonderful people" and "our kind". Occasionally she wagged her finger, saying, "No, no!." In doing that she was not guilty of gossiping, but her varying tones indicated her preferences.

It was many years later that Yseult heard what Mrs. Hamilton said about her own parents.

CHAPTER THIRTY-EIGHT

It was after one o'clock by the time Yseult and Brendan walked into the kitchen to eat dinner. Martha was on the phone, taking a message and nodding as she spoke.

"Your mum just walked in," she said and held the receiver towards Yseult.

Yseult continued walking towards the table without responding.

Martha hesitated. "Mrs. Ffrench, Rachel is on the phone."

"I'm going to eat my dinner," Yseult said, taking her seat at the table.

Martha didn't know what to do. She held the receiver away from her ear. "Mrs. Ffrench, Rachel missed the train this morning. She'll be home on the half six train –"

Yseult interrupted her, speaking clearly and loudly, "Tell her she can walk home."

Yseult was not going to explain in front of all and sundry that she had sat like a ninny in the train station, waiting twenty minutes for a girl who hadn't the manners to call. What hope had Lugdale of surviving with that mentality?

Rachel would never appreciate the value of work. The mooing cows irritated her, the calf nuts made her hands dry. Rachel would step over a sick calf rather than treat it. She wasn't an early-morning person, and most pitiful of all, she refused to eat the meat from the farm.

Martha was still on the phone. "I'll pass on the message – the half six train today."

"Bloody vegetarian," Yseult sighed quietly.

Years ago, the likes of her daughter would have been locked up in an asylum. Who in their right mind makes a decision not to eat meat? When Yseult was a child, there was a man who had a notion about falling leaves. He'd run at the sight and sound of rustling leaves. That boyo was sent to the local mental institution. In Yseult's opinion, there was little difference between a woman's rejection of certain foods and that poor barking madman from the 1920s. The likes of Rachel and her finicky, pale-faced, nutrition-lacking friends should have seen the poverty in Ireland that Yseult had seen. Those freaks wouldn't be long putting a fine cut of steak into their mouths then instead of finding fault with it. Now that the world was gone more idiotic, they were making these people sound interesting. Yseult didn't believe Rachel was happy as a vegetarian – nobody could be happy on such a substandard diet. It was enough to make Yseult sick.

When Yseult had back surgery, she was confined to her bedroom for weeks. Rachel convinced her that she needed a new diet to build up her strength. So, desperate to get well, Yseult ate what Rachel gave her. Rachel bought soya milk which seemed ridiculous when they produced a quarter of a million gallons of milk a year on the farm. The soya milk was sweet and heavy. Beans and nuts were a large part of the diet, and Yseult was wholeheart-edly sick of it in the end. The very first day that she got enough strength to walk down the stairs, Yseult she got enormous joy out of ripping Rachel's ridiculous food plan in several small pieces and flinging them in the bin.

"Enough," she declared to Rachel when she questioned what she was doing.

Idly, Yseult wondered what Rachel was doing in Dublin. She knew there was more to her weekend than attending a lecture on cheesemaking. If Rachel was not careful, her fiancé Laurence might have second thoughts about his bride-to-be. Yseult didn't want to think about a catastrophe like that. Rachel was still beautiful – however, if she didn't put the brakes on her lifestyle she'd look old and tired before she knew what had happened. Only then would she realise that nobody wanted her.

Yseult stuck her fork into a pork chop in the serving dish and slapped it onto her plate like the men did.

The two farmhands came into the kitchen and joined the others at the table. There was something delightful in watching men and women eat hungrily after a good morning's work. Yseult reflected again on the great tricks of the trade she had learned from her time with the O'Neills. They believed in feeding their workers or neighbours who were helping "as decently as if they were kings," Mary O'Neill said. "When you're eating 'tis the best time to get to know people and the workers do better on a full stomach." There was always a strong ritual of eating together at Mary O'Neill's. It was more than just the food. There was a sense of unity between workmen and family and neighbours around their table. There was a warmth there that was new to Yseult. Mary's mother would bake every day – bread, scones and tarts. She also made her own ice cream. Everybody seemed welcome. Even the big lurcher, Sadie, was allowed into the house. She'd sprawl contently in front of the fire. Yseult had to admit, it was one the nicest houses to eat in, far better than some of the exclusive restaurants she had eaten in since then.

"This is very nice," Brendan said to Martha. "You're a good cook."

Yseult looked up to see Martha blush.

"Where did you learn to cook?" Brendan asked.

Normally Yseult would cringe at that kind of flirtatious conversation. Today she enjoyed the simple normality of the day.

Martha told them how she had worked in hotels all her life. This was her first time working in a house.

"So far so good," she said.

Yseult acknowledged that Martha was hardly going to say she hated it, hated the daft abrupt old lady and cracked carry-on.

Yseult listened to the conversation around her as it went from eating dinners to football to drunk-driving and the local circus.

"There are lions and monkeys," one of the workmen said.

They talked about the size of the lion, the paws and teeth.

"Is the circus in the same place?" Yseult suddenly asked.

"Curtain's Field," Brendan said to her.

Yseult began to recall her first circus in Ireland. "There was a dwarf dressed in horns," she said and the men laughed at the idea. "He did acrobatics on a trampoline. A pony ran in circles with a black dog on his back, then the devil dwarf swung from the trapeze." Yseult threw her eyes upward as she recalled it.

MARY O'NEILL WAS AT THAT SAME CIRCUS. YSEULT WATCHED MARY leave her seat midway through the dwarf's performance. Intrigued, she watched her go to the back of the tent and crawl under the canvas. Clearly Mary had entered without paying – now she had seen enough and simply up and left. Yseult thought it daring – she'd love to have been with her.

Their picnics and outings with the Hamiltons were all very nice but eventually tiring. Yseult's preferred company was Butch Slattery. She plagued him to take her fishing and help him train his greyhounds, and a few times he obliged. She loved his greyhounds, the structure of a greyhound's body, its physique. When it moved she'd watch every rippling muscle in awe.

"You'll be a great doggie woman yet," Butch said.

During her first few weeks of slipping the greyhounds he never got her name right. "Hold the dog by the collar, tight, and don't let her go, Assault!"

BUTCH AND NELLIE TOOK PORTIA AND YSEULT TO THE FAIR THAT April in 1921.

Yseult watched Mary O'Neill and her parents stop to admire the horses. Mary sized the animals up like a man. She pulled each horse's lips apart to judge its age and walked slowly down the length of the animal, rubbing her hand along its body, regarding it closely.

There were races – one for girls and one for boys.

Yseult would take the opportunity to shine. Let Mary O'Neill sit up and take notice of Yseult Ffrench from Lugdale Estate. That day Yseult had no notion of stopping to yawn during the race. She'd show Mary O'Neill who was the best.

Yseult and Mary left the rest of the group behind as they sprinted down Curtain's Field with Mary O'Neill passing the finishing post first.

"Ya done well," Mary O'Neill said breathlessly after the race.

"I didn't win," Yseult's said, her voice shrill with disbelief that she had lost and equally surprised that anyone would congratulate the loser.

"You nearly did," Mary said and began to walk away.

Yseult quickly said, "How's your stallion?"

"He's grand," Mary said. "They're coming from all over for him to service their mares." She continued to walk away.

"I live near you," Yseult said, keeping pace with her. "I live in Lugdale." Since her arrival to Ireland, Yseult had noticed how certain people were impressed with her home.

Mary didn't respond.

"Do you remember? I came with my sister and our farm manager to see your stallion. We had cake and lemonade with you."

"I remember ya," Mary said indifferently.

"We must arrange to meet sometime," Yseult said, imitating her mother when she extended invitations.

Mary O'Neill paused to regard her. "You live in Lugdale. I can't go down there."

"Of course you can," Yseult said. "Why not? We're neighbours." Just because Mary O'Neill lived in a cottage and she in a great big manor, they could still go fishing and hunting together. "You have a lurcher and I have a golden retriever. We can go hunting together."

"Your people wouldn't be long accusing me of poaching your

streams and lands," Mary said. "Let you come up to me." And she nodded her head with finality as if that ended the matter.

Yseult was so excited she found herself unconsciously imitating her. "I will," she said and realised she'd spoken with a Kerry accent.

On the way home Butch and Nellie talked about the fair, the neighbours they'd seen, who said what and then they talked about the race.

"Assault, you met your match with the young O'Neill girl," Butch said. "She's faster than ya."

Yseult didn't care any more about the race. At the first opportunity, she'd sneak across the estate and up to Mary and her friends who fished and hunted, trained greyhounds and had the most coveted stallion in the country.

CHAPTER THIRTY-NINE

Yseult wouldn't let her daughter walk the eleven miles to Lugdale, although it would do her no harm at all to drag her bags up the hill in her expensive high shoes. She would collect Rachel, she'd take her to a hotel and have tea, do something nice to take her own mind off the past.

She went to her bedroom and took her going-to-town clothes from the wardrobe.

There were times when she'd like company, someone to chat to about the ordinary everydayness of life. Occasionally she liked to get dressed up and have her tea in the local hotel. There was little to do on the farm at this time of the year except stare at the dark evenings or gape at the junk on the television. Life had changed, nobody called to anybody's house any more. Although Yseult hadn't ever had many friends. For most of her life she'd kept herself to herself as Nellie Brown would say. Normally she wasn't good in crowds. She found people and too much interaction to be a kind of a nuisance, making conversation wearisome. Unlike most, she seldom needed people. The only person whose company she'd like now was her sister Portia. It was strange that she wanted Portia's presence after all these years.

Portia lived in Jamaica.

"So I won't be having afternoon tea with her," Yseult said aloud as she held her clothes up to the light.

Rachel was not due back on the train for another three hours. Yseult would go to town early, she'd pay the vet's bill, get that old scrounger to knock a few bob off it. Then she might behave as Rachel behaved and "treat herself to a top." Women her daughter's age loved to treat themselves to a top, or blouse, or jacket, or a spa day. Rachel's voice rose an octave when she mentioned treating herself. "Treat myself to a blouse." It had an air of authority and self-importance, a hint of "don't deny me my indulgence". Their treats were endless. Rachel went to Limerick to buy her make-up, she talked with her friends about the softness of the foundation, how easily it went on her face. They talked about matt make-up and skin toner, as if it were paint for walls they were discussing. Yseult had to admit, their soft foundations made them look as if their faces hadn't seen a day of hardship. Yseult didn't believe in wasting money on such things.

"Tops! Blouses!" she said aloud in the raised voice Rachel used, clothes that would never see the outside of a wardrobe after four outings or fall asunder after five.

"What treat would you like, Yseult?" she asked herself as she sat at her dressing table.

Slowly she applied her own make-up. It was a new brand, one that Rachel had given her and said suited her skin. Rachel was good at that type of thing, although there was only so long any woman could deliberate over make-up or tops, or blouses. Rachel's make-up made Yseult younger, not prettier, but there was a vague throwback to the years when she was a tall, dark, handsome woman. Yseult had never been pretty or delicate. She was taller than most Irishmen in the 1930s when she was in her prime. She had sallow skin – "Worse than the Enrights from the heart of the bog and they're burnt from the sun and wind," Nellie Brown would say as she'd scrub her face till it hurt. Nellie would say, "'Tis a quare dirt on you tonight – 'tisn't comin' off." A day in the sun would make Yseult look Spanish or Italian, especially with her black unruly hair that was kept short all of her adult life.

Yseult took a deep breath and placed her hands on the mahogany dressing-table.

"What do you want, Yseult?" she said again.

She could see the squad car driving up the avenue. It continued round the side of the house.

She did not want to deal with them again.

Yseult remained sitting at her dressing-table, looking at her reflection. A few minutes later the phone by her bed rang. It was someone in the house ringing through to her bedroom. Yseult didn't pick up the extension.

At her age there was nothing material she wanted. She wanted pain-free days. She wanted to be independent as long as possible. She wanted the farm to do well. She wanted her mind to remain quick and alert. She wanted painkillers, strong soothing painkillers for the difficult days.

Yseult put on her lipstick. She'd used the same colour for the last few decades despite Rachel encouraging her to experiment. Yseult told Rachel she'd leave experimenting to the younger age group, God knows they did enough of it.

Yseult wanted her daughter to get married as soon as possible. Hopefully Rachel's fiancé would rein in her antics, curtail her many courses and treats, her weekends away, her spa days and her nonsensical talk of building a cheesemaking factory or turning Lugdale into a boutique hotel.

Yseult put on her jewellery and fur coat. The full-length fur was her type of clothing. It cost the price of a milking parlour forty years ago and remained as good as the day her husband had bought it for her. It had lasted a lot longer than her marriage or the muck that Rachel bought.

She wanted Rachel to have a child. Only with a child would Rachel become less obsessed with herself and her treats and her tops and her make-up that was only sold in a city over an hour away.

Yseult felt the cold pearls. They were older than the coat, older than Yseult. They were over one hundred years old. They came from Jamaica. Her father claimed he knew the boy who fished for the pearls and he knew the woman who had strung them together. Arry and Okeke were their names. It was strange how she could remember their foreign names.

She wanted to stop recollecting the past, but since she established that the skeleton was concealed in 1923, little remembrances were dawning on her.

YSEULT RECALLED THE FIRST TIME SHE VENTURED ON HER OWN UP to the O'Neills' house to meet Mary, armed with Butch Slattery's fishing rod and a cutting from a bright pink Rhododendron from their garden.

Mary stood at the front door, staring from the Rhododendron to the fishing rod.

"I thought you might like to add our Rhododendron to your garden – it's from India," Yseult said awkwardly. She had heard Nellie Brown asking permission to take a slip of the Rhododendron plant and gathered it was sought after.

For a moment Mary said nothing, only looked at the proffered flower and cutting.

"'Tis very strange to have someone knocking at the front door," she eventually said, "and 'tis even stranger that 'tis yourself holding Rhododendron in one hand and your fishing rod in the other!" And she laughed.

Yseult so desperately wanted company other than Portia's and the Hamiltons' that she had taken Butch Slattery's fishing rod without his permission. She intended returning it that evening.

When Yseult realised how peculiar she must appear, she too began to laugh.

"'Tis very nice," Mary added more seriously when she examined the flower. "The colours of our Rhododendrons are blue and light pink – yours have a great deep colour."

The O'Neills' cottage was a strange higgledy-piggledy affair. It appeared small from the outside with two windows at each side of the front door. There was a narrow corridor and another room at the back, then behind that another room, and on the right of the kitchen was another room. They walked through the house and out the back door.

Mary compared Yseult's flowers to her own.

"The leaves are nearly the same," she noted.

She examined the buds and stem in a slow thoughtful way, feeling the texture of the stem and leaf between her fingers. She went to the edge of the garden and planted the slip immediately. She talked more about the plant while her hands worked busily with the small shovel and clay. The lurcher stood beside Mary looking inquisitive.

"It all depends on the earth," Mary said.

"I caught a trout this morning," Yseult lied when Mary stood back to admire her new plant. "I'm going now to catch another, if you'd like to come."

That afternoon they caught four trout. They returned to Mary's home, washed and gutted the fish and then fried it on the stove. The fish tasted all the better to Yseult because she'd caught it. There was something primal that thrilled her in catching and eating her own food.

The following day Yseult returned to Mary's house with Ginger. They set off with traps and Mary's big lurcher, Sadie. They caught and killed three rabbits. Mary thought it hilarious that Yseult didn't know how to skin a rabbit.

"You've the life of Reilly down there in Lugdale," Mary said as she slit the rabbit behind the ears, stuck her fingers inside and pulled the fur off as if it were a mere outer garment.

"'Tis only that," Mary said when Yseult commented on it. "'Tis his fur, like our coat during winter."

The following day Mary's mother had a sandwich ready for Yseult. It was filled with her portion of the meat from the rabbit.

Each day after her lessons Yseult ran across the field and up the steps to Mary O'Neill's, taking great care she wasn't seen leaving the estate.

Mary O'Neill's father was tall, thin and tanned. To differentiate him from the other O'Neills, he was known as Rusty O'Neill. Some said it was because of his skin colour and others because of his occupation with rabbits. Each day when Yseult arrived at the O'Neills' house, Mr. O'Neill would be on his tea break. He'd sit with his quiet wife Eileen on a bench he'd made in the garden. Once she saw him with his arm around Eileen's shoulders. Yseult found the affectionate gesture strange. Each day he used the remaining tea in the pot for the plants.

Unlike a lot of local men, Rusty O'Neill was able to read. Yseult saw him reading the newspaper and there were books on a shelf in the kitchen. Their walls were not covered in holy pictures. Instead there was a picture of a boat and another strange picture in a frame of a man holding a snake.

"Hapi was the snake's name," Mary told Yseult. They were eating scones in the kitchen. "He used to eat mice and rats."

Yseult was intrigued.

Mr. O'Neill sat behind them, looking up at the picture as they discussed it.

"When one Hapi died they got another snake and called him Hapi too."

It impressed Yseult when Mary's father encouraged their fishing and hunting. He gave them bamboo sticks as rods that he'd grown specifically for fishing and gave them fishing hooks made from safety-pins. Equally Yseult thought it peculiar and nice when Mary found a wild hen's egg in the ditch and kept it for her father.

"Dad will love this for his tea." Mary had smiled affectionately when she thought of her father.

Yseult could not think of anything her father loved apart from Lugdale and the old letters from Jamaica that he drooled over.

"My considerate little girl," Mr. O'Neill said when she showed him the egg. He put his arm around her shoulders and planted a kiss on her head.

THE GIRLS' DAYS VARIED FROM FISHING TO SWIMMING IN THE streams, catching pheasants and hunting, all free from the land. On

Friday nights when her parents went to the Hamiltons, Yseult could spend longer unaccountable hours with Mary.

As time passed, she grew more daring. One Friday evening she accompanied Mary and her father into town on the pony and trap with rabbits to sell at the train station. Awestruck, she listened to the women and men who bargained with Mr. O'Neill: "Gimme three for the price of two – I've a house full of hungry children!"

Initially she thought they were shameless to admit they were poor and had hungry children.

"No shame at all in being poor," Mary said to Yseult. "The shame is when money is flung around without thought."

The women crowded around his cart. "Go on, Rusty, take a half crown from me!"

Sometimes he relented and other times he remained firm.

"I will not. I've a houseful to feed myself."

On their way back to Mein, he bought them an ice cream each.

ANOTHER AFTERNOON YSEULT AND MARY ROAMED HIGH INTO THE hills on their bicycles to find a stream with the best fish. They had tea in a cottage owned by a man who claimed his mother was the oldest person in Ireland.

Just as they entered the house, Mary stopped and whispered to Yseult, "Say your name is Bonnie and you're new to the area. Don't be mentionin' that auld talk of Lugdale for fear they'll shoot the pair of us."

The man of the house let them peep into a back bedroom to see the woman who was rumoured to be one hundred years of age. They looked at her lost shrivelled eyes in a small face with wrinkles so deep they were black.

On the road home they howled with laughter at the name Bonnie and Yseult sang out of key in the most guttural Kerry accent which sent the pair of them into further fits of laughing.

. . .

Occasionally one of the girls from the tenants' cottages accompanied them.

Yseult remembered standing in a stream in the Stack Mountains one afternoon. There was something lovely and happy about the day that she couldn't identify.

Yseult said aloud that she preferred Ireland to England.

"Of course ya do," Mary said. "'Tis the best place in the world."

At night Yseult scrubbed her hands and nails before dinner. When their father enquired about their day, Portia talked about her lessons and her preferred songs on the piano, the sponge cake she had made with Nellie Brown and the novel she was reading.

Yseult talked about her pony Hazel and Ginger the retriever, and what she had seen in the woods. She gave details of the birds and how many rabbits she had seen. She told them she had fished. She told the truth about her day, omitting the fact that Mary O'Neill was with her, or that they had roamed high into the mountains on their bicycles.

Yseult didn't know why she felt the need to lie about her new blossoming friendship with Mary O'Neill. She could have got permission to leave the estate to go to Mary's house as it was so close to theirs, but she didn't. She was afraid their suspicious minds would put an end to her first flurry of a happy friendship. Afraid she'd be condemned to spending her days with Portia baking cakes, giving piano recitals and waiting for Aunt Lydia's pictures to dry.

During those dinners in the first few months of their arrival in Ireland, Aunt Lydia listened quietly to Yseult's account of her day with narrowed eyes.

Yseult suspected that Aunt Lydia knew the truth.

Yseult stood at the window watching the squad car as it slowly drove down the avenue away from the house. She wondered if they could see her in the rear-view mirror. The lamp on her dresser was switched on. She didn't care if they saw her watching them.

"To hell with them," she whispered.

She leaned across her dressing-table and took from her jewellery box one single gold coin minted in 1860. Queen Victoria was on the front, wearing a high headdress. Her frumpy side profile was clear. On the back was a coat of arms. For a moment she thought about the coin found close to the skeleton. She toyed with the coin and felt the weight as she watched the Garda car leave.

She wanted the Garda forensics to bring to a conclusion the story of Mr. Doe as soon as possible.

She did not want the deceased to have any connection with her family or her lands, or any of those who went before her.

CHAPTER FORTY

In the train station carpark, Yseult began to think about Rachel while she waited for her train to arrive. As mother and daughter they couldn't have been more different, both emotionally and physically. Rachel was like her father, Archie, pale with a round smiling face, clear dimples and deep-set blue eyes. Her hair was the only vague feature that resembled Yseult's. Rachel had long thick dark curly hair. Rachel's hair was an asset now when women wore big pumped-up manes. Some nights it was so pumped up Yseult asked if she'd stuck her finger in the electricity socket.

Normally when Yseult thought about Rachel she was filled with uncertainty, but since Rachel's engagement to Laurence, the looming cloud of uneasiness wasn't as dark as before. There was hope for her giddy daughter who was happiest regaling her friends with stories, shopping and partaking in all of those frivolous girlie pastimes. She was flighty and dramatic, expressive and emotional. Serious situations were often dealt with in an inappropriately jovial manner. Even news of the occasional death was received with delight. Rachel would speculate on who'd attend the funeral and what she'd wear. An out-of-town funeral and over-nighter was a real treat. She'd come home filled with the joys of life and would tell Yseult all that occurred.

When Yseult had her back operation, Rachel spent her days on the phone talking about it. She loved talking about the dramatics of the rain and floods the morning Yseult went to hospital, and the post-surgery recovery. Nothing was omitted from the saga, all told with a comical bent – even Yseult's stumbling into the kitchen and ripping up the healthy diet Rachel had taken the time to write.

In the end, Yseult told Rachel to shut up.

That too was met with hilarity and plenty of amused eye-rolling at her intolerant abrupt mother.

Hopefully, Rachel would get pregnant soon after the wedding. It would help her focus on something other than herself. Lugdale would have an heir. At least Rachel's fiancé was steady. He was so steady that Yseult was still surprised by Rachel's choice. Maybe Rachel had been playing dumb when Yseult cautioned her about finding a man who'd suit Lugdale. Laurence was not handsome, he was tall, thin and all nose. He was everything Rachel was not. He was grounded, consistent, a hard worker and a tremendous bore. Laurence loved Lugdale. He loved the house and gardens, he particularly loved the paintings, especially Major Frederick Stratford-Rice's portrait. It was painted in 1795. Laurence was so taken with the painting that each time he came to their home Yseult noticed how his eyes delayed to admire it. He suggested she have it valued. Yseult had no interest in that type of thing – the price of the painting was irrelevant. Hopefully it would always hang on the walls of Lugdale instead of being part of some auctioneer's lot at an antique sale. Laurence's attitude to farming was similar to Rachel's – he didn't like farming or manual work. Yseult could overlook that.

His mother was Church of Ireland and very well connected. Laurence was a doctor, as was his father and grandfather. Yseult felt the need to acknowledge he was a humane doctor, one who didn't like to see his patients suffering. He was sympathetic and personable. Not only was Laurence kind to his patients, he was kind to Yseult.

He understood her back pain and went above and beyond the call of duty to assist.

Rachel liked the fact that Laurence was connected to the Grosvenor family. Rachel was an elitist – all of her friends sounded as if they were somebody of importance. Sally was not just a restaurant owner, she was a renowned celebrated chef. Margo wasn't just a journalist, she was an award-winning writer. Rachel's Dublin friend whose name Yseult couldn't remember wasn't just an interior designer, she was a *prestigious interior decorator*. At that point Rachel always mentioned some singer whose house she had decorated and how the singer had flown her to New York. Yseult thought it was nonsense and said so. "She was hired by a singer to tell him what colours to paint his walls and where to fling his matching cushions. The world is gone mad."

The interior-designer girl stayed recently. Yseult hated the way Rachel showed her around the house. She said she'd love the job of overhauling Lugdale. They talked about the cottages on the fringes of the estate, how she'd love the opportunity to decorate them. She thought they were quaint and spoke disparagingly about the previous tenants.

"Imagine the dirt and squalor they lived in," the interior designer said.

Yseult told the interior designer the previous tenants kept their cottages clean, cosy and welcoming. The old occupants were hard-working. Yseult didn't bother explaining to Rachel's friend that people had great pride in their work and their homes. They maintained their leased lands and homes as if they owned them. Yseult could still recall the children from the tenant farms. Josie Broderick, Mairéad Nolan, the Lawlers, the Hartnetts. Each of the eleven Hartnett children had red hair of various shades: carrot-red, auburns, copper and strawberry.

BUTCH SLATTERY DELIVERED THE RENTS EACH WEEK WHILE HER father filled up the accounts.

"The Red Hartnetts," Tobias said, filling in the rent book.

The first time Yseult saw this rent book, her father was sitting at his bureau as Butch Slattery handed over the rent he'd collected from the tenants. Butch explained that John Hartnett had only half the money this week. She couldn't recall the reason why they were behind in the rent, she only remembered her father accepting their excuses.

"That's fine," her father said. "I want to appear to be a kind landlord. The risk of these men and their red children burning me out of my house is too high."

They talked about other tenants, who were late with the rent and those who were on time.

Yseult never heard a word mentioned about the O'Neills. At the first opportunity she sneaked a peek at the tenant rent book. She wanted to ascertain how much land the O'Neills leased and how often their rent was late.

Rusty O'Neill's name was not listed in their father's rent book. There was one O'Neill family who lived in Kilflynn but none in Mein.

"We own our own land," Mary O'Neill said when Yseult cautiously broached the subject. "We answer only to ourselves."

They were gutting fish in one of the O'Neills' sheds. Yseult remembered Mary waving her hand around the shed with such pride anyone would think she was standing in Lugdale's entrance hall.

"Please God I'll work hard and buy more and more land," Mary said, flicking one of the fish heads to the waiting cat.

Yseult was disconcerted at the news that the O'Neills were one of the small independent units in the locality. They were not susceptible to changing rents although Yseult heard her father say the rents would remain the same until Ireland's wars ended. There was no son in the O'Neill family to inherit the farm, only Mary and her older sisters who were married locally.

"I'll marry a man who'll work hard with me and we'll be happy," Mary concluded.

To anyone else that would have sounded childish but Yseult

didn't doubt Mary's determination to remain where she lived and to marry for common sense rather than love.

"Will you marry?" Mary asked Yseult.

"I don't know," Yseult said honestly.

"You'll have to marry a Proddy like yourself," Mary said matter-of-factly, "and there aren't too many to pick from."

Yseult agreed and watched Mary count the fish.

"One, two, three, four," she said, with her skillet knife pointing at the house. "Five, six, seven, eight," pointing towards the haybarn.

There was enough fish to feed Mary and her parents and the man they referred to as Fonsy who Yseult had never laid eyes on. There was also enough to feed the four men who were hiding in their barn.

That afternoon Yseult had seen the men edge along the hedge towards the O'Neills. They had the furtive gait of rebels on the run. It was not the first time the O'Neills allowed rebels to hide in their barn.

"I hope there's enough," Mary said, looking at the fish.

There was always enough food in the O'Neills' – enough for the rebels, any callers and Fonsy, the rumoured lunatic.

YSEULT NOTED THE GREAT DIFFERENCES BETWEEN THE O'NEILLS' home and her own. Each week she heard her parents' friends discuss Ireland's troubles and the men they called the Shinners, the Sinn Féin supporters. They mentioned murders, men in Knockbrack, Hedley's Bridge, and a local massacre. Outside of Lugdale the world seemed in chaos.

Eavesdropping, Yseult heard Mr. Hamilton's voice: "There are Irishmen with more passion for their country than passion for the flesh. Their thirst for victory is immoral."

Yseult learned that her father gave jobs on the ships to the local unemployed men.

"It will clear out the men from the area and make me appear like the compassionate squire," Tobias said.

He donated a prize of a pig at the local raffle.

Yseult didn't need to eavesdrop to hear how unhappy her mother was.

"How long are you going to continue with this farce?" her mother asked her father. "I miss London terribly. I miss my family and friends."

"Your family doesn't want you living in the same country as them," her father said calmly. "You've made a mockery of me."

Despite her mother's apparent dislike of her father, he attempted to be nice to her. On her birthday a few weeks after their arrival in Ireland, he gave her a gold necklace with emerald diamonds.

"For you, my dear," he said as he presented it to her.

"Thank you." Yseult's mother glanced at the jewellery and placed it on the table beside her. All evening she didn't look at it again.

Later Portia held the necklace to the light and wished for something exactly the same. "Someday it will be mine," she said, returning it to the velvet-lined box, "because I'm the oldest."

On hearing that, her father looked at Yseult and raised his eyebrows ever so slightly. She knew her father intended the gold-and-emerald jewellery for her.

Later that night Yseult heard her parents arguing.

"You cast my gift aside as if it were the leftovers from something unpleasant," her father said. "They cost quite a penny."

"The price of a slave?" her mother retorted.

"How dare you!" her father said. "I earned my money just like the rest of them, yet they gossip and whisper their lies about me. What a joy Ireland is, far removed from their selective attitudes."

She heard her mother scoff. "That's rich coming from a man like you."

"Really? And what right has a woman like you to treat me with contempt? None of your own kind would dare marry you."

She heard the silence that followed, then the crackle of the gramophone and the upbeat sound of jazz.

.   .   .

HER FATHER EVENTUALLY RETURNED TO SEA.

"I'm sure we'll still be here when you get back," her mother said. "Growing more insane in this forgotten little outback."

The house heaved with relief. He would be gone for at least three months.

Thus began the pattern for the next year. He spent three months at sea and one month in Ireland.

Yseult thought about Mary O'Neill's parents. There were no emerald gold necklaces or 533 acres of land. There wasn't a Big House or servants or children wishing their father would leave for a few months. The O'Neills seemed happier sitting in their exotic flower garden, fostering a lunatic and feeding their rebels than Yseult's parents.

YSEULT WATCHED RACHEL APPEAR AND WALK HURRIEDLY TOWARDS the car with her overnight bag on her shoulder.

"What's the story with the human remains?" Rachel said as she got in, her eyes wide and dancing with excitement. "My God, when I heard the news I couldn't believe it! I was like, stunned, totally stunned."

"You were so stunned that you missed the train home and didn't take the time to tell me."

"Chillax, Mother," Rachel sighed. "How are you?"

"Very well."

"Any pain?"

Rachel needed to have something to consume her, something exciting to think and talk about. Similar to un-sad funerals, the excitement need not be happy excitement, just any type of excitement. Since the excitement of the engagement ebbed away, recently she had got it into her head that Yseult was not well. There was back pain and weight loss. Yseult had a series of tests but nothing showed up on the results. There was a CAT scan and more bloods, and still nothing. It was plain old back-trouble and old age. Rachel wouldn't accept it – there had to be more to it.

"No pain," Yseult replied.

She felt the need to categorically deny the presence of pain and quell any notions of a sinister sickness that might be consuming her. Rachel was expressive, everything was discussed. She'd spend her days telling all and sundry about her mother's illness, manufacture a sickness and put labels on debilitating disorders until Yseult would begin to believe there was something wrong with her. The actual fact was that Yseult had back pain from years of wear and tear. Every eighty-one-year-old person had little and large ailments that would continue to worsen until the lid went onto the coffin.

"So where's the body?" Rachel asked as they drove off, getting back to the more topical issue.

Yseult need not worry tonight about playing down her pain – Rachel was too consumed with the skeleton on her land.

"It's a skeleton," Yseult corrected her. "It's just around O'Neills' bend."

Rachel opened her mouth and eyes so wide that Yseult could have laughed, except it was not a laughing matter.

"On our land," Rachel gushed. "Who is he?"

"I've no idea."

"What have the Gardaí told you?"

"Nothing – they're trying to establish the facts. Nobody knows anything yet."

"I'll talk to them tomorrow," Rachel said in a business-like tone. "They'll probably tell me stuff they won't tell you."

"Don't you tell them *stuff*," Yseult matched Rachel's tone, "that I wouldn't tell them."

"I've no notion of behaving in your paranoid secretive manner," Rachel countered.

They went to the hotel on the outskirts of town to eat.

"Deliberate, like, it has to be a murder," Rachel said. "A murder on our land, this will make an interesting story."

Rachel couldn't eat when her sandwich arrived. She barely mentioned the weekend in Dublin or the cheesemaking workshop – she only mentioned a wedding dress she had seen.

"Totally stunning," she said, closing her eyes and tilting her head back as if dazzled by its beauty again.

Instead of eating she ordered a wine and speculated some more about the skeleton: who was it, how old was the tree, why was the tree planted, what species of tree?

All of her talk brought them back to the same response from Yseult.

"We don't know anything," she summarised.

"You've lived here all your life – you must have your suspicions?"

"It could be a skeleton from the war, or a medieval skeleton or possibly a man from the Viking age."

"Or it could be an old servant," Rachel added, "or it could have something to do with Frederick in the entrance hall, or William in the drawing room," she was referring to the family portraits, "or it could be someone else related to us?" She paused as if thrilled at the prospect.

On the way home, Rachel said she hoped it wasn't an ordinary death like a murder from the war. "Something with a bit of mystery would be more interesting."

Yseult shook her head in exasperation. She wished the skeleton had turned to dust and ashes whereas Rachel wanted to piece the skeleton together in the hope it would speak and tell a sordid tale.

CHAPTER FORTY-ONE

Yseult had been thinking about retirement when the Gardaí arrived. There was a woman on the radio who divided her time between Lanzarote and Ireland – she was talking about her network of friends abroad and her Irish friends. She described her apartment in Lanzarote overlooking the beach and the constant sunshine. It sounded dreadful to Yseult, all that packing to sit gazing at the sea. Then she thought of the problem of getting monthly medication abroad, like her painkillers. The woman on the radio didn't mention any medical issues or the language barrier when conversing with her doctor in her sun-soaked Lanzarote.

"Hello, Mrs. Ffrench," the Garda said.

Yseult raised her eyes. "Is Spanish the language in Lanzarote?" she asked Brendan.

"I think so," he said uneasily, looking at the Garda.

"Are you thinking of moving, Mrs. Ffrench?" the Garda was bold enough to ask.

"Only when I see a man of the law in my kitchen before I've had time to digest my breakfast," she replied, tossing crusts to Laddie. Normally she didn't believe in giving the dog her scraps from the table but today she'd do anything rather than give the Garda her full attention.

"It's only a courtesy call," he said with a smile.

Yseult felt he was enjoying tormenting her. She'd like to have said that to him. There was a word for it, people who got pleasure from another's pain. Sadist.

Yseult remained sitting throughout the conversation that ensued, looking indifferently at the Garda. Brendan and Martha remained in the kitchen while the Garda stood at the end of the table. Yseult was relieved Rachel was not up yet. She'd unwittingly tell him all she suspected, even adding her own unfounded suspicions.

"We're trying to establish the age of the skeleton," the Garda said. "Our forensics should establish that quite quickly. The archaeologists will comb the scene for artifacts. The fact that a coin was allegedly found close to the skeleton makes them think there might be more relics in the vicinity. And they've found some buttons."

"Buttons?" Yseult repeated. "What relevance has that?"

"The buttons indicate that he or she lived locally. According to sources they were the standard copper buttons used for decades. It probably confirms that he or she was wearing clothes from Ireland."

Yseult stared at him open-mouthed. "Dear God, did you think he might be a nude alien? Of course he lived locally!"

The Garda reddened.

Brendan spoke. "What happens now?"

"We'll remove the skeleton and then Forensics will carry out a series of tests to establish more details, like the cause of death, the sex of the skeleton, the age." He looked at Yseult. "If anyone would like to volunteer DNA samples it would give us a clearer picture."

Yseult stood up. She had heard enough. Clearly Garda O'Riordan had heard old rumours. As she put on her jacket the Garda continued talking.

"We can also identify where the deceased lived, if they lived abroad."

"Really, can you tell that?" Brendan asked.

"Yes, the forensics drill holes in the teeth because teeth absorb the environmental atmosphere. Every part of the world leaves a signature."

Yseult paused on her way out to the door.

"Even a person who'd been to Mars," he said.

"Good afternoon, Garda," Yseult said as she left the room.

YSEULT TOOK A PAINKILLER BEFORE RIDING HER GELDING OUT OF the stables. She liked to ride out a few times a week, but it wasn't always possible. There were days when her back pain almost brought her to a standstill. Every movement was torturous. Without the painkillers, death would have been attractive. At this stage of her life she didn't take part in the hunt, but occasionally she followed it in her jeep. She loved the suspense of seeing where the scent took the dogs, over how much terrain and double dikes, how long the fox would outmanoeuvre the beagles. It was suspense and exhilaration at its best.

Today Yseult took the horse through the back fields, up to higher ground and away from the archaeologists. After an hour she ended up in the chapel grounds, feeling refreshed. She dismounted and patted the horse on the neck.

"Just you and me together for a few hours, Barney," she said. "You're as handsome as ever." He was a black full Irish Draft. Spending money on well-bred horses had always been one of Yseult's indulgences. She bought Barney six years ago, he was a great purchase. She took crushed barley and oats from her pocket. "You might be my last," she said as she rubbed his neck. "We'll grow old together." She took a moment to watch him eating the oats before tying him to the old cast-iron hitching post at the side of the chapel.

NELLIE BROWN USED TO REBUKE YSEULT FOR THE AFFECTION SHE had for her animals. "Kissin' your dogs and horses. Pity you're not nicer to humans."

"You're not human," was Yseult's bold response.

Yseult's first pony, Hazel, broke her leg. It was so long ago she couldn't remember how old she was. She remembered her father was home from sea, nearing the end of his spell in Lugdale before he left again. It was one of those scenes that regularly flashed through her memory. Sometimes the memory stubbornly sat in her line of vision and refused to move from her sights. It always seemed as if it happened only recently.

Yseult was devastated at Hazel's break.

Her father said it wasn't a bad thing. "You're too fond of her."

He saw Yseult's love for the pony as a failing.

"It's only an animal," he reminded her as he took the pony from the stable with his shotgun.

He loaded the gun and passed it to Yseult.

"If you want to manage an estate as great as Lugdale you must be able to separate your mind from the love for your pony."

Yseult wanted to wrap her arms around the pony and protect her from the brutality of the mere suggestion.

"She is your animal – you must take responsibility," her father said.

Yseult made the mistake of looking into her pony's brown eyes. They blinked, she fired.

Yseult folded up the memory and tucked it away. She could never discard it. That memory and many more defined her, they kept her keen and apart. Without them she would never have survived. Her estate would never have lasted when so many of her kind bailed out, opted for city life or fled from the *savage* Irish.

Yseult turned her attention to the little chapel. It was built in the grounds of Lugdale by her ancestors to accommodate their Church of Ireland congregation in 1750. She used the key to enter the side door. Most of her extended family were baptised and married there. With only twelve pews, it accommodated seating for roughly 50 people. Some of her ancestors were buried in the vaults of the church, their names etched on their tombs. Yseult looked at the names: *Major Frederick David Stratford-Rice 1759–1821.* The remains of the stern old men who adorned the walls of her home were now interred in the walls of their private chapel. Those who made the greatest impact were interred inside. The others were taken out the front door, up a small hill and into the private cemetery on the outskirts of the forest.

She went back outside and slowly ascended the hill, following the route to the cemetery. The trees were old and loomed high. At both sides of the overgrown path they joined at the top, shielding her from most of the light. The day was so still and the forest so secluded Yseult could hear the twigs crunch beneath her feet. She opened the small cast-iron gate wide and walked through.

There wasn't any order to the graves. Some of the headstones no longer stood upright, the shifting earth inclined them forwards and backwards. The circular headstones signified the men who were buried standing upright and facing Lugdale Estate, surveying all they owned. Even in death they laid claim to the land that was taken from the Irish and granted to them by the English. Yseult didn't pause to pray. She walked around the cemetery until she found Lydia's grave. She was buried beside her son, Henry. They had arrived to live in Ireland in 1891.

Lydia and Henry's grave was as overgrown as the rest of the cemetery. They were buried at the back, out of sight. Yseult noted that even in death Lydia kept Henry hidden.

According to Nellie Brown, Lydia's son Henry had been a happy man. He and his mother lived simple lives after they returned from Jamaica. "They even liked the dirty auld rain," Nellie said in disbelief. "Did ya ever hear the likes of it?"

Lydia was very protective of Henry – she wouldn't let anyone see him. When the police came to the house to warn Aunt Lydia about the Irish rebels burning the Big Houses of the Anglo-Irish, she wouldn't let even them see Henry. At one point she pretended he was dead. Nellie Brown blessed herself when she told that to Yseult.

Yseult stepped onto the grave and looked at the earth beneath her feet. She bounced on the balls of her feet.

"That's a bit silly of me," she said.

Recently Yseult had watched a documentary about a serial killer. Detectives used newly-developed equipment that could detect where the killer's victims were buried. They stood over the suspected burial sites and were able to tell if the body was below them. Yseult thought about that machine now. It would be nice if she could determine if Henry was buried beneath her feet in Lugdale's small cemetery. There were only small rumours, clearly rumours the Gardaí had heard when they suggested the skeleton was not Irish, and although he commented on the unlikelihood of a Mars alien his suggestion of world-wide environments would include Jamaica. It was probably foolish to suspect the corpse was Henry's though his death was shrouded in mystery. Nellie said when Henry died nobody saw him, only Lydia and an out-of-town undertaker who laid him out. When Yseult asked why Aunt Lydia used a different undertaker, Nellie suspected it had something to do with Henry's body. "I suppose she didn't want anyone to see his little useless legs."

There was a rumour that he hadn't died at all but lived in a cottage in the woods away from prying eyes. Just then Yseult remembered discussing it with Portia, their hearts racing at the thought of the crippled boy living in the woods in a cottage and Lydia fattening him like in the *Hansel and Gretel* story.

Yseult looked at the headstone commemorating Henry's life.

"The darkness is past and the true light now shineth for him who lieth here."

Aunt Lydia obviously took the time to choose a biblical reading that reflected Henry's difficult life.

AUNT LYDIA DID KNOW ABOUT YSEULT'S FRIENDSHIP WITH MARY O'Neill. At any hour of the day or night Lydia could be seen roaming the fields and woods with her camera and walking cane. Occasionally she used a pony and carriage to access higher ground from where she would take photographs.

One evening, as Yseult was rushing home from O'Neills', she skipped down the last few steps without breaking her stride and took three long steps across the lane, put her right foot on the second-last rung of the gate and threw a leg over the top. She loved the last sprint across the back meadow.

"Yseult, you're as fast as Butch Slattery's greyhounds," Aunt Lydia said.

She was standing in the lane with her walking cane.

Yseult slowly stepped down from the gate and tried to think up a plausible excuse. "There are lovely blackberries on the side of the hill …" she began.

"Don't worry, my dear, your secret is safe with me." Aunt Lydia smiled. "I saw you and Mary O'Neill fishing at Dash Bridge."

Yseult felt the need to explain. "Mother and Father might object – that's why I didn't mention her name."

They walked back to Lugdale together, commenting on the day and the sight of the meadow dotted with neatly piled haystacks.

"Have you seen the man who lives with the O'Neills?" Aunt Lydia asked.

Cautiously Yseult looked at her. "No. But one of the girls from the cottages said he was a cross between an animal and a human. Is it true? Is he terrifyingly ugly?"

"Some say he's not human at all," Lydia agreed. "They believe he's the ghost of Killian O'Neill who was sentenced to death on the hanging tree. Others say he's the ghost of a man called Falvey, the previous owner of the O'Neill house."

"Have you seen him?" Yseult was curious.

"Yes, and I don't believe he's a ghost."

"Is he a lunatic?" Yseult asked. Several times she had tried to picture him, imagining claw-like hands and teeth like a greyhound's gnashing incisors.

"I don't believe he is," Aunt Lydia said. "The poor man has just seen more than his mind can take."

Yseult wanted to ask more. She wanted to ask if Aunt Lydia had seen more than her mind could take in Jamaica. She had been warned never to mention the Caribbean to Aunt Lydia. Their mother had warned Portia and Yseult that they were never to pry into anyone's life, especially Aunt Lydia's. Her parents didn't elaborate which made Yseult more interested. So she had asked Nellie who told her that Aunt Lydia had returned to Ireland after a terrible incident – but she didn't know what that was.

When the adults talked about Big Houses being burned by the rebels, Aunt Lydia didn't seem in the slightest frightened of being murdered in her bed. "I'd rather be burned under Lugdale's roof than under the sweltering sun of another country," she said. She never mentioned the incident in Jamaica, only referring to the Caribbean climate as "hot, sticky and unkind".

Whatever happened to her, she had no desire to travel outside of Ireland. She was content with the confines of Lugdale and the rugged terrain.

"In the end my body will be taken to the cemetery in Lugdale where the Irish mist will keep my old skeleton moist."

Yseult noticed that Lydia was preoccupied with Tobias and his beginnings in Cuba. She quite often asked him a question about his background over dinner. It was done so sneakily that Yseult doubted her father noticed.

"The climate of the Caribbean is completely unsuitable for a lady such as yourself," Tobias said to Lydia one evening.

Aunt Lydia had a way of looking at Tobias – she'd tilt her head and regard him. "No, our skin colour does not suit the intensity of the sun. But Cuba must have suited yours."

Yseult noticed her father hesitate before speaking. He smiled and then spoke, "Yes, that's right."

"Your parents? Were they Cuban?"

Her father hesitated again. "My parents were Spanish. My father was a shipping agent. My mother died when I was a child."

Aunt Lydia nodded slowly. "Yes, I think you said that."

Under Aunt Lydia's persistent promptings over dinner, Tobias gradually revealed bits and pieces about his life in Cuba. Their house was large and by the sea, the sun always shone, he spoke Spanish, and his mother died soon after his birth, his father travelled the world and left him in the care of servants and an English tutor. Eventually his father, Nicolas, was killed during an insurrection in Jamaica.

Yseult noticed that her father was sometimes inconsistent about his past. She guessed Aunt Lydia must have noticed this.

They talked about Italy one evening.

"I love the Italian language," Aunt Lydia said. "The Italian winter climate makes travelling so pleasant, although my days of travel are over."

Tobias agreed.

Lydia then asked Tobias a question in a foreign language. "*Has visto mucho de la familia de tus padres en España?*"

Tobias responded at some length.

Aunt Lydia nodded.

"I'm guessing you just spoke in Spanish?" Emilia said.

Aunt Lydia laughed. "Yes, I asked Tobias if he returned to Spain to see his parents' family. He said no – his father was an only child and his mother's family lost contact after her death. He never knew his mother's extended family."

But one day Yseult overheard Tobias telling Butch that the sun setting in the Caribbean was much nicer than in Ireland. In the Caribbean the sun was a great big orange ball, he said, and it appeared to drop into the sea quite quickly. He told Butch that he and his cousins never appreciated it at the time.

CHAPTER FORTY-TWO

From her bedroom window Yseult used her binoculars to see the skeleton finally removed from her land. She watched the Garda car drive slowly down the lane, followed by the vehicle carrying the skeleton. She saw the squad car almost stop halfway up the lane, then it drove closer to Mary O'Neill's hedge. They were avoiding a large pothole she had yet to repair. As the cars slowly progressed down the lane Yseult thought it made a sad sight. A man buried beneath a tree, his body concealed for seventy years. A deliberate act to hide a murder. The deceased was utterly silenced for all these seventy years. He couldn't retaliate the night of his death, couldn't defend himself against his killer.

Brendan was waiting by the open gate. He spoke to the Garda and then made the Sign of the Cross as the van containing the skeleton passed.

Yseult was sorry she had lingered at the window and witnessed them removing the deceased, sorry she had considered the man. She was sorry for so much this evening, sorry she was forced to recall yesteryear with such melancholy over the last few days. Her father always said the past caught up with every man. He was old and melancholic when he said that. Yseult did not want to know about his past, the same way she refused to dwell on his beginnings. When she heard small tit-bits, she was as adamant to deny his origins as he was. Would she end up like her father, alone, locked in horrid memories with nothing or nobody to turn to only the mountains and Mary O'Neill's happiness and many heirs taunting her?

Yseult went directly to the study to light the fire. The Gardaí could do whatever they wanted to the skeleton. She was not about to leave any documents lying about her house to have someone raking up the past.

Yseult found Rachel sitting at the desk on the phone.

"It was great fun, we must do it again sometime. Richard said he'd visit over the coming days." She nodded her head. "Great, I'll look forward to it."

She hung up and got to her feet.

"I'm so busy," she smiled.

"Where are the keys to my archives?" Yseult asked. She dragged a chair across the room and sat in front of the archives. Then she tore a black bin-liner from a roll, opened it and left it at her feet. Today she'd begin decluttering the study.

Rachel paused before speaking. "Keys? The archives? I don't know," she said, reddening, and then she patted her pockets as if she might find the key on her person.

Yseult knew she was lying although she had no idea what she'd want to see in the archives. Old diaries, letters, logbooks were all too ordinary and boring for her daughter. In fact, calling the drawers "archives" was pretentious.

"Why are you asking me?" Rachel said then. "The archive drawers are open." She nodded impatiently towards the opened drawer.

"I had to force them open." Yseult said sulkily. She wasn't going to explain how she'd opened them with a nail-file, a trick she learned as a child.

"What are you doing?" Rachel asked.

"I'm clearing out this study once and for all." Yseult found a diary her father kept from 1911. She began to flick through it hurriedly. She'd read it years ago. There was nothing personal in it, only details of shipping and cargo from his company. He referred to shipments of sugar, rum, bananas, sugar, citrus, wine and thankfully there was no mention of slaves. She tossed it into the plastic bin-liner beside her. There was another diary from 1915, she added that to the bin-liner too.

"You're not throwing those out, are you?" Rachel was all agog as she watched her mother.

"Why not?" Yseult asked without raising her head.

"Seemingly those books are very valuable. Laurence said they could contribute to a museum, in years to come and –"

"Laurence said?" Yseult gasped incredulously. "How does Laurence know what is in my archives?"

"I showed him – is there something wrong with that?"

"Does Laurence have the keys to my archives?" Yseult asked in a raised voice. She was indignant that anyone would go through the drawers of her study. Laurence might be engaged to her daughter but going through her study and reading family documents was an altogether different matter. The quicker she did this clear-out the better. She tossed another rent book into the bin bag and added a bundle of yellowing letters.

"Of course he doesn't." Rachel turned away.

Yseult suspected that Laurence had the keys. He was prone to that same affected nonsense as Rachel. He fancied himself as a historian.

"I have to go into town," Rachel said. "Brendan needs me to deliver bloods to the clinic." She adjusted the collar of her jacket. And I've a few things to get – some books I ordered and other jobs."

Yseult was looking at the letters from members of her mother's family who lived abroad. The same letters her father drooled over when he first moved to Lugdale. She picked a random letter. It was dated December 1824.

Yseult couldn't concentrate with Rachel talking.

"The books I've ordered are on boutique hotels in Europe. Houses like Lugdale that open for the summer months and host inti-mate weddings."

Yseult suddenly raised her head. "Close the damn door and keep in the heat."

16TH DECEMBER 1824

My dear Alice,

Thank you for your recent letter. It lifted my spirits. I thought of you today when I looked at the calendar and know how wonderful Lugdale is at Christmas. I shall keep you close in my thoughts on the 25th.

There is a cabbage tree in Jamaica. To get the cabbage they must cut down the entire tree and only use the leaves from the very tip. It seems such a waste. I'll save the next tree for Christmas Day to feel closer to you.

It does not feel like Christmas in Jamaica. The sun and heat is ever-present. My eyes are slowly acclimatising to the sights and scenes here although at times it is difficult to believe what I see and hear.

As a country, Jamaica is in its infancy. This country lacks culture, there is no theatre or museums of any description. The people remain the crudest; not only the blackies but certain white people. A great many white men lack morals. They take a "wife" from their slave community. There is little to no organised religion here and most do not see the need.

The blackies are quite uncivilised and godless. One of the domestic slaves lost her child last week. The same slave had lost two children previously. She mutilated the dead infant, fearing the spirits were sending the same child back each time, and by mutilating the baby she believed she was scaring him away from returning and dying again. I pray God will send me some assistance to begin Christianising these heathens.

The climate and people have a most extraordinary effect upon me that is most unusual for me. There are times when everything is not only uninteresting but disgusting. I feel a sort of inward revulsion that I have never had before. I try to buoy my spirits with work in the garden with my little Irish boy, Art, who collects pearls from the waters. I fight against this nauseating disposition but it is not always easy. I try to argue that I know such privilege, I should not feel as I do. My son Blair is growing and newly born Ernest is alive and thriving each day. Edward is well and remains greatly interested in Jamaica and his planta-tion. I have so much to be grateful for. However, religion does not offer me the solace it normally does.

I pray that my mood will have lifted with my next letter.
Yours sincerely,
Victoria

"DEAR JESUS!" YSEULT GASPED. SHE ROLLED THE LETTER INTO A ball and tossed it into the bag. "Such whinging, I never did hear the likes."

There were hundreds of similar letters. Yseult flicked through only a few. They were filled with similar whimpering accounts which vexed her.

"Rubbish, rubbish, and more rubbish," she said as she scooped up every letter and stuffed them into the bin bag.

Yseult worked quickly. She moved from one drawer to another, packing the contents into the black sack. By lunchtime she'd emptied most of the drawers. She sighed in relief. In the centre of the floor were three filled bags of old letters, documents, books, tax documents, farming journals, news clippings, pictures, vets' receipts, and a receipt for glasses for Nellie Brown.

FOR MONTHS NELLIE'S EYESIGHT DETERIORATED. FINALLY, SHE USED the wrong detergent to clean the china and their tea tasted like ammonia. Yseult's mother insisted that Nellie should get glasses.

"Everything is right again," Nellie marvelled several times a day when she first got the enormous milk-bottle glasses that greatly changed her appearance.

A year after their arrival in Ireland, it was Nellie Brown with her new glasses who forced Yseult to tell the truth about her friendship with Mary O'Neill. It coincided with the Christmas holidays. As Yseult was sitting down to her lunch, Nellie caught her by the ear and marched her into the butler's pantry.

Yseult shrieked, "Let go of me, you daft woman!"

"Daft, am I?" Nellie said. "I thought I was gone a bit daft in the head before I got my spectacles but I seen ya properly this time!" Her eyes appeared bulging and frightening behind her thick glasses.

"How daft will your father be when he hears you're behavin' like a street-hawker selling rabbits at the train station?"

"It wasn't me! The girl of the O'Neills looks like me," Yseult said, cupping her sore ear with her hand.

Nellie suddenly looked doubtful. "Well, maybe it wasn't you selling the rabbits – I didn't think even you'd be bold enough to do that."

"Apologise to me," Yseult said.

"I will in me hat! I was wearing me glasses when I seen ya cycling down the Fennor Hill!" Nellie raised her voice, as if recalling it added to her disbelief all over again. "*On the main road!*"

Yseult didn't say anything to this. It would be easier to explain cycling on the road than selling rabbits at the train station.

"The pair of ye freewheeling on yeer bikes at a hundred miles an hour and holding hands." She stretched her arms across the small pantry and beamed in imitation. "Not a care in the world and the pair of ye laughing like Billy-oh at the dangerous antics." She looked sharply at Yseult. "Them O'Neills are grand people but they're not from here. What's more, they have a lunatic living with them, a quare fella who only comes out at night."

That night at dinner, as they relayed their day's events to their father, Yseult waited to find a gap in the conversation to mention Mary O'Neill's name.

Aunt Lydia was asking her father about Cuba again. She would never let it rest.

"Your hometown Bayamo is quite rural," Aunt Lydia said. "I imagine the houses are neat and practical in that part of Cuba. Are they?"

"The Spanish influence is all over Cuba," Tobias said. "My home is Santiago de Cuba."

Aunt Lydia nodded. "Oh yes, you said that. Santiago de Cuba, only a short boat journey from Jamaica."

Yseult remembered that Aunt Lydia had made the same observation when her father was last home two months before.

Yseult said, "I made a new friend. Mary O'Neill is her name. She lives at the top of the hill." She resumed eating her soup. She wanted to appear vague and, hopefully, if the matter came up again, at least she could say she'd told them about Mary O'Neill.

"That's splendid, Yseult. It's good to understand the local tenant farmers," her father said. "Actually I must familiarise myself with the locals when I find the time. Is your friend Ned O'Neill's daughter?" He was referring to his tenants in Kilflynn.

Yseult hesitated. She felt the need to give Mr. O'Neill's Christian name rather than his nickname. It would seem more respectable. She smiled, pleased she'd had the foresight to think of that.

"No," she said. "Leon O'Neill's daughter."

Her father moved his head back slightly as if surprised with the name. "Leon O'Neill?"

Aunt Lydia was blowing on her soup. She paused, holding her spoon in mid-air. Her head bent forward, her eyes narrowed as she looked at Tobias.

Tobias opened his mouth to speak. Yseult waited, and then as if changing his mind he resumed eating.

CHAPTER FORTY-THREE

The Garda was propped against the counter, talking to Rachel in the kitchen. When Yseult saw him she felt like turning on her heel and leaving again. Martha was serving up the dinner to Brendan and the workmen. Yseult dithered for a moment, reluctant to eat her dinner while the Garda was present. However, she felt the need to supervise Rachel to see what tumbled out of her careless mouth. She went in and took her place at the table.

"I do all the administration side of the estate," Rachel said. "I look at innovative ways of progressing. You could say," she paused,

"I'm the Business Development Manager."

Yseult sighed loudly.

"I also write articles for *Women and Health Magazine*," Rachel said. "Your wife probably reads it."

"I'm not married," he said. "Yet."

"Your future wife probably reads it," she replied, matching his tone.

They were openly smiling at each other.

"And you're doing a course in cheesemaking?" the Garda said.

"Yes, we're very forward-thinking on Lugdale. We're always looking at various options for progressing. We have all of the raw materials for cheesemaking – 120 herd of cattle and several other milk-producing animals including goats."

"Really?" he said, sounding impressed. "I thought it was only cattle."

"Cattle and a lot more. Lugdale also has the forest at the back and the lake, and a river running through it."

"Dear God!" Yseult moaned aloud.

Rachel hadn't an ounce of sense. The Inland Revenue was only aware of half of her stock. Being conservative with the truth was a must for Yseult. All of that lot were the same – the Gardaí, tax inspectors, Inland Revenue. She could just imagine the Garda down in the pub discussing the size of the farm.

"It's all about continuity and progression," Rachel continued. "At the moment we're enquiring about Aubrac cattle. Obviously we'll need to buy a few cows and a bull."

We're enquiring about Aubrac cattle! Rachel had spent ten minutes trying to dissuade Yseult from the idea. She tried to tell Yseult she was sick and it was time to wind down instead of investing in more stock. Rachel had been inordinately forceful until Yseult told her in no uncertain terms to mind her own bloody business. And here she was chirping away as if she would be pulling on the wellington boots, eager to attend the next mart.

"Yes," he said, turning towards the window, "you have some fine-looking cattle. I saw a bull in the lower field, a frightening-looking thing."

"We need the bull." Rachel smiled when she said that.

Yseult felt like taking out her hearing aids.

The Garda nodded. "I assume for continuity the bull plays his role."

"We also have a ram," Rachel added, "for obvious reasons. And," she began to laugh, "a boar for our sows."

The Garda began to giggle. "You also have poultry, chickens and a –" The Garda was nodding, encouraging Rachel to continue.

"Rooster!" Rachel said.

They both erupted into fits of childish giggling.

Yseult slammed her knife and fork on the table. Was there any end to this nonsense?

"It's a beautiful estate," the Garda said, ignoring Yseult. "I was telling your mother that I'd never been here before."

"Thank you. It was built centuries ago and has remained in my family since then."

"Wow!" the Garda said. "And were all of the men Ffrench?"

"No, Stratford-Rice was the family name. My grandmother married my grandfather Tobias Ffrench in England and they came to live here in 1921. Mother was eleven at the time." There was a pause and then Rachel said, "I'm sorry!"

Yseult turned around to face them, curious as to what Rachel was sorry about.

"Where are my manners?" Rachel had her hand on her chest as if remembering something. "Would you like a coffee, or maybe a drink?"

"Coffee would be lovely," the Garda said, taking off his jacket and putting it on the back of a chair.

"I can show you around later, if you like," Rachel said as she boiled the kettle.

What next? Yseult thought. As if it wasn't bad enough that they had to contend with the law trudging through her land with their greedy eyes trying to find the guilty party, now Rachel wanted to invite them into their home.

"Actually, there's a book on the estate. It was printed a number of years ago. We'll take our coffee to the study and chat there."

"*No!* " Yseult bellowed.

Everyone looked at her, startled by her raised voice.

Yseult had three black bin-liners of old documents and books ready for burning in the study. She could just imagine the Garda having a good look at them while Rachel rolled her eyes in that flirtatious manner. She'd probably tell him to help himself and take whatever he wanted down to the Garda station.

Lowering her voice, she added, "I am using the study this afternoon."

Rachel made an exaggerated expression of shock. "Fine, we'll use the drawing room."

Yseult didn't finish her dinner. She left the table and went immediately to the study. She stood and thought for a moment. Then she locked the door from inside, opened the window wide and tipped the bags outside. She left the house and walked to the farm tackroom where she got a wheelbarrow, with Laddie following and watching her curiously. Returning to the study window, she put the black bags into the barrow and wheeled the barrow directly to the furnace. Would Rachel have the *innovation* to think of that?

Their furnace was once used to heat the pipes in the greenhouses. As Yseult lit the first of the old documents and added the first fistful of letters, she realised the furnace would now be used to destroy the correspondence so sacredly stored by her ancestors. Their horrid irrelevant reminders could heat the pipes one last time.

While the Garda and Rachel had their tête-à-tête in the drawing room, Yseult began to stuff the documents into the opening as fast as her old 81-year-old body would move. A few papers escaped and almost blew away with the wind. She gathered them and decided to slow down, allowing the furnace burn a little at a time. While she waited with increasing impatience she picked up one of the documents from the ground. It was a receipt for payment for a white stallion in 1922 – Coconut Boy, her father's horse. She remembered the stallion. Yseult leaned against the wall and willed the fire to burn faster. She wanted to be rid of the reminder flapping in her hand and all the other reminders.

BUTCH SLATTERY SADDLED COCONUT BOY FOR THE BIGGEST hunting day of the year, 26th December 1923. They'd enjoyed their second Christmas in Lugdale. Their governess had returned to her family in England for the Christmas holiday and Yseult remembered being free to roam with Mary O'Neill. Her mother's cousin had come to visit with her daughter a few days before Christmas. Apart from one small incident when her cousin referred to Tobias as a "half-breed", she recalled it as a peaceful happy holiday.

The morning of the hunt her mother looked very smart in her riding outfit. Aunt Lydia took a picture of Emilia while Portia and Yseult watched, infected with the excitement.

Tobias was the only person who wouldn't enter into the spirit of the morning. Instead he asked Butch about Leon O'Neill.

"He's not from here," Butch said quietly. He was cautiously saddling Tobias's horse. Coconut Boy was a flighty stallion.

"Where's he from?" Tobias asked.

Butch didn't answer immediately – he was too preoccupied with the horse.

Tobias's hunter was a stallion with too many quirks. He was nervy and occasionally bold. According to Butch, he was too unreliable for the hunt. Yseult had heard Butch say Tobias wasn't the right man for a horse that unpredictable: "Himself needs a quiet obedient animal."

"I don't know where they're from," Butch said, soothing the horse as he spoke. "Maybe Donegal. Grand fellow. He owns a mighty stallion. They come from all over to get a service. Finest stallion I ever saw. Leon might know what to do with this lad." Butch indicated Tobias's temperamental horse.

"How much land does Leon O'Neill have?"

"About thirty acres."

"How did he come to buy the land if he's not from here?"

"He worked at sea for years. Some say he made his money in foreign lands and that's why he's so dark, too much sun."

"Dark?" her father said.

"He's like the Enrights of the bog. A bit of sun and them lads look like the darkies of Africa," he said. "Although the Enrights probably have a bit of turf dust in their skin that makes them look darker."

"Are you saying he's a darkie?" her father said with an angry edge to his voice.

If Butch noticed her father's sharp tone, he didn't show that he did. "Never seen a real darkie up close so I don't know. He's not pale and he's not yellow either. He'd be tanned all year round." He was keeping his voice low so as not to upset the horse.

Her father stood with his hands on his hips, looking towards O'Neills' house. "Who did he buy the property from?"

"The house and lands belonged to a man called Falvey. He was a sailor as well. I think Leon and Falvey came to some agreement. Leon and his wife moved into the house, and Leon's wife nursed Falvey when he was sick. He only died about ten years ago."

Tobias didn't speak. He continued to look up at the cottage.

"There's a quare fellow living with them," Butch said.

"A quare fellow?"

"Some say he's a lunatic from the madhouse," Butch said, "If you could believe it, some say 'tis the ghost of Falvey."

"How long has Leon O'Neill lived here?"

"They moved here about twenty years ago. He's a rabbit-trapper by trade. They call him Rusty. He's good with horses and, would you believe it, he's great with flowers. He has hundreds of flowers with all the colours of the rainbow. I never did see anything like his garden."

"Is he a Shinner?"

"I wouldn't be surprised. He's a decent fellow," Butch said, summarising Leon O'Neill.

Her father remained standing at the stables, still looking up at the O'Neills' house.

"Your horse is ready, sir," Butch said, handing Tobias the reins.

As Tobias approached Coconut Boy, he shifted uneasily.

"Go to him easy and hold him steady," Butch said. "A bit of coaxing and he'll be as good as Leon O'Neill's stallion."

Butch helped Tobias up and then passed him the reins. The horse moved sideways and kept going until he banged into the stable wall.

Yseult held in her laughter at the sight of the horse moving sideways, like an elegant woman dancing the foxtrot. It looked comical.

Her father cried out in pain with the impact against the wall. "My damned shoulder!"

"He'll steady in a few minutes – coax him a bit," Butch said.

Her father tightened the reins, and the horse fought against the restriction. Tobias took the whip out and hit him on the neck. "Damn you! This animal is only good for..." he said between gasps of breath as he tried to hold on, "shooting!"

"Take it easy, sir!" Butch called out.

"Stop it, you useless animal! " Tobias bellowed.

Yseult could see that Tobias had no control over the horse. Butch was right – as he said, her father had "bad hands for a rider".

The horse began to kick. Her father quickly jumped down, staggered and fell. He rolled out of the way as the horse bucked higher.

Tobias quickly got to his feet and ran at the horse in anger.

"Stupid dumb horse!" He began to whip the horse's neck as it bucked higher. *"Yuh monsta', wat de hell, neva seen more stupid horse! Me give to yuh de bullet! Shoulda shot yuh de day me got yuh! "*

Yseult, Portia and Aunt Lydia stood still watching the scene unfold, trying to make sense of his actions and the peculiar English he spoke.

CHAPTER FORTY-FOUR

Yseult was woken by Rachel. She was standing by her bed, shaking her awake.

"You were dreaming," Rachel said. "I came to tell you I'm going out for the evening – a pal of mine has arrived."

"What did you wake me for?" Yseult hated being woken. She especially hated being shaken awake. After burning all of the documents from the archives, she was exhausted. She snuggled deeper under the duvet and closed her eyes in annoyance.

"You're such a grumpy old lady," Rachel said. She began to look in Yseult's jewellery box. "While you were sleeping we've established the year the man was murdered."

Yseult pulled back the covers to look at Rachel. This was not the time for Rachel's drama. She was dressed up, all in black, her hair like a lion's great mane it was so plentiful. "What?" She had removed her hearing aids before she went to bed.

"You're always telling me I waste money," Rachel said, raising her voice. "Your hearing aids are stuck in that box untouched and, as you said, 'they cost a pretty penny' so you'd want to listen to your own advice."

"Speak louder," Yseult said, realising again how deaf she was.

"The tree was planted around 70 years ago – the Garda told me," Rachel said over her shoulder. She was distracted by the jewellery box. She pulled out another drawer in the box.

"What are you doing in my jewellery box?" Yseult demanded.

Rachel didn't stop. "I'm looking for that old gold coin. You know, the coin with Queen Victoria's head, dated sometime in the 1800's."

"Why?"

"Because it sounds as if it could have come from the same period as the coin that was found with the skeleton. That lovely Garda told me there was a picture of Queen Victoria. It's dated from 1870 which would be her reign."

"I got rid of that coin," Yseult lied. "It was worthless."

Yseult had some sixth sense about the coin. Of course she didn't bin it, it was probably worth money. The next time she'd go to Dublin she'd sell it to one of those coin collectors or art dealers. It was hidden in her fur coat pocket in the wardrobe.

Rachel put her hand on her hips. "Dumped it?" she repeated. "Have you gone mad?"

"Well, I put it in one of those charity boxes. It was ages ago." As she thought about the coincidence of the coin discovered by the skeleton and the coin that her father gave her, she felt a cold chill.

"That ends that," Rachel said, disgruntled. She stepped away from the jewellery box and began to examine Yseult's curtains. "Those curtains have not changed since I was a child. Your room could really do with an overhaul."

"Good idea," Yseult said cheerily. "You can redecorate my room if you're not too busy being a tour guide for the local Gardaí and a 'Business Development Officer' for the estate."

Rachel was fingering the curtains with a look of disgust. "I have no role on this estate. Anything progressive I've ever suggested has been shot down. If I told the Garda the truth, Martha the cook and cleaner has a more relevant position than I do."

"If you like we can give Martha her marching papers and you can do the cooking and cleaning."

"Don't be so ridiculous," Rachel said, standing back for a better look at the walls. Anyway, when the archaeologists wrap up you'll have your estate all to yourself again. Right – I have to collect a friend of mine from the train station – Richard Fields from Scotland. You remember Richard – he's the art expert." She checked her watch. "We're meeting Laurence in town."

"Is Laurence here?" Yseult asked.

"Yes," she said, then shouted over her shoulder, "Would you please use those damn hearing aids!"

Yseult got out of bed to watch the lights from Rachel's car meander down the avenue. Rachel was great for having friends staying. She treated Lugdale like a hotel. A few weeks ago it was the interior decorator. The week before it was the restaurant owner and chef – Sally was her name. She wore copious amounts of make-up and might as well have been a professional wine-guzzler. She and Rachel drank the house dry. This week an art dealer. What did Laurence think of all of this? Would he too treat Lugdale like a hotel? What kind of a husband would he make?

"Will he stare at the sky?" she asked aloud in a Kerry accent.

WHEN YSEULT THOUGHT THERE WAS NOTHING NEW TO EXPLORE IN the hills of North Kerry, Mary O'Neill took her to a woman who'd tell them about their husbands-to-be. She was a fortune-teller who read their tea leaves in exchange for a few trout they'd caught. Mary addressed her simply as "Tea-Leaves."

"You'll live to be a fine age," Tea-Leaves told Mary. "You'll marry a man who is left-handed. A silent man who can't be bothered making idle chat."

Tea-Leaves took Yseult's cup and examined the leaves from every angle. She was silent, her mouth firmly closed as she deciphered the shapes in the clusters of tea leaves. "You'll have a daughter who'll be beautiful," she then decidedly said. "You'll marry a man who won't be much good with his hands but he'll have brains to burn. He'll be the type who loves staring into the sky."

Mary O'Neill had erupted into laughter when she heard it.

They called to Tea-Leaves several times after that. Yseult was always hoping Tea-Leaves would see a different man in her cup. But a different man never presented himself to Tea-Leaves.

"Your husband is still in the cup, he's still staring into the sky," she'd say with her rolling accent.

Mary got endless hours of enjoyment from it. When visitors called to Lugdale and Yseult reported to Mary on the guests, if there was a young man their age Mary would ask with a serious face, "Does he stare at the sky?"

Regularly Mary made references to a local odd-ball with a peculiar walk, his head always tilted backwards, "'Tis him is your husband, staring at the sky."

All these decades later, Yseult didn't know if Mary's husband was left-handed. She only knew of his strong hands for working.

Yseult recalled those carefree innocent days with Mary O'Neill. While her father was away at sea and during the night when the house slept, Yseult used to steal out. The first night she did it, she only checked the rabbit traps with Mary. Then she stayed out longer and ventured into the forest. They lamped rabbits with Mary's dog, Sadie, and Yseult's Ginger. She was terrified initially and then it became easier but remained as thrilling. During one of their nights stalking deer in the Stack Mountains, she came face to face with Fonsy, the lunatic who lived with Mary O'Neill. He was small and hunched, and unable to speak. When he saw Yseult he fled. The next time she saw Fonsy he didn't run away. Yseult and Mary lit a fire in the wood and fried their catch. He took the fish Mary offered. Under the light of the fire she briefly saw Fonsy's face before he edged into the forest with a limp and his right hand dangling uselessly by his side. He was darker than the Enrights of the bog and his face was more frightening than the one-hundred-year-old woman they'd seen at the top of the mountains.

Yseult asked if he was a lunatic.

"There are quarer people roaming the country than poor auld Fonsy," Mary said.

Yseult asked why his face was so dark.

"Don't be askin' quare questions," Mary said.

It wasn't a quare question, Yseult thought, yet she didn't confront Mary the way she tackled her governess or her mother or sister.

The only information that Mary volunteered was that Fonsy could read and write as good as her father but he couldn't speak and he couldn't use his right arm.

"It's dead – he had an accident and can't feel anything. Poor auld Fonsy," she was wrapping the uneaten fish, "he'll eat this later." She smiled kindly as she thought of crippled Fonsy.

Several times after that they met Fonsy. He grew more comfortable in Yseult's presence. He'd sit for longer in their company and smile at their antics.

Once they went on their ponies high into the mountains with her father's gun to shoot deer. When Yseult aimed and fired she believed she'd come into a new higher realm of life. On those nights in the woods under the silhouettes of mountains and trees against the low hanging moon and the pant of the dogs and nature bubbling all around her, Yseult thought she could never be happier. There was endless joy in the rugged lands of Kerry. The "savage Irish" and their terrain was more amenable than she could ever have envisioned.

WITHIN THE WALLS OF LUGDALE HOUSE, THERE WAS A DIFFERENT atmosphere. Tobias returned after a two-month absence.

He was all the more curious about Leon O'Neill yet he wouldn't go to his house.

"He has three daughters. Fine-looking women. The youngest is a lot like your Yseult," Butch said when Tobias asked more questions about Leon O'Neill's family.

"In what way?" Tobias asked.

"She looks like her. Go on up to Rusty," Butch called Leon O'Neill by his nickname, "he's a grand fellow."

Tobias didn't go up to Leon O'Neill. Yseult thought that strange – her father was never reluctant to call on anyone.

A few weeks later they were returning from their church service in their carriage at a leisurely pace. On the road coming against them was Leon O'Neill and his family on their pony and trap. Yseult knew they were going to town to have dinner in Mary's sister's house. The O'Neills alternated their Sundays between Mary's married sisters' houses. Yseult could see Mary sitting forward to look for her in the carriage. As they passed, Tobias and Leon looked at each other. Although their passing was brief, their eyes locked.

After they'd passed, her father looked over his shoulder. Leon O'Neill was doing the same. Tobias faced forward and cracked the whip until the horses were going so fast that Yseult had to hold onto her seat.

"That's enough," Emilia said.

Tobias wasn't listening. His eyes were fixed on the road ahead as he whipped the horse.

THAT SUNDAY, TOBIAS SHOT HIS STALLION. HER FATHER DID NOT have Leon O'Neill's gentle nature or Butch Slattery's patience to coax the horse along. When Coconut Boy threw him again, he swore and whipped the horse until he galloped wildly around the yard.

Tobias staggered to the house and got his gun.

Butch Slattery pleaded with Tobias not to shoot him – it would be a shame to kill the animal.

Tobias wasn't listening. His hands trembled with rage as he loaded the gun. The first bullet hit the stallion's hindquarters.

Yseult fled to the stable to be with her pony, Hazel. She imagined Hazel dancing in circles, upset with the fracas. But she couldn't stop herself from looking over the stable door at the scene. The second bullet knocked Coconut Boy to the ground. When he was neighing and writhing in pain, Tobias reloaded with the same rage and shot him in the head.

In the safety of her stable with Hazel, she wrapped her arms around her pony and cried quietly into her neck. She brushed

Hazel's mane until her sobbing subsided and the chaos outside her stable died down. When she wiped her eyes she saw Aunt Lydia looking over the stable door. Yseult didn't have a tissue to wipe her nose, so she sniffled loudly.

Aunt Lydia didn't offer any words of comfort, just hobbled away quietly.

CHAPTER FORTY-FIVE

Yseult found movement difficult. She went to the kitchen. When she was alone she opened the cutlery drawer. She stretched her hand in and felt about. There was a new blister-pack of painkillers at the back. Yseult took one immediately and returned to bed where she slept for a few hours. When she finally got up it was after eleven. Was this a sign of her ending, an old woman who grew increasingly house-bound? One who drifted through her days wishing for her bed?

It was late morning when Yseult slowly descended the stairs. When she passed the drawing room she heard Rachel's voice.

Yseult stood outside the door, listening.

Rachel's voice was loud and animated. "She's so anal it's painful. Sometimes I ask myself is that what I'm going to turn into? Am I doomed to play the part of the stiff bitch for the rest of my days? I mean, every woman needs to get screwed senseless once in a while. When I think of a woman who needs a severe fucking shag, I think of her. So fucking prissy it's disconcerting."

Horrified, Yseult thought Rachel must be talking about her. Would her daughter speak like that about her own mother?

"How do you know she's not getting it?" a male voice asked.

"She's too masculine."

"She can't be that bad," the male said.

Yseult could feel the heat in her face and her heart beating faster.

"She's vile," Rachel said. "She has a moustache at the moment."

Yseult sighed with relief. Rachel was not talking about her. She was talking about Laurence's mother. It was strange – Yseult had the same opinion of Vera Webster. She thought of her as being prissy and uptight, although she'd never dare use such language or verbalise her thoughts, not to herself and certainly not to another man.

Rachel continued, "Vera has a small dark moustache and hairy legs. She wears skin-coloured tights so you can see all the hair on her legs. Sex with her must be like mounting a hairy bear."

"As opposed to a bald bear?" the man said.

Rachel laughed. "I hope to Christ she gets a good waxing before the wedding. I'd be mortified with such a hairy mother-in-law."

"Does Laurence's mother like you?"

Yseult held her breath while she waited for Rachel's response.

"I think she does, although she's a bit freaked by this business of the skeleton. Vera likes the idea of Laurence living in Lugdale. I think she likes me as a person, but," she paused, "she's such a snob. She alluded to my grandfather's pedigree more than once."

"What did she say?"

"She asked a few silly questions – if my mother ever went to the Caribbean to see my grandfather's family, were any of my grandfather's family alive, would they be attending the wedding, that kind of thing."

Yseult seethed outside the door. Why did people find the need to discuss these matters all these years later? Nothing had ever been certain. Why was Rachel talking about this? How dare she discuss it? Yseult had refrained from ever dwelling on her father's origin. She certainly never needed to air her opinions or suspicions.

"Did Laurence's mother know your grandfather?" the other person asked.

Just then it occurred to Yseult that Rachel had said something about an art dealer from Scotland. He didn't have a Scottish accent.

"Vera knew Mrs. Hamilton who was a family friend of my grandparents. Mrs. Hamilton said my father was little more than a crude half-breed –"

Yseult stepped into the drawing room, affecting surprise.

"Hello," she said, looking at Rachel and then her male friend. "I didn't know you were in here."

"Hello." The man stood up.

"Mother, do you remember Richard Fields from Scotland?"

He shook her hand. "How do you do?"

"How do you do?" Yseult nodded and smiled.

There was nothing more to be said. They stood in silence, surveying each other.

Then Yseult left, closing the door softly behind her.

A FEW NIGHTS AFTER HER FATHER SHOT HIS HORSE, THE HOUSE WAS restless.

Portia feigned sickness. "I hate this gloomy country," she cried in her bedroom. "At least it was better in England when Father was never home!"

Nellie Brown behaved as if Portia was really sick. She rubbed her back and told her to ask her Guardian Angel to help her.

"No fear of you hating Ireland or ever being sick," Nellie said to Yseult affectionately.

Yseult was unable to admit that she cried during the hullabaloo in the stables, and that all day she'd felt out of sorts.

"Ye're great girlies! Now you go off to sleep," Nellie said, "and all will be well in the morning."

Yseult returned to her own bedroom. Unable to sleep, she left her bedroom and went out on the landing. She could see the light beneath her mother's door. Her father and Aunt Lydia were still up. She tiptoed down the stairs and followed the sound of their voices.

They were in the dining room.

Standing behind a screen in the alcove closest to the opened dining-room door, Yseult could clearly hear their voices.

"I know it's true," Aunt Lydia said, her voice angry. "You are an imposter."

Yseult waited to hear his voice or a movement. There was nothing, only Aunt Lydia's whispering rage.

"I know who you are. From the moment you entered Lugdale, I've known. Each night I've listened to your contradictory stories about your childhood and your nonsensical notions."

"How dare you!"

"You tried to play me for a fool. Did you think I wouldn't recognise you after thirty years?"

"Yet you continued to question me," Tobias said.

"Initially I doubted myself – thinking my mind was playing tricks on me – but as time went on my suspicions grew. You grew careless and betrayed yourself many a time. How could a man born to Spanish parents who was raised in Cuba know so many details about Jamaica and Mein?" Lydia's voice was quieter. "When I saw you whip the horse, your resemblance to Blair was the most damning confirmation. You share the same ugly nature."

Yseult was surprised that her father was not objecting. Why didn't he call Aunt Lydia a liar?

"They say you are an imposter, a man pretending to be an aristocrat. They have got it wrong. You *are* the son of an aristocrat – a brutish one – the son of Blair Stratford-Rice. Only such a man could become the callous slave trader you were."

When her father spoke his voice was quiet – it was almost pleading. "You speak to me like this yet you were kind to me in Black River," he said. "You accepted me."

"I had to accept you," Aunt Lydia retorted. "I despised you then and despise you now. I despised how you treated Henry, despised how cruelty came so easy to you. Despised how you took your cargo from Jamaica's seafront."

"I made my money like most of the British aristocracy, who are at pains now to conceal the original source of their income!" Her father's voice rose. "It was all legal at the time!"

"I know how you began to amass your fortune. You claimed to be Nicolas Ffrench's dead son and took his boats and money. I heard Nicolas Ffrench's screams the day of his death. They killed and fed the 'French Prince' to the crocodiles, a death Art would have gladly given you!"

"Stop it," Tobias said.

When Aunt Lydia spoke again, her voice shook. "I know some of your dealings were not only against the law but against your own blood."

"I did what I had to do," Tobias said.

"It takes a certain vile breed of a man to do what you did."

Yseult could hear Aunt Lydia standing up and walking across the room with her walking cane.

"The fact that Lugdale is in your hands revolts me. The fact that my niece now belongs to you. *You*," she said with contempt, "are like Blair, that wanton brute."

Tobias didn't speak.

Aunt Lydia continued, "Like Blair, everything you touch will become corrupt – your wife, your children, Lugdale."

They stepped into the hall. Yseult couldn't see them – only their shapes illuminated onto the walls of the entrance hall, multiplying their sizes. They appeared large and menacing as Lydia venomously whispered insults.

Tobias finally spoke. "Your sort think you're superior –"

"Our sort?" Lydia interrupted him. "You're welcome to this cursed house and all its cursed acreage, to pretend you're one of our sort!"

She slapped him in the face.

It was the crisp sound of the slap that shocked Yseult.

YSEULT WAS STANDING IN THE VERY SAME SPOT AS SHE WAS THE night that happened over half a century ago. She put her hands on her head, feeling suddenly trapped.

She went to the kitchen, poured a glass of water and took two painkillers. She made a mug of tea and left the kitchen.

She paused again at the drawing-room door.

Their conversation had progressed from sex with hairless bears to place-names.

"'Kil' is the English version of 'cill' in Irish which means church or churchyard," Rachel was explaining. "Kilflynn, Kilgarvan, Killorglin."

"What does Lugdale mean?" he asked.

"Frederick, the first owner of Lugdale called it after his home in England."

"So Lugdale is as English as it gets," the Scottish chap observed.

AUNT LYDIA HAD MOVED OUT OF THE MAIN HOUSE. SHE TOOK UP residence in one of the vacant cottages on the estate after her fight with Tobias. She took with her the bare necessities including her camera, the materials for printing the pictures and some clothes.

Initially Yseult thought it was a temporary arrangement. Each night she expected Aunt Lydia to arrive dressed for dinner.

When Portia asked why Aunt Lydia was living in the cottage, Emilia said, "She doesn't really like Tobias."

Tobias returned to sea and Aunt Lydia remained where she was, living in her cottage on the fringes of the estate. It was very strange to see her sitting by the stove in her cottage, her clothes drying on the overhead rack. Aunt Lydia made the cottage homely. There were always large flower arrangements on the table and the fire was always lit. She refused to take any hand-outs from Lugdale. Emilia suggested they send her dinner each night. Aunt Lydia declined. She bought furniture from a carpenter in town, she had curtains made by the dressmaker. Strangest of all, Aunt Lydia acquired a rocking chair that came from Mary O'Neill's house. Yseult recognised it.

"A dear old friend gave it to me," Lydia said when Yseult asked where she got it.

Yseult asked Mary O'Neill if her father had given her aunt a rocking chair.

Mary was direct in her response. "That's between my father and Lydia."

Yseult made no further remark about the peculiar sight of Aunt Lydia in Leon O'Neill's rocking chair, flicking through her many photographs, some of which she framed and hung on her walls.

"I must admit that it's a pleasure to see pictures of ordinary mortals and pretty landscapes rather than the severe portraits of the military men in my family," she said, smiling at her newly hung pictures.

One of her pictures was very similar to a picture that hung in Mary O'Neill's. When Aunt Lydia saw Yseult looking at it she explained that the picture was from Jamaica.

"That man's name is Art O'Neill. He's holding Hapi, a resident snake in Mangrove House."

It was a strange dreamlike image taken by the window with a shaft of sunlight over the man's head.

"If Lydia would like to live in the cottage, it is Lydia's choice." Tobias said when he returned from sea to find Lydia had not returned to the main house. "Probably the best solution."

Although he behaved defiantly, Yseult felt he remained troubled.

EVERYBODY SEEMED UNEASY, EVEN FONSY. YSEULT SAW HIM ON THE side of the hill, peering down at Lugdale's stables where her father stood in the yard talking to Butch Slattery. When Fonsy saw Yseult he shuffled away, stopping at the top of the hill to peer down at the yard again before moving off.

Another day she saw him closer to the house. Yseult and Mary O'Neill were collecting duck eggs in the hedge beside the lane to the bog when they saw him on the other side of the hedge.

Then Tobias came riding by with Butch Slattery. The girls quickly crouched down behind the hedge.

They were only separated by the thin hedging from Fonsy. He was on his hunkers, looking up at the horses. His eyes were wide and frozen.

Tobias was talking about the forest. "Maybe I should plant more trees – the winters can be long and cold."

Slowly Fonsy covered his ears and shut his eyes tight.

That day Fonsy returned dripping wet with the smell of the sea from his clothes.

Mary told Yseult, "He was trying to swim away."

"To where?"

Mary shrugged.

CHAPTER FORTY-SIX

Yseult dressed for town. She had only three painkillers left and didn't have a prescription. It was pointless checking the cutlery drawer – her benevolent friend had not called. While passing the entrance hall she saw Rachel and her male guest looking at the portrait of Major Frederick Stratford-Rice. His hand was on the small of her back.

"At least fifty grand," the male said. "I'll take a few photographs of this one too and send them to him."

Yseult didn't speak to them.

When she'd passed she heard the man whisper, "Did she hear us?"

Rachel said, "Hopefully not. She's hard of hearing and usually doesn't wear her hearing aids."

Just then Yseult remembered he was the art expert. Not just any old art expert, he was a *world renowned art expert*. What could he and her daughter have in common? More pretentious nonsense. The more she thought about it, the more her back pain intensified and beads of sweat dampened her forehead.

On her way into town she tried to delay taking the painkiller. It seemed best to wait until her nightly dosage but the pain was unbearable and she was beginning to perspire. She hated the clamminess she experienced when she tried to refrain. Finally when she stopped at traffic lights she couldn't wait a moment longer and took a tablet. At the crunching sound of the seal breaking she knew her pain would be over in a few minutes. That warm sensation would envelop her and all would be fine again.

The chemist girl did not have a local accent although she was local. "Born and bred," as she said. Yseult heard her speaking in a countrified accent to the other customers. There was a lot of "whisha" and "yerra", but she spoke to Yseult with pronounced words that clearly did not come easy to her. Yseult liked her despite her silliness and aspirational carry-on. She spoke to Yseult as if they were friends, each time taking her into the back room while she prepared the tablets.

The chemist girl always warned Yseult about the dangers of the tablets.

"You can get fond of them, unintentionally like," she once advised.

It was a ridiculous thing to say. Nobody got fond of anything intentionally. That was like choosing an addiction. I think I'll become an alcoholic, or I'll get intentionally dependent on drugs. Naturally she didn't say that to the chemist girl. She needed the chemist girl with the varying accents who often gave her extra pills. "Just in case you get a very bad day."

As she packed Yseult's prescription, she'd say as if talking to herself, "You die if you crush them. Goes straight to the bloodstream and bam! Your number's up."

When Yseult lost her prescription the previous month, the chemist girl looked her squarely in the face. "Highly addictive," she cautioned again.

Yseult normally wouldn't listen to that type of patronising nonsense from anyone. She had reached the hearty age of eight-one without the chemist girl. Normally Yseult would have said in an equally direct manner, "Enough" but she didn't. The chemist girl was very nice to Yseult and Yseult was charming. Needs must!

"You're so much nicer ..." the girl had said on Yseult's third visit, then bit her lip. 'Than what I've heard about you,' was implied.

Yseult arrived at the counter. The chemist girl nodded solemnly, her expression of sympathy overdone.

"Mrs. Ffrench, how are you, my dear?" she asked, almost breathless with concern.

"Not too good," Yseult said. "The pain is dreadful."

"Terrible business on your land. I hope you're OK?"

"It doesn't help the pain." Yseult needed to exaggerate the symptoms. "I have my prescription somewhere here." She pretended to look in her bag. "I thought I put it here," she said, opening one of the compartments. "Maybe it was here." She unzipped one of the pockets in the bag. "Dear God, don't tell me I've lost it!"

"Don't worry," the chemist girl said, offering her a chair. "Would you like me to look?"

Yseult handed over her bag. She watched the chemist look in all of the pockets.

"No, nothing." She looked at Yseult. "I'll give you a few to tide you over until you see your doctor and get another prescription."

Yseult sighed in relief.

"I met Delia recently," the chemist girl said as she packaged the pills. "She sends her regards."

Yseult couldn't remember who Delia was.

The chemist continued, "Delia was only talking about Burgess Hall over the Christmas."

Then Yseult remembered. The chemist girl's mother-in-law's husband's cousin went to boarding school with Yseult. The chemist girl loved referring to it.

"She was talking about the Christmas plays in Burgess Hall," she continued.

"Terrible place," Yseult sighed. "The only noteworthy accolade I achieved during my three years in school was a tennis trophy."

She had told the girl this several times before but nevertheless she gave a loud hearty laugh as if hearing it for the first time.

Yseult asked her if she could change the batteries for her hearing aids.

"Of course." She said her mother had hearing aids – again, not for the first time in their periodic exchanges. "I was hoarse from shouting at her," she said, reverting to her normal country accent.

When she'd finished, she handed her the hearing aids and the pills. Yseult thanked her and left. She was a good girl, even with her fluctuating accents.

On the way home Yseult thought about her days in boarding school, a time when she had unaided hearing, strength and a never-expressed vulnerability.

YSEULT AND PORTIA WERE SENT TO BURGESS HALL BECAUSE TOBIAS said Yseult was running wild with the tenant farmers' children. In the same breath he forbade her from ever visiting Mary O'Neill's again.

"Portia is as bad," Tobias said. "Praying like a Catholic and behaving every bit as superstitious."

For three years Yseult attended Burgess Hall. She was an unwilling and unremarkable student. She made friends with the Fitzgerald sisters from Charleville in Cork with whom she remained friends until their deaths. Apart from that she believed she gained little from her school days.

Yseult wouldn't be telling the chemist girl her other memories from Burgess Hall. She would always associate the loud din of tuneless music with her mother's death. She was in the music room adding to the cacophony of instruments when the headmistress called her outside the room, where Portia was waiting. When she saw Portia's tearstained face she knew something bad had happened. To the sound of screeching violins and pianos keys, Yseult was informed that her mother had died.

The headmistress accompanied them home. Yseult remained disbelieving until she arrived in Lugdale and saw her mother's corpse. Although her colour was not their mother's, she appeared better than when they last saw her. Friends who viewed the body said she looked "at peace". For years after that, each time Yseult attended funerals, she always thought of her mother, 'at peace' eventually. They said she died from an infection. Yseult could not understand how someone could die from an infection.

Tobias was bereft, his crying unlike anything Yseult had ever seen then or since then from a grown man.

"Your poor father loved your mam," Nellie said that night. Even she seemed embarrassed at Tobias's bawling.

Tobias broke with the tradition of a private funeral. Instead he opened Lugdale's doors and welcomed friends and neighbours. He sent word out to the workmen that all were welcome to the funeral. Most of the tenant farmers arrived, cap in hand, and whispered words of sympathy. There was no explanation for his generosity.

Leon O'Neill and his family didn't call.

Aunt Lydia refused to enter Lugdale House.

The throngs of people expected didn't come and Nellie Brown said she never saw such waste of food. When the visitors left and there was only Tobias sitting at his wife's remains, Yseult crept silently down the stairs. She could hear him cry and mumble. She peered through the gap in the open door and she heard him speak a foreign language. It was not Spanish or French.

"Nwunye m," he sobbed. "Olileanya na nwa r anw."

When the funeral was over and the mounds of leftover food were fed to the pigs, the girls were relieved to return to school where the pain of their mother's loss was lessened with the routine of school.

DURING THAT FIRST YEAR IN BURGESS HALL, YSEULT wrote to Mary O'Neill. Each week she gave her an account of life during 'her incarceration'. Mary responded with a few short polite replies before her letters stopped.

The first summer Yseult returned to Lugdale, she continued to trap the rabbits on her estate but didn't accompany Mary O'Neill to sell them. The childish days of behaving like a street-hawker were gone.

"You're too good to sell them," Mary O'Neill said. "Is that it? 'Tis beneath you?"

"I don't need to sell them," Yseult said.

Of course it was beneath her. In Burgess Hall Yseult had learned what mattered. Love mattered, manners mattered, and money bought everything except breeding. Yseult realised she came from a class where breeding mattered. People like Yseult who mattered did not sell rabbits with their cursed fleas biting at her flesh. Esteemed people like Yseult mattered. People like Mary O'Neill should not have mattered.

"Your accent has changed," was Mary's response. "The auld school must make the accents more high-falutin."

Yseult laughed at Mary's response. Yes, maybe her accent had become stronger. In the past she wanted to be like the other children and had used the local dialect. Burgess Hall taught her she was not like the tenant farmers – however, she could enjoy the same pursuits.

In truth, Yseult was conflicted. She wanted to set aside Burgess Hall's principles and trap the rabbits with Mary O'Neill. She desperately wanted to sit at O'Neills' table and eat the cooked rabbits that Eileen O'Neill served, and sense the old familiar warmth. She wanted to go hunting in the dead of night with their dogs and leave the grief for her mother behind – they'd only take the sounds of the whispering night and camaraderie with them. She wanted her simple life back, before her mother's death and before Burgess Hall.

"I will trap Lugdale's rabbits," Yseult continued. "You can sell them at the train station at a fair price and give me a percentage."

Mary walked away. "Keep them. I'll trap and sell my own rabbits. They'll probably taste nicer than the Lugdale's rabbits."

Yseult was angered at Mary's rejection.

When she returned to school, Yseult showed Trudy Fitzgerald one of Mary's letters that she'd kept. Trudy pointed out Mary's poor writing and bad grammar. Yseult began to read out the letter in Mary's accent. She wanted Trudy to laugh at her friend's poor education and bad handwriting.

"Girls like that," Trudy said, holding the letter by the corner, "don't matter."

Some part of Yseult knew Mary would always matter.

But she wanted to ridicule Mary, to hit out at her. Mary thought she had it all but she really had nothing. Yseult would be a better farmer. She could separate her mind from the animal. She'd shot her pony Hazel. Would Mary O'Neill be able to do that?

During those months Yseult learned to supress the tears of grief and loneliness, behaviour she never unlearned.

Portia spent her time with Aunt Lydia and Nellie Brown when they returned from Burgess Hall for holidays. Yseult spent part of her holidays with Trudy Fitzgerald and her sister in Charleville and the rest of her time in Lugdale, working with Butch Slattery.

Tobias spent months at a time abroad with his ships, much to delight of everyone at Lugdale.

Nellie Brown was wonderful for keeping them up to date on all of the news. She told Yseult that the lunatic the O'Neills kept in their house was dead.

"He flung himself in the sea," she told her. "For weeks Leon O'Neill and his wife and Mary went to Fenit with friends, hoping to find his body."

"Did they find him?" Yseult asked.

"The only thing they found was his shoes and coat on the pier. The sea hasn't thrown him up yet."

"Maybe he didn't drown," Yseult said.

"Well, if he didn't drown he wasn't a lunatic but a ghost who's still haunting Mein and I doubt he's a ghost because nobody has seen sight nor sound of him for this past two months."

Yseult was very sorry to hear it. She pictured his sheepish dark eyes and lame gait. Despite appearances he was a gentle creature, one whom Yseult had grown fond of.

"Poor Fonsy," Yseult said. "I wonder what happened."

Nellie told Yseult that the lunatic was "gone soft in the head."

He was seen in Fenit staring at the boats or staring into the sea. One night he jumped in and one of the men from the pub pulled him out.

"The O'Neills must be kind people that they'd be so concerned for a lunatic. I suppose people can get attached to any quare yoke," Nellie concluded.

Yseult finally met Mary on the verge of Lugdale forest. Mary was walking a greyhound.

"I was sorry to hear about Fonsy," Yseult said. "Do pass on my condolences to your parents."

"I will to be sure," Mary said.

They talked about the greyhound. Mary told her she was walking her six miles a day. She'd won a sweepstake at Tralee track.

"Are all the family well?" Yseult asked.

"They are," Mary said. "But I don't want to break The Prairie's stride," she said, referring to the greyhound. "I best keep going."

"I must call up and see them," Yseult said.

Mary stopped walking. "Don't call up."

Yseult waited for her to say something more.

Mary shook her head slowly. "There's too much bad blood."

"What kind of bad blood?" Yseult asked.

Mary didn't say anything, only remained looking at Yseult.

"Why won't you tell me?" Yseult asked.

Mary stretched her hand down to pat the dog. "I won't tell ya cos if I did it would keep the bad blood flowing for lots more years. Let it alone, Yseult." And she walked on.

Yseult swore Mary O'Neill would never get the chance to do that again.

CHAPTER FORTY-SEVEN

The archaeologists left. They packed up their tools and tent and finally decamped. They didn't leave as much as a dirty tissue behind them. Yseult scrutinised the area and the tree with Brendan.

"It'll make good wood for burning in six months when we've dried it," he said happily.

Yseult got the impression Brendan was as relieved to have the farm back to normal as she was.

"I wonder did they find anything?" he said vaguely.

She watched him toe some of the soil around the tree.

Yseult didn't answer. They got into the jeep and drove away.

Yseult expected to feel better with the farm back to normal but she didn't feel better. It was as if it could never be righted.

When Yseult got back to the main house that afternoon she was tired and sore. When alone in the kitchen she put her hand into the cutlery drawer to see if her kindly donor had left her something for the pain. She couldn't feel anything, only her rising alarm. She lifted the cutlery-holder higher and patted the bottom of the drawer. She felt panicky. She could not live with the pain or without the pills. There were two tablets in her pocket, not enough to last twelve hours. After that? What happened then? Nights of hell, sickness – she'd done it before and never wanted to experience it again.

"Dear Jesus," she muttered.

"Mother, are you alright?" Rachel was behind her.

"Yes, fine," Yseult said, closing the drawer immediately.

Yseult saw Rachel looking at the cutlery drawer. She didn't want Rachel to know about the pills, and she specifically didn't want her to know about her Pain Days. It was pointless discussing her pain issues with Rachel. The small pills were the only thing that alleviated the pain and the past that was suddenly as clear as the roots of the unearthed tree.

"Are you staying home for dinner tonight?" Yseult asked.

"No, Laurence and I are meeting a pal from Dublin. He'll stay here for a few nights. He's American," Rachel said informatively.

"So the other chap is gone?"

"Yes, he left this morning. Marshall from Atlanta will call today before he returns to America. You met him before."

Yseult wasn't listening. She was thinking about the pills and how she'd survive the day and night. Even the mere thought of a sleepless night was enough to aggravate her.

"He has a lovely southern American accent," Rachel continued. "He's an architect."

"A multi-award-winning architect whose reputation is global," Yseult said, beating Rachel to it.

"That's him," Rachel said. "He loves Ireland. He visits at least three times a year. He says we're mystical."

"What does Laurence think of the male company you keep?" Yseult suddenly asked.

"Mother, every girl has male friends," Rachel said.

"You and that Scottish chap seemed quite close examining Lugdale's paintings like a united little couple," Yseult said. At times like this, she knew she should not talk. When she was in pain it was the wrong time to discuss Rachel's behaviour.

Instead of launching into long defensive rhetoric, Rachel began to laugh.

"I saw you," Yseult continued in a shrewd voice. "The pair of you in deep conversation in the entrance hall with his hand on your back."

"Mother," Rachel interrupted her, "Richard Fields is gay. Richard is as gay as blinking colourful fairy lights perched on a gay Christmas tree."

"For God's sake," Yseult said. She couldn't understand how people were so open about their lives. Everything was discussed.

"Would you rather I had no friends?" Rachel asked. "You and I alone all day?"

"No," Yseult agreed. "Absolutely not."

PERIODICALLY YSEULT LIVED ALONE IN LUGDALE WITH HER father. In the first few years after she finished school it was easier. Tobias was rarely in Ireland. He'd stay for a month before returning to sea for two months. The new Free State Irish government tried to force out the plantocracy by penalising them with enormous taxes. The farm ran at a loss, but Tobias managed to pay Lugdale's hefty tax bills.

When Tobias was in Ireland he bored his guests with his talk of the wealthy and influential people he'd met.

"Lord Haverthone met me in London during my last stay – I told him about my thriving estate," he told the Hamiltons who indulged him with pained smiles.

As far as Yseult could see they were laughing at him. Lugdale's 533 acres was a backyard compared to some of the estates in England.

He still insisted the family dress for dinner each night. He continued to mimic a class that he did not belong to.

Mary O'Neill was courting a local farmer. By all accounts he was as hardworking as Mary.

The O'Neills had bought two more fields that Butch Slattery knew about.

"And then we don't know about what other lands they bought," Butch said. "Those O'Neills never sit still."

Portia moved to London. She wrote occasionally but rarely

returned. Aunt Lydia remained alive and haunted. With each passing year they expected her death.

Nellie encouraged Yseult to visit her aunt. "She won't be here next Christmas," she'd say.

But the following Christmas Aunt Lydia was still alive and Nellie made the same prediction as the previous year. "For sure she'll be gone in twelve months' time."

The first year that Yseult finished school she enjoyed the outdoors by attending all of the horse shows, hunts, greyhound meets and local fairs. The Fitzgerald sisters were regular visitors to Lugdale and Yseult was a frequent visitor to their Charleville home.

On St Stephen's Day, Lugdale hosted the hunt. Yseult was the appointed Hunt Master. She rode upfront, guiding them through her terrain. She remembered that day's hunt was not great. As they were returning to Lugdale that evening, they chanced upon a fox. The hounds pursued the fox over their back meadow and up the side of the O'Neills' Hill and into one of their fields. There was a moment when Yseult hesitated. She could see the freshly planted hedging in a field with a flock of sheep. Yseult thought about Mary O'Neill, a simple peasant who thought she was better than Yseult Ffrench. Yseult cracked the whip and followed the hounds. The final stage of the hunt through the O'Neills' land proved to be the finest part of the day. The double dykes and steep hills were an exhilarating surprise. Eventually the fox outwitted them. Yseult was happy enough to watch him scurry away. He'd provided a great end to the day.

The following day, Yseult was having her hair curled for a party at the Hamiltons' when she saw Mary O'Neill trotting down the avenue on her horse. Yseult went immediately to the back door to meet her.

Mary dismounted, hitched her horse to a fence and came to the door.

"Hello, Yseult," she said, eyeing her bouncing hair. "You passed through our land on your horses and trampled on the new hedging."

Yseult was so taken aback at the sight of Mary and how quick she was to air her grievance that she said lamely, "we were following the dogs."

Mary paused. "Don't be blamin' the dumb animals, Yseult."

Yseult was momentarily speechless.

"I don't care what you were following, I want my hedging repaired."

Yseult gathered herself together. She pulled her shoulders back. "Excuse me," she began.

"There'll be no excusing you till you send someone up to repair my fencing or give me fresh whitethorn to plant." Mary nodded her head once, indicating the message delivered before turning away from the door.

"As if you and your kind have not thieved from this estate!" Yseult said, raising her voice, as Mary walked away. "You've helped yourself to my streams and my forest!"

Mary didn't look over her shoulder. She unhitched her horse, mounted and trotted away.

Yseult was shaking when she stepped back into the kitchen. Who did Mary O'Neill think she was to come knocking on her door looking for payment for wild hedging? It was more than the trampled wild trees or Mary's tone, it was the act of challenging her.

Yseult obsessed over her altercation with Mary O'Neill during her party at the Hamiltons' and for most of the following day. She noted how Mary had remained calm. Unpleasant confrontations didn't perturb her. She merely wanted her hedging repaired. The little unknown peasant farmer expected Miss Yseult Ffrench to fix it. How preposterous!

Yseult didn't fix the O'Neills' hedging. But it did not end with Mary O'Neill's visit to the back door.

Butch Slattery planted trees on the boundary of the cottages. The following day thirteen of the trees were uprooted. When Butch told Tobias, initially he was baffled and then angry.

"It's thievery, call in the law," Tobias said.

Butch played it down at the mention of the law.

One of the farmhands was quick to suggest it was the O'Neills.

"They're spitting fire since the hunt trampled their hedges. I'll bet you'll see the trees on their land."

"They wouldn't be stupid enough to steal trees from Lugdale and plant them openly on theirs!" another said.

Tobias remained quiet.

Yseult didn't know why she felt the need to say nothing about Mary O'Neill's visit or following the dogs.

That afternoon Tobias summoned Yseult to his study. "The O'Neills took our trees to replant their hedging. Don't ever take the horses through Leon O'Neill's lands again." He was clearly shaken. "Don't ever bring that man upon me."

She waited for him to continue. They stood awkwardly looking at each other. Tobias's discomfort was so tangible that if she had any affection for her father she would have done something to soothe his peculiar fears.

Only afterwards did she overhear a second-hand account from Butch as he relayed the events to one of the farmhands.

"Meself and Himself," when Butch referred to Tobias he indicated the house with his thumb, "we were out for our morning ride when Rusty appeared out of the furze like a slow-movin' hedgehog smoking his pipe at his ease. Himself nearly had a seizure at the sight of Rusty. The next thing Rusty stops Himself and says, 'I took your whitethorn trees because Yseult and her hunting friends barged through my hedges. It took us half a day to round up some of the sheep.' As calm as ya like, Rusty says, 'The county is big enough for the two of us.'"

Yseult knew there was more to it than sheep that escaped or broken fencing. By this time it was clear to her that the men had known each other before. Leon O'Neill's past was as vague as her father's.

Butch continued, "What strikes me as strange is that Himself said nothing in response. He didn't demand that O'Neill call him *sir* or Mr. Ffrench. He looked like he was the small man and O'Neill the big fella. 'Tis right strange."

. . .

AT TWENTY-ONE YEARS OF AGE YSEULT DECIDED TO TRAVEL. SHE was tired of hearing her friends talk about foreign countries and exotic cities.

The night before her departure she reluctantly visited Aunt Lydia.

Aunt Lydia's cottage was clean and orderly. There was a local girl whom she paid to call to her once a day with her main meal and to do some cleaning.

"I've been expecting you," Aunt Lydia said. She was sitting at the table looking at her photographs. Her sight was so bad she used a magnifying glass to scrutinise the pictures.

"I hear you're going to see the world."

Lydia would probably be dead by the time Yseult returned. The thought didn't perturb her in the slightest. There had never been any warmth in their relationship with Lydia always blatant in her preference for Portia.

Yseult joined her at the table.

"The cuckoo," Lydia said, showing Yseult a picture of the bird. "Each year I take his picture – sometimes I like to think it's the same cuckoo." She compared pictures of the bird from last year's photo album and the year before. "I know it's foolish of me," she said, yet she continued to compare the images.

That last night Aunt Lydia had more than photos of the cuckoo. There were pictures from Jamaica and photos of Tobias and Emilia together. There were very few photographs of Yseult – she had always hated having to stand still for so long – any movement would make the picture blurred.

There was a picture of Emilia, a close-up photo of her laughing.

"She was wonderful but so foolish." Aunt Lydia picked up the photo and smiled. "Your father loved her," she admitted as if to herself. "They first met in Jamaica when Emilia was a young girl visiting me during my marriage to Blair. Tobias was invisible to Emilia then. At that stage, they were worlds apart. He could only admire her from a distance." Lydia put the photo down again.

There was another photograph of Tobias, a close-up picture of his face.

"These people from Jamaica look like Father," Yseult said. She looked at some of the close-up pictures of the coloured men and women. "Who are they, Aunt Lydia?"

Aunt Lydia plucked a picture of an old white man from her collection. "That man is Art O'Neill. He lived to be over eighty years of age. It seems he comes from the mountains around here. His father was hanged after he shot and killed Frederick, the owner of Lugdale at the time. He was hanged and the boy was sent to Jamaica as an indentured slave."

Yseult felt uneasy.

Lydia continued, "That is his daughter Arry and that is her son Okeke."

"And these people?" Yseult slowly lifted another photograph.

"That is Art O'Neill's son, Chinwe, and his daughter."

Aunt Lydia slid a picture of a boy towards her. "Okeke at his grandfather's cabin."

Yseult looked at it. "He looks like Father … and …" She was about to admit his likeness to herself but stopped.

Aunt Lydia remained quiet.

She placed the photographs of Arry and Okeke beside Tobias.

Yseult pushed her chair away from the table. She refused to believe Aunt Lydia's suggestion. She left that night, hoping Lydia would indeed be buried in Lugdale's cemetery by the time she returned.

CHAPTER FORTY-EIGHT

Yseult lay on the bed. She wasn't fit for much. In the last few hours she'd used the bathroom more times than she had in the last six months. Her body contained nothing – it seemed as if everything had flushed through her. She turned off the electric blanket, a short time later she turned it on again and put on her bed jacket. She had trouble breathing, every movement left her breathless. She tried to sleep but her limbs were too restless. Her legs seemed to jerk. She turned on the light and tried to read. Her bedside reading material were magazines. She never read in bed, it was always her place to sleep. She'd like to have opened her mouth and screamed for her pills but only crazy addicts behaved like that. She thought of the girl in the chemist shop and one of her warnings, "If a person becomes addicted to morphine tablets, the withdrawal pains are horrific. *Horr-if-ic*," she added, dragging out the word. "Morphine is the same family as heroin."

The chemist's advice was pointless, Yseult thought. She had back pain not a morphine addiction.

She lay in her bed and rocked. She fought the spasm and moaned. She noticed the sickness was worse than the back pain. Maybe she *was* addicted? It didn't really matter. At eighty-one, nothing really mattered. For three hours she endured the *"horr-if-ic"* withdrawal symptoms.

Eventually she heard the car door close and knew Rachel had returned. She could hear their voices upstairs. Rachel was showing her American guest to his room. Laurence's voice was there too. She thought they'd never stop talking and go to bed. When there was silence she stepped out of bed and stood outside her bedroom door. At last, she thought, descending the stairs and ignoring the dizziness. In the kitchen she checked the cutlery drawer. Her hand found the fresh blister-pack of pills.

"Thank you, Laurence," she sighed. "You're the best doctor and the best future son-in-law."

She took three immediately and returned to bed.

WHEN YSEULT LEFT LUGDALE TO SEE THE WORLD IN THE 1932, HER first port of call was London.

She became reacquainted with her cousins and spent two happy months accepting invitations to hunts and balls, polo matches, horseracing and parties. She saw the enormous estates and great English houses her mother referred to. She noticed how the females in her mother's family were married to men who'd proudly served Queen and Country in the battlefields. They were gentlemen unlike her father.

While in England she pieced together her parents' story.

Her unmarried mother became pregnant but Portia's father was "unavailable" to marry. Tobias was friends with Uncle Cyril who arranged a marriage between Emilia and him. It was whispered in Emilia's circle that Tobias was eager to enhance his social standing. He was impressed with status and pedigree rather than money. Yseult didn't need to hear that Tobias knew about Emilia's pregnancy. That was evident in his preference for Yseult.

Yseult spent two nights with Portia in Cambridge. She was engaged to an English engineer and talked enthusiastically about life in London, the plays she'd seen, the new jazz music she enjoyed, the fashion, her friends and her plans for her future in England. Ireland or Lugdale was not mentioned. When Yseult talked about news from home Portia became distant. When Yseult tired of her returning a blank gaze, she asked if she'd any plans to visit Ireland.

Without speaking, Portia shook her head.

Yseult understood.

After visiting England, Yseult went to New York, Chicago and Washington DC. She then accepted an invitation to the Caribbean. She visited Cuba, the playground for wealthy Americans. She saw the town where her father claimed he came from. There was nothing to see and nobody to ask about her father's Cuban or Spanish ancestry.

After Cuba she visited Jamaica. There she noted their dialect and recognised the language Tobias lapsed into during his rages. She felt the dreaded baking sun and admired the scenery that Aunt Lydia referred to. She rode out, swam in the warm water, played croquet and ping pong.

Yseult saw the remains of Mangrove Plantation where Aunt Lydia spent the years of her marriage to Blair Stratford-Rice. Her hosts showed her where the original house had stood. The family cemetery was lost to wild overgrowth. She waded through the knotted plants and choking branches. She scraped the clay from one of the stones in the ground: *Beatrice Stratford-Rice 1829–1831*.

Yseult asked them if they knew what became of the last owner of Mangrove Plantation.

"He was murdered callously by his overseer's young boy forty years ago." They made it sound brutal. A robbery by Blair's overseer, who'd served the family for seventy years, and his young son. The robbery didn't go according to plan and the overseer was shot – then the overseer's young son shot Blair.

None of those who gave the account could remember the overseer or his young son. However they could remember Blair as a handsome charming man and his regal wife.

"A tall woman who used a camera," one explained. "She and her crippled son witnessed her husband's murder. In the aftermath they fled the country."

Yseult asked what had happened to the overseer's son.

"Nobody knows. Some say the boy escaped with some gold coins. Some believed he drowned, others felt that he'd been captured by the law, killed and his body discarded."

"Drowning was too good for him," her host said.

Yseult noticed how emancipation freed the slave but her hosts and the whites she met lamented the days of slavery and the whip.

Yseult listened to their accounts impassively. They were aware that the last owners of Mangrove Plantation were distant cousins of Yseult's. She didn't inform them that Lydia, the tall willowy woman, was still roaming the Irish countryside with her camera.

Yseult tasted the sumptuous food: crocodile, black crab, ring-tailed pigeon, calipever and mountain mullet. She noted each dish and watched the young men stalk and kill the crocodiles.

Yseult and her friends met an educated coloured elderly man called Ignatius Duffy who spoke good English. They had a meal at his inn on the seafront where he explained he'd been educated by his white father who was of Irish descent. His mother was black and for four generations his family had lived in Black River. He had inherited the inn from his father and enjoyed regaling his customers with stories of the locality and the history of Black River.

He praised the English for freeing the slaves before the Americans who were so divided about slavery.

"Although free, the coloured man is still treated like a slave," Mr. Duffy said. "Some are still conditioned to accept slavery and some whites will never accept the end of slavery."

He talked about the psyche of the Jamaicans, the guarded soul and spirit, their unwillingness to trust authority, and the omnipresent results of slavery.

In a guileless manner Yseult asked about the last owner of Mangrove Plantation.

"The last master of Mangrove Plantation was a gambler who placed the wrong bet on the wrong son," he said, surprising Yseult. "Blair Stratford-Rice promised his overseer seven gold coins for seven decades of service. When the overseer went to the house to collect the coins, Mr. Stratford shot the overseer dead. The overseer's young son had followed him to the Big House, fearing there was trouble ahead for his father. It was believed that the overseer's young son shot Mr. Stratford and fled with the coins."

"'It was believed'?" Yseult asked, picking up on his tone.

"Yes, it was believed – but that was not the truth. Mr. Stratford's son, a crippled boy in a chair, shot his own father."

Yseult's friends laughed at the account, believing that Mr. Duffy's coloured skin made him biased against the white planter.

"Why would he do such a thing?" Yseult asked.

"Every day the domestic staff saw and heard Mr. Stratford call his son a half-man and a coward because he couldn't walk. Mr. Stratford-Rice took his son's wheelchair and made him crawl around the grounds of the house. The only people who showed the boy some kindness were the overseer – an Irishman called Art O'Neill – his son Leon and the grandson he raised who was called Akeem."

The group smiled, doubting the account.

Mr. Duffy sensed they were mocking him but he continued directing his conversation at Yseult. "Mr. Stratford-Rice backed the wrong son."

"There was another son?" Yseult asked.

"He had several daughters and one other son with a mulatto, who proved to be as cruel as his father."

Yseult waited for him to continue.

"This son was also a grandson of the overseer. Yes, relationships could become complicated in those days, with the masters having children outside marriage by their slaves or by the local women. Okeke was that grandson's name. He would be my age if he is still alive. For a few years he was educated and then he worked for Mr. Stratford-Rice. When times were hard Mr. Stratford-Rice went into the slave-trading business. They brought slaves from Cuba and sold them to countries that continued slavery. Sometimes when their cargo was low they took some easy pickings from the shores of Black River."

Yseult looked out at the seafront. She knew what she was about to hear. She didn't want to hear it but couldn't leave.

"Okeke took Art O'Neill's grandson, Akeem, and sold him."

For several moments nobody spoke.

"There is a story that Blair Stratford's wife, Lydia, hated her husband as much as their crippled son did. Fearing that the truth would be revealed – that her crippled boy had killed his father – she fled, taking the only witness, the overseer's son, Leon O'Neill, with her."

"It's all a bit farfetched," one of the group said.

"I know it to be true," Mr. Duffy said.

"What about the gold coins?" someone asked.

"Ah, yes, the coins. The overseer's wife, Ngozi, was in possession of one gold coin. Years later when the talking about Mr. Stratford-Rice's death faded, two more coins resurfaced. With them, the overseer's sons bought good land from Mangrove Plantation where several generations of Art O'Neill's family lived. Some are still there."

"And the other coins?"

"My grandfather got one gold coin," Mr. Duffy said. "He was known as Irish Ignatius. Occasionally he was known by his profession as Ignatius the Slave Trader. His father was also a slave trader. Blair's wife, Lydia, wrote to my father from Ireland, imploring him to help her find the boy sold by Okeke. My father changed with age. He regretted his dealings. At night he said all he saw were the slaves and all he heard were their pleas. Lydia sent my father a gold coin to find Akeem, the grandson of Art O'Neill. My father gave Okeke the gold coin to help him find the boy."

"Did they find him?" Yseult asked.

"Yes, I believe so. Miss Lydia wrote to thank my father for his help. She said the boy taken from these shores was found in Morocco. He was no longer a boy but a man who'd been worked into old age." He turned a penetrating look on Yseult. "Only with freedom can we tell you the truth and only with time will this account be accepted."

YSEULT SAW SEVERAL MEN IN BLACK RIVER AND IN EVERY TOWN AND city of Jamaica who were similar in appearance to Tobias.

She noted the names of the villages and towns: Irish Town and Dublin Castle in the hills of St Andrew's, Irish Pen and Sligoville, Clonmel, Kildare, Waterford, Longford Road, Killarney Avenue, Sackville Road, Kinsale Avenue in Kingston. She heard the Irish surnames, the Lynches, Murphys, Maddens, Walshes. She noted the many Patricks, Seáns and Peggys.

"Apparently 25% of Jamaicans claim Irish descent," one of her English friends told her.

She went to an auction in Kinsale Avenue in Jamaica and was shown a map dating back to the 1700s. She was told it originally came from the plantation in Black River where Aunt Lydia had married. The map belonged to one of her ancestors. Yseult studied the antique map and found Jamaica, then Ireland. Her finger hovered over The Kingdom of Kerry and Lugdale, her Kingdom. She noted the wide expanse of water separating them. One great tide separated Yseult from her beloved horses and dogs, the cooling rain and the enigmatic Lugdale she pined for.

The same day she bought her boat ticket home, satisfied the world was more or less the same everywhere. People lived and suffered. Some prevailed. All eventually died.

CHAPTER FORTY-NINE

Yseult hesitated by the door. There was a voice she recognised but couldn't identify.

"Those forensic fellows will be able to identify the skeleton." It was the deep hoarse voice of an older man.

She could hear Brendan and Martha's voice, then the old voice was back again.

"They'll do a series of tests and probably take the DNA – they might even take auld Yseult's DNA."

Behind the door Yseult raised her eyes at this. She could count on one hand the number of people who addressed her by her Christian name but she still couldn't identify who this one was.

"That's if she's human and has DNA like the rest of us," he continued. He had the voice of a smoker.

"I don't know," Brendan said.

Good old Brendan, noncommittal and loyal as ever, Yseult thought.

"Then the Gardaí and those forensic lads will say, 'Yseult, we found your husband – he's not off living the life of Reilly in America but dead in your bog'."

Yseult could hear a spurt of laughter from Martha.

"We found his skull has been thrashed to smithereens with a strange implement."

Just then it dawned on Yseult: it was Roger Colgen. She hadn't seen him in years. He was the old vet's son. As a boy he often came to Lugdale with his father. He had been employed as an Artificial Insemination agent for years. Colgen was a difficult character, argumentative with and without drink. She'd thought he'd died. It must have been over ten years since she heard he had liver disease. Yseult would like to see what he looked like now – the last time she saw him he was yellow. Obviously he was still quite alive with his same dirty gossiping habit.

Yseult listened as he continued in the same vein, "The Gardaí will say, 'We believe your poor husband, Archie, was whacked to death with your bank book – he wasn't making money for you so you beat the living daylights out of him.'"

That fellow thought he was hilarious. No doubt he'd said all of that before to a different audience. Colgen was a gossiping nobody, his age and knowledge of the local area his only attribute.

"Archie Sinclair, Yseult's husband, was a grand fellow." Colgen's voice was serious. "I remember when he first visited Lugdale. I knew all belonging to Lugdale. I might even know who the skeleton is. I've been coming to this estate all my life and many a great party I attended. By Christ, Yseult could knock back the porter. She and poor Archie. Did you know Archie?"

"No," Brendan said.

"He was a … what do you call it … a fellow who studied the stars and space … an astronomer. That's it, he'd spend his nights staring into space." He laughed. "Can you imagine auld Yseult romancing a fellow who'd spend his days staring at the stars? 'Twas a howl."

Yseult didn't mind that kind of gossip, she almost enjoyed it. Her abrupt manner and ownership of Lugdale made her a good talking point. Although she was surprised at his reference to Archie. Their marriage was so brief, nobody else could remember her husband.

"It's so romantic," Martha said.

"Nothing in the slightest romantic about it," Roger replied. "Yseult was getting auld and needed his sperm."

There was silence.

Yseult was tempted to barge into their little chat and tell Mr. Colgen that his wife and children fled from his abusive behaviour.

She didn't. She remained where she was, reminded again why she detested the likes of Roger Colgen.

"Poor Archie," he sighed, wanting to continue the conversation.

Yseult couldn't help thinking about Archie with the same sympathetic thoughts. She had used Archie. He was one of the few people she felt genuine regret about.

"But there was another fellow before Archie," Colgen said. He spoke so quietly Yseult had to lean closer to the door. "They say he was the love of Yseult's life. I remember him. Brent Thistlewood."

As he announced the name Yseult barged into the kitchen. She could not allow him go on.

"Hello," she said abruptly, without addressing anybody in particular.

When Roger Colgen stood up to greet her and extended his hand she looked blankly at him.

He was indeed yellow.

"Mrs. Sinclair, it's been a long time," he said.

"Hello," Yseult said vaguely. "Mr. Enright, isn't it?" She plucked the name out of the family from the bog who were dark-skinned.

"It's Roger Colgen," he said, smiling at her.

"Colgens from Ash Street?" Yseult said as she switched on the kettle.

"No, from Kilduff."

Yseult nodded before moving on. "Brendan, did you price the slats?"

While Brendan talked about new slats Yseult could see Roger slowly sitting down. As Nellie Brown would say, 'Colgen, stick that in your pipe and smoke it, you Mr Nobody'.

"We'd better get back to business," Brendan said to Roger.

Yseult stood at the sink with her back to them. She heard them discuss the straws for the Artificial Insemination procedure and then she heard his chair scrape on the tiled floor, his voice drifting out the back door. Yseult noted the ignorant old buffoon didn't even thank Martha for the tea.

YSEULT WAS VAGUE ABOUT YEARS. THERE WAS LIFE BEFORE LUGDALE, life after relocating to Lugdale, there were the war years, the school years. However, 1934 was a year imprinted in her memory. Yseult returned from her travels at the beginning of the hunt season 1934. She shod, groomed and clipped her gelding. She became reacquainted with old friends and ignored their scolding for not keeping in contact. She wasted no time in returning to her country pursuits. She attended everything from dog shows to horse shows, greyhound racing and coursing meeting, the races, and pheasant shooting. There were times when she idled away a few afternoons fishing alone in the Stack Mountains.

Lydia was still alive.

"Not many older than Miss Lydia," Nellie said. "Will any of us see it?"

In 1934, Mary O'Neill got married to her hardworking farmer. According to Nellie Brown, "A grand fellow, a farmer from Kilflynn. He don't say a whole lot. Comes from good people."

Nineteen thirty-four was the year Yseult briefly found love. She identified nineteen thirty-four as The Year of Brent "Superb" Thistlewood.

She met him while staying with the Fitzgerald sisters in Charleville. She accepted a challenge to ride a large flighty mare for the hunt. Trudy Fitzgerald claimed that the best of men found the mare difficult. From the moment Yseult mounted the temperamental horse she knew it was risky. There were moments during the hunt when Yseult felt ecstasy and terror simultaneously. She could read when the mare was about to get hysterical and flighty, and relished the challenge of controlling her. Passing through a river she fell off but held on to the reins and climbed on again. After the bugle was blown with the homebound signal, she was jumping a deep dry dyke when the mare threw her again. She slid to the bottom of the dyke that was over eight feet deep while her mare trotted away. Yseult looked up at the horses' sturdy bellies as the other riders passed overhead. The yelp of the dogs wafted into the distance, leaving Yseult alone to find a way out. Despite the mare finally throwing her, Yseult felt she'd done well. Nobody had completed the hunt on the mare and she was only a stone's throw from the house. Yseult tried to climb out but couldn't find a groove into which she could place her foot. She was searching for over-hanging branches or something to help her out when she heard horses appoaching.

It was Mr. "Superb" Thistlewood. Yseult had first met him before her travels. He'd just returned from America and used the word "superb" a lot. Although Yseult and the Fitzgerald sisters referred to him as Mr. Superb, they were all secret admirers. So much had happened since they'd last met that Yseult couldn't remember his first name.

"Miss Ffrench, I've brought you back your nemesis," he said, indicating the mare he was leading. He dismounted, tied up the horses and passed the end of his hunting crop down to her. "Hold tight." He moved backward until Yseult was pulled from the dyke.

"Thank you, Mr. Thistlewood, I'd probably be languishing in this dyke for the entire night if you hadn't rescued me," Yseult said.

"Highly unlikely, Miss Ffrench – I'm sure you would have been missed," he smiled.

"Thank you," Yseult said.

"You can repay me with the first dance tonight," he said playfully.

She gave him the first dance and many more.

The following weekend she returned to Charleville. They went to dinner and later went alone in his new motorcar for afternoon tea at the local hotel. They overheard a middle-aged countrywoman loudly asking the price of a pint of milk. The following week they returned to the same hotel and the same woman was discussing the same thing.

"Whisht, Billy, tell me, how much is the price of a pint of milk?"

They thought it hilarious. During their courtship they'd often recall it. At the height of one of their many debates or trivial arguments, he'd raise his hand to stop Yseult, "Whisht, tell me, how much is the price of a pint of milk?"

And so began the only romance that ever really mattered. She loved him. Even his failings were endearing. He was conceited. He deemed every nationality beneath the superiority of the British.

"All of these small nations will rue the day they left the British Empire," he said, "including the papists in this country."

Brent proudly traced his ancestors to the Siege of Limerick in 1691. They enjoyed healthy debates, although both sides liked to win.

Yseult was never one for looking at the past or deliberating over the what-if's. What if she'd never gone to Burgess Hall and met the Fitzgerald sisters? What if she hadn't fallen into the dyke? What if her father had a lighter skin colour and was more refined? It was utterly pointless.

Brent visited Lugdale twice. Thankfully her father was absent both times. She took him through the forest for walks, they went riding in the woods, and she showed him the sights, the chapel and cottages. She told him about the fortune-teller, about Nellie Brown's sayings. She glossed over her mother's death – like so many dark fragments of her life, she was unable to discuss it in depth. Instead she told him about her father's Cuban origins and his esteemed shipping company. Yseult put off Brent's visits when her father was in Ireland. Brent would see through her father and question her own pedigree at the sound of her father's name-dropping and over-doing the English traditional customs. The idea of it made Yseult cringe.

"I believe your father's an interesting old boy," Brent said.

Finally on New Year's Day in 1935, Lugdale hosted the hunt. Yseult was obliged to invite Brent. Tobias greeted the guests as the servants dished up the drinks and nibbles.

That night over dinner they discussed the hunt, the house and Tobias briefly mentioned his beginnings in Cuba. Her father had not aged well. His skin was coarse, his white hair appeared a great contrast to his brown colour. The lines on his forehead and around his mouth were deep. He looked like a sailor wearing a gentleman's clothes.

Brent made a few observations before a distance developed between them. "Your father … he is foreign in appearance."

Even as he aired his observations, Yseult tried to tell herself that the relationship was waning prior to Brent meeting her father.

"He is Anglo-Caribbean … yet he's not altogether Anglo," he said. "And I hear he spends a great deal of his time abroad … in Morocco, North Africa … countries where reform for slavery is slow."

His questions confirmed he'd heard the rumours about her father: the imposter, the half-breed, and the outrageous rumours that her father was a slave trader.

"Your sister Portia … she's not at all like your father."

It was as if he was fiddling with a rip in a tablecloth, idly tugging it until it was irreparable.

"Your mother, Emilia Stratford-Rice, she had quite a reputation."

If Brent Thistlewood had spoken to Mary O'Neill like that she'd have told him in her guttural accent and bad grammar to "Take me as I am or get outa me house, ya devil-maker!"

Yseult finally said, "This is Lugdale, unyielding and unapologetic."

Brent left and nothing ever replaced him.

CHAPTER FIFTY

Yseult had felt awful all day. It was a Pain Day. At noon she took some painkillers and returned to bed. She had a restless sleep, several times waking to the sound of her own voice. She thought there was somebody in her room whom she spoke to. Her dreams were chaotic. When she woke she was groggy. Midway down the stairs she stopped walking and held onto the banisters. She was breathless and dizzy. She took a deep breath before continuing. At the bottom of the stairs she sighed with relief and wiped the perspiration from her brow. She needed to feel in control, yet each day she felt as if something else were taking over. It was a vicious cycle of pain and pills, and pills and pain. As a show of control, she'd left the remainder of the pills on her bedside table. It was silly to carry them in her pocket. What had happened to the independent old tyrant she had been?

As she approached the kitchen door, she could hear Rachel's voice. "Ireland is changing, the wedding industry is booming."

Yseult stopped to listen. She rested her hand against the wall to catch her breath.

"We have the capital – three of the portraits would kickstart our business," Rachel continued.

"Would you consider selling them?" someone asked.

"Not all of them," Rachel said.

Over my dead body! Yseult thought. She was too exhausted to stand and too weary to hear any more. Just then she didn't care. Rachel was sitting opposite another man.

"There you are," Rachel said. "I thought you'd died and gone to heaven."

She was too tired to think of a clever reply. "I was only having a nap for God's sake."

"Since when does a nap last twenty-four hours?" Rachel asked. "You've been sleeping for a full day."

Yseult remained composed. It had happened before but she wasn't going to admit it.

"Obviously you needed the rest," Rachel said and then turned to her friend. "Do you remember Marshall Lewis from Atlanta?"

He rose to shake her hand. Only when he stood up to his full height did Yseult remember him. He was too tall. Marshall made small talk about his trips to Ireland. He did that the last time too.

"I was infatuated with Ireland even before I visited your lovely home," he said. "I'm enjoying it so much I'm considering moving in."

Yseult remained looking at him. She could tolerate the Yank for a few days – a longer stay than that would be rude.

"Mother, he's joking," Rachel said.

Just in case he wasn't, Yseult said, "Remember, familiarity breeds contempt."

The American laughed, as if she too was joking.

"Will you bring me a pot of coffee to the study?" Yseult said to Rachel. Slowly she left the room.

She heard the man say something and then Rachel interrupted him, "I don't know. She bought hearing aids but rarely uses them. She hasn't the patience for that sort of thing."

Yseult pictured Rachel rolling her eyes when she said that. She pulled the door behind her but didn't altogether close it. She remained where she stood. For a moment she didn't think she had the strength to walk across the entrance hall to the study.

"This business of the skeleton is having a terrible effect on my mother," Rachel continued. "She's very private. Now the whole town is talking about her."

Yseult stayed put. She felt awful. It was more than lethargy. Maybe she was dying, maybe she had some terminal disease that she hadn't heard about. It was more than her usual back pain – it was her skin and kinky hair, her origins, her exposure. Everything seemed out of focus except Rachel's voice.

"The worst thing of all has happened now." Rachel paused. "The forensic team have established that the skeleton was a black guy, possibly a slave from the Caribbean or Morocco."

"You're kidding," the American said.

Yseult put out her arm to support herself. She moved her other hand to her head to remove her hearing aids – she couldn't bear to hear any more – yet Rachel's voice continued and she listened on.

"Seemingly, the forensics can tell from the condition of his spine that he endured torturous labour. He lived in the Caribbean and Africa. He was roughly a middle-aged man. Isn't it an interesting story? When I change Lugdale to a hotel I'd like walks through the forest for our guests. We could have a plaque and make up a lot of interesting details about his life – you know, like give him a name, describe his work as a slave. It would have an international effect."

The irony was not lost on Yseult: she had spent her life eavesdropping, now she couldn't bear to hear any more yet she was unable to move.

"They're making wild suggestions that the skeleton is a slave whom my grandfather killed. Someone else suggested there were several slaves kept in the cellars of Lugdale and my forefathers worked them all to death."

"Are you not worried about the negative effect of that on your hotel plan?" the American asked.

"I won't be depending on the locals for their business," Rachel said dismissively. "Anyway, I've given my DNA, a goodwill gesture. So has Mary O'Neill and a few of the other farmers."

Yseult was aware of Rachel's voice but it seemed miles away, as if she were at the bottom of a tunnel.

· · ·

WHEN YSEULT RETURNED FROM HER TRAVELS SHE HAD VISITED AUNT Lydia. She found Lydia thinner, paler and more vague. She had the air of someone who wasn't really present. Her eyes regularly looked over Yseult's shoulder and out the small window of her cottage. The sight of her cottage walls adorned with scenic photographs and her haunted watery blue eyes unsettled Yseult. She felt she was intruding.

"Which countries did you visit?" Aunt Lydia asked.

Yseult gave a run-down of her travels. She told her about England and Portia, America and her preferred cities.

"You finished with Jamaica?" Aunt Lydia looked at her curiously.

"Yes."

Yseult waited for Aunt Lydia's standard reaction to any mention of Jamaica.

"Dreadfully hot," Lydia said.

Yseult agreed. She knew that Aunt Lydia could never love her. She reminded her of the two people she most hated in life: Blair and Tobias.

AFTER THAT, ONCE A MONTH, YSEULT CALLED TO LYDIA'S COTTAGE. And at last Lydia talked about her last days in Jamaica. On that occasion Yseult felt sure that Lydia was confusing her with Portia.

"When we left the pier for the very last time in Jamaica, I held Henry's hand and swore I'd never return," Lydia abruptly began. "But our companion, being native to Jamaica, always wanted to return there but never did." She smiled fondly.

Yseult knew not to ask who he was. Instead she asked why the boy didn't return to Jamaica.

"He was accused of a crime he didn't commit. He would have paid a heavy price if he returned." She frowned at Yseult. "But I told you that story."

"Yes, you did," Yseult said in a voice she hoped sounded like

Portia. "You were brave to bring him with you," she added, hoping Lydia would reveal more.

"Our act was the cowardly one – he was the brave one," she said. "He rescued me and Henry many times in Jamaica, and many times since then he has come to my rescue."

"Maybe he could return to Jamaica now?"

"I believe he prefers our wet climate these days."

Yseult thought of Mr. Ignatius Duffy's story in the inn on the seafront in Jamaica.

Lydia surprised Yseult by continuing, "Only last week he referred to his last sighting of his home in Black River and how he promised himself he'd return. He laughed at his naivety."

"He settled into Ireland eventually," Yseult said.

"Yes, after spending years trawling the seas and working on those ships."

"Did he like working on the ships?"

"No, I don't believe he did." Aunt Lydia looked over Yseult's shoulder and out the small window into the distance. "Poor boy was looking for someone. He trawled the seas with rough sailors and violent seas between Ireland and Morocco until he found what he was searching for." For a few moments they sat in silence.

Yseult spoke. "He was so young. How did the boy survive without his family?"

"He survived like his father survived when he was sent to Jamaica as a boy, and he survived as the slaves survived when they were captured, and survived as I did during my years in Jamaica. There is always a will to adapt and to live." Lydia never mentioned anything personal about Jamaica again.

In 1935, at seventy-eight years of age she died. Yseult had not seen her for one month prior to her death. Portia didn't come home for the funeral. Aunt Lydia was laid out in her cottage and there was very little order to the funeral. A few neighbours called. Leon O'Neill, his wife, and daughters came with flowers. Yseult offered them whiskey. Silently they gathered round Lydia's coffin. Leon O'Neill put his hand on Lydia's as if he'd lost a family member.

Before leaving he leaned forward and gently kissed her forehead, his face creased with sorrow.

Aunt Lydia left the contents of her cottage and a photo album from Jamaica to Leon O'Neill. She left her land in Jamaica to Portia. Tobias and Yseult were not mentioned in her will.

CHAPTER FIFTY-ONE

Yseult was on her bed. She remained still, trying to recall what happened. She couldn't remember walking upstairs. She was not in bed but lying on the covers, wearing her clothes. She remained still as she listened.

"I can't believe she burned everything," Laurence said.

"I was curious about how she disposed of the archives and then I saw a few sparse bits of pages fluttering in the garden," Rachel said. "She used the old furnace for the greenhouses."

"Wow, that's a pretty penny gone up in flames!"

There was silence. Yseult thought they'd left her alone. She brought her hand to her head and moaned.

Rachel appeared in front of her. "You fainted," she said. "You know you're not well."

Laurence appeared at Rachel's side. "Would you like anything?" he asked. He had his hand in his pocket. "Are you in pain?"

Yseult looked at him. Rachel didn't speak but looked without moving her head at Laurence and then back to Yseult.

Yseult saw that Rachel's glance was filled with knowing. She knew Laurence had been supplying her with morphine tablets.

"Yseult," Laurence asked again, "would you like anything?"

He kept his hand in his pocket, like a dog owner with a treat to reward a dog, or a mother bribing a child, or in this instance keeping a difficult future mother-in-law quiet.

Yseult was sticky and clammy, in a moment she'd be cold again. The painkiller would help.

"A cup of tea would be nice," she said.

Laurence left the room to make the tea.

Rachel sat on the edge of the bed. "You know you're not well," she repeated.

Yseult thought it strange that the doctor hadn't diagnosed her with anything. Her breathing had worsened, though Yseult felt it was another age-thing. A few months ago there was a series of tests – X-rays, a CAT scan – all cost a fortune but nothing showed up. Her own diagnosis seemed to prove correct. She had plain old back pain.

"I'll be fine," Yseult sighed.

Rachel's hand was on the duvet. Yseult noticed the engagement ring glistening and that she was wearing the pearls from Jamaica. Opportunistic, that was Rachel. Impatient and opportunistic.

Suddenly so much became clear. Rachel was waiting for her to die so she could do whatever she liked with Lugdale. The art expert was discussing the paintings, how much money they'd get. The architect had a purpose, the interior decorator was happy to over-haul the interior of the house and the cottages. The chef, a girl who wore too much make-up and knew how to knock back the drink, gave her input. Of course, it all made sense. Except that Yseult had no notion of dying. She'd be like Tobias and linger until everybody else was on their knees.

Yseult pointed at the pearl necklace and bracelet. "I see you've been helping yourself to my jewellery?"

"I hope you don't mind."

"The pearl, a freak of nature," Yseult said out loud.

Rachel regarded her closely.

Yseult couldn't remember who told her that a pearl is formed when an irritant becomes accidently lodged in the soft inner tissue of an oyster. As a defence mechanism, a fluid is used to coat the irritant. Layer upon layer of this coating is deposited until a lustrous pearl is formed.

"An accident of nature," she repeated, looking at the pearls.

Laurence returned with the tea and set it down beside her.

Rachel helped Yseult to sit up.

Yseult lifted the tea to her lips but didn't drink it.

Laurence raised his eyebrows slightly.

He was humane but how humane?

"You'll be fine," he said. "Nothing a good night's sleep won't fix."

Yseult stirred the tea.

Laurence hovered by the window, watching her.

Without drinking the tea, she set it aside and looked at her pearls on Rachel's wrist and neck.

TOBIAS GAVE YSEULT ALL OF HER MOTHER'S JEWELLERY A FEW months after Aunt Lydia's death. Like a vulgar sailor he told her how much each piece cost except the pearls.

"Sixty pounds in 1924," he said, handing her a gold bangle. "All the way from India and your mother barely glanced at it."

Yseult tried on the bangle.

"These cost a nice price," he said, handing her some earrings. "Diamonds from Morocco. I used to deal with an American in the bazaar. Twenty-five pounds, if memory serves me."

There was a silk handkerchief. Yseult asked what was in it.

Tobias opened the handkerchief. It held one gold coin. "I don't know why I kept this," he said, more to himself than Yseult.

Tobias held it in his hand. It was minted in 1860 during Queen Victoria's reign. Her Hanoverian features were on the front of the coin.

"Where did you get that?" Yseult asked.

"A Jamaican-Irish man called Ignatius Duffy gave it to me."

"Was it a gift?"

"No, it was in exchange for information on a boy he was trying to find …" His voice trailed off. He stared at the coin.

"Did you find the boy?"

"Yes, the boy was returned to his family." Tobias flipped the coin over.

"A happy ending then?"

"No, not really," Tobias said. "The boy was a man and too damaged for anything at that stage."

When Tobias removed the pearls from the box he sighed loudly. "Pearls are the oldest gem, revered long before history was written," he said as he held the ivory set to the light to examine them. Only then did his mood change. He didn't see the pearls in monetary value. "I knew the boy who picked these pearls from the bottom of the Caribbean Sea and the woman who strung them together." He remained quiet and thoughtful. "It's strange how little keepsakes make us remember with such vividness," he said, fingering them.

Yseult had never been curious about her father. He exaggerated and told lies to hide the truth about his beginnings. Listening to him was a waste of time. But that day she felt compelled to ask.

"Can you remember the boy's name?" she asked.

Her father looked at her before answering, "Okeke was his name. Arry was the woman who strung them together." He sighed.

"Many lifetimes ago."

"Were they brother and sister?" Yseult asked, playing dumb.

"Mother and son," he said.

"From Jamaica?"

"Yes, Arry was born in Jamaica to an Irishman and a slave called Flora. Arry died from cholera."

He shook his head and returned the pearls and the gold coin to their boxes but didn't give them to her.

"For another day," he said.

SOMETIME IN THE MID-1940s, NELLIE BROWNE COLLAPSED IN THE kitchen. She was brought to the local county home where she lingered infirm for three years before surrendering to death.

A few years later, Yseult saw Butch Slattery walking through the back meadow, a field where the grass was tallest. She couldn't remember the year. She did remember it was the height of summer. Yseult could remember the glare of the sun. The grass was so long and the summer breeze so strong that Butch had the appearance of a man wading in water. His hands were open. He appeared to be allowing the tips of the grass to caress his palms. Then the grass swallowed him from sight. Yseult had to use the dogs to locate him. By the time she found him he was dead, lying in the grass clutching his chest. Butch Slattery was ten years younger than her father who was almost seventy years of age at that time.

Her father paid for Butch's funeral. Tobias watched the congregation of sympathisers and commented on some of the locals. He mentioned how they'd prospered or failed, he discussed the little snippets of gossip, and commented on their appearance. When Leon O'Neill arrived with his wife and family, Tobias didn't pass any comment.

EACH YEAR TOBIAS PAID LUGDALE'S TAXES AND RETURNED TO SEA. At sixty-five, he sold his ships and returned to Lugdale for good. His seafaring days were over, he declared. He began to use a walking cane – he was clearly aging albeit slowly.

Occasionally he'd look in the direction of Lydia's cottage. "I'm as bad as old Art, staring hatefully at the enemy."

When Tobias turned seventy years of age he had a big party in the house. He sent out invitations to all of his friends and acquaintances. Yseult did not know why he bothered continuing the charade at his stage of life. His old friends, the Hamiltons came, members of their church, and a few families new to the locality who were impressed with Lugdale. They laughed heartily at his stories and applauded his antics.

When Yseult was alone with Tobias at the end of the night he said, "You need to find a husband, produce an heir." He made it sound coarse.

Had it never occurred to him that he was her obstacle to finding a husband? Brent Thistlewood would be working out of his study if her father had remained at sea. Yseult would be as good as Mary O'Neill with a flock of children ready to take the reins.

Mary O'Neill's mother died. Tobias remained watchful but never discussed her. Yseult joined the sympathisers. She brought a bottle of whiskey and a cooked ham. Leon O'Neill and Mary accepted Yseult's condolences.

"Thanks for coming, Yseult," Mary said. "The lads will give you a drink."

She accepted a glass of whiskey and noted Mary's husband and four young children. One boy was sallow like her with curly dark hair, the other children were pale and Irish like their father.

Yseult stood on the fringes of the gathering and listened to the sympathisers. They talked about Eileen O'Neill's life. "Is she from Malin?"

"I don't think so," someone else said. "Leon worked on the ships when he was a boy. Eileen's father worked on them too. That's where they met." Someone else said the same thing.

"She's not from here," another said.

"Don't matter no more, she's here long enough to be one of us," another said.

The small cautious community had finally accepted Leon O'Neill and his wife.

Yseult stayed for the rosary. Afterwards, she left using her old way down the steps and across the lane and returning home through the rear meadow to Lugdale.

THE NIGHT OF EILEEN O'NEILL'S FUNERAL YSEULT QUESTIONED HER father. Tobias was in the dining room, eating alone. He remained alive like the dark weeping stain on the wall of the entrance hall of Lugdale.

"Were you acquainted with Leon O'Neill prior to moving to Ireland?" Yseult asked.

"Possibly. I've met so many on my travels I cannot recall each one."

"Was Leon O'Neill from the Caribbean?"

"I've no idea where he's from," her father said.

"Were you from Cuba or Jamaica?"

"My story has never changed."

"I know all about it," Yseult finally said. "You are Okeke."

He looked at her squarely. "I am Tobias and I have yet to write my will."

Yseult knew it was a silly threat. Tobias had groomed her for the estate from the moment they stepped off the carriage on their first day in Lugdale.

As time passed, Tobias developed a slight tremor in his left hand. She noted how slowly he moved. Yseult looked for signs that his end was nearing.

"Damn you, old age," he'd sigh impatiently when the knife slipped from his hand.

At thirty-nine Yseult was unwed. She'd look at her father and will him dead. She recalled her pony Hazel, how he'd handed her the gun and ordered her to shoot.

Brent Thistlewood got engaged to a debutante. She read it in the *Irish Times*. There was a picture of his chiselled features and young unscathed bride-to-be.

Her father remained, the son of a slave who became a slave trader.

"You'd want to hurry up," he said to Yseult, "or everything will have been pointless."

Yseult knew what he meant. She didn't need her father to remind her to find a husband.

Yseult had known Archie Sinclair most of her life. He was a regular at some of the parties she attended. He took part in the hunt but did not shine as a horseman or share Yseult's love for animals. Archie was a quiet unassuming man. If Nellie Brown had survived she'd have said, "He's no match for you, Yseult." Only when she was nearing the end of her thirties did it occur to Yseult that he was the type of husband she needed. More importantly, Archie was familiar with her father. He was accepting and broadminded enough not to query another man's origins. He was immune to the gossip and put little value on class. He was a romantic who was passionate about astronomy.

Archie got a teaching post in a Church of Ireland boy's school in town. He moved into Aunt Lydia's old cottage with his scant belongings and enormous telescope. Yseult listened as he enthusiastically talked about the many planets and comets, referring to the life cycle of stars that took millions of years. Yseult could only listen for so long – she was more interested in the planet beneath her feet.

He was from Dublin, the second son of a jeweller. There was nothing remarkable in Archie Sinclair. However, something about his demeanour complemented Yseult. He was an uncomplicated contented man and easy company. Apart from the room in Lugdale's house that was closest to the sky, Archie had little interest in ownership of the estate.

The day he married Yseult, he was unassuming in his wedding suit. It was 1950, women could own land, they could vote, a new era was dawning. Their wedding guests raised their glasses in a toast.

There were two miscarriages before they were blessed with Rachel. Archie chose the name. He'd suggested between pregnancies that they go to the Atacama Desert in Chile to study the stars. Yseult said she'd consider it, knowing she had no interest in living beneath the clear Chilean skies as an exile. She said she wasn't well, the farm needed her, her father needed her and it was a bad time of the year. A few months after Rachel's birth, she encouraged him to travel to Chile alone.

"You never loved me," he said mournfully the day of his departure to Chile. "You are Lugdale's bride."

Ten years later, Archie died suddenly at fifty-two in Chile. There was no mourning period for Yseult. Very few could recall him.

CHAPTER FIFTY-TWO

Yseult was unsure if it was day or night. She was unsure how long she had been sleeping. She was unable to open her eyes. Somebody was holding her wrist. There were other voices in the room. Her wrist was released and carefully placed across her abdomen.

"Her pulse is very slow." Laurence's voice was unsteady. "Jesus Christ," he gasped, "I knew the end was close but I wasn't expecting it so quickly."

"It's easier this way," Rachel said.

"Christ!" Laurence gasped.

"How long more?" Rachel asked.

Yseult could not hear a reply.

"Laurence, she's not getting any better," Rachel said. "You said this was the best course. How long more?"

"Yes, tonight," Laurence said. "A matter of hours in fact."

"Why not now?" Rachel asked.

"Jesus Christ," Laurence whispered, his voice laden with emotion, "would you like me to strangle her right now to suit you!"

Yseult opened her eyes, she tried to speak. She saw Rachel approach her bed.

"Water," she finally said. "It's too hot."

Laurence told Rachel to turn off the heating while he lifted the water to her lips. Yseult saw his doctor's case. It was opened on the chair beside her bed. Rachel didn't turn down the heating. She remained where she was, looking impassively at Yseult.

Yseult lay back and closed her eyes. A child willing a parent dead goes against nature, against the order of life, against instinct, yet it had happened. Lugdale was a place where the current ran upstream and the order of life was never as it should have been. Like the pearl within the oyster, she'd always hoped something beautiful would evolve from her corrupt beloved Lugdale. Just then she acknowledged she was as cruel as Tobias, as cruel as Rachel.

IN 1945, WHEN TOBIAS TURNED SEVENTY-FIVE, HE HAD A STROKE. He spent three weeks in hospital. Each day she expected his death. She got her hair done, and got the housekeeper to abandon all jobs except cleaning and polishing. He didn't die within the week. Three years of dust was gathered and wiped from the antiques before he succumbed to death. For three long years he lingered. It was Archie who kept him alive with conversation. He appeared morose and regretful at times.

One night her father did the unthinkable and suggested giving some lands to the O'Neills.

"*Over my dead body!* " Yseult shouted loudly. "Have you lost your senses?"

"I need to right the past," he said unapologetically.

"*What past?* " she demanded.

Only when she saw him wincing did she realise she was shouting. He never mentioned it again.

It was during her marriage to Archie that she got her best glimpse into the truth of her father's past. Archie was gentle and encouraging. He had many lengthy discussions on life and various cultures, the customs of Africa and the indigenous tribes. Tobias was forthcoming with Archie's inoffensive non-judgemental manner. It allowed Tobias to trust in mankind. Possibly for the first time in his life he felt safe enough to unleash the stories he protectively guarded. Several times he mentioned Arry, her stall in the market and her fighting spirit. He also mentioned Arry's mother, Flora.

"She was a slave who couldn't cope with captivity. She was found dead in a barn."

"How did she die?" Archie asked.

"Her death certificate said she died from 'A visitation by God'," Tobias said.

"Interesting," Archie said. "We'd need a more elaborate explanation these days. Did Flora have any other family? Did the rest of her family share her resistance?"

"No, Flora was unique. Her mother was a slave from the Igbo Tribe in the Ivory Coast. She was known for the flutes she made from bamboo shoots."

Yseult noted all of his references to Jamaica and the regular names that came up. She never told Archie how she had ascertained that Art O'Neill was her great-grandfather and Arry was her grandmother. She never admitted that she shared the same blood as crazy Flora.

"Are you afraid of death?" Archie once asked.

Tobias looked from Archie to Yseult, and then said clearly, "It is the living I'm afraid of."

Her father remained. Most days he sat by the fire. Silenced and unable to impress Lugdale's callers, he became morose. Rachel's birth gave him a little hope. When Archie left he became even more despondent. He kept in his pocket the pearls that had been picked from the Caribbean Sea. Occasionally he held the Victorian gold coin.

When she asked to see the coin he reluctantly handed it to her.

"Is it expensive?" she asked, thinking it might be some priceless piece of gold he liked to finger to make him feel titled.

He shook his head and took the coin back from her.

Towards the end of his life he began to leave the house at night and ramble around the estate. Most of the time he walked the lane that divided his land from the O'Neills to the birch tree on the border of the bog. Once Mary O'Neill found him sitting at the tree. She brought him back to Yseult late that night.

"I'd have brought him up to our house but …" Her voice trailed away. "Forgiveness don't go that far for some wrongs."

"Forgiveness," Yseult had scoffed.

"He has some notion about that tree," Mary said when she found him again. "You'll have to lock the door at night and put the key away till morning."

Yseult didn't lock the door on Tobias. There were colds and flus, cuts and bruises from his rambling, but not death.

RACHEL WAS TALKING, THE CURTAINS WERE OPENED. IT WAS DAYTIME. Yseult shifted in the bed. They stopped talking.

"Are you alright, Mother?" Rachel asked, coming to her side.

"I want to sit up," Yseult said.

They stood at either side of her and helped her to sit up. Rachel stood back to look at her. It was Laurence who puffed the pillows and left his hand lingering on her shoulder.

"My father was asked towards the end of his days if he was afraid of dying," Yseult began.

An uneasy smile crossed Laurence's face. Rachel remained unmoving.

"He said he wasn't afraid of dying … that it was …" Yseult paused before looking at the couple.

Why would she tell them she knew they were about to hurry along her death, their murderous intentions whitewashed with gracious humanity?

Her father was aware of how Yseult wanted him dead. Yseult never dared admit it until that moment. That she had wished her father dead, that she was as ruthless as the wild animals who refused to feed the offspring whose death was imminent. Was it shame? Or hate? Or something ruthless that passed through her veins, something that came all the way from Jamaica?

"What am I?" Yseult asked aloud.

"Yes, Mother?"

The offspring of slaves, Irish indentured servants, a small slice of aristocratic English and an unending desire to remain.

"Drink your tea, Mother," Rachel said. "You'll feel better."

Yseult began to cry.

Rachel looked at her disbelievingly.

Nobody had seen her cry for over seventy years. Just then she didn't care – she felt her shoulders shake. She didn't need to hide it. She sat in her bed with her fluffed pillows and cold tea and cried. Why was it that so much occurred to her late in life? Why was it she only saw empathy at the last hour? Suddenly Yseult considered the boy on the boat to Jamaica. She felt for the slave called Flora who died in a barn. The little footprints each left brought her to this bedroom on this strange February morning, her daughter willing her dead, as she had willed her own father's death. At this time of her life was she ready to concede defeat and take the final dose of morphine that would stop her heart?

Yseult saw it happening from the upstairs window. She noticed Tobias had been out again at night. He staggered into the wind and fell. This time, she didn't go to help him. Instead she remained where she was and watched. She saw him face down on the back lawn below her window. He rolled sideways and raised his head. He looked towards the house, towards the window where she stood. She watched him stretch his hand towards her, yet she stayed there watching him. Slowly she descended the stairs, reliving her anger. She thought she heard thunder, then shouting. For an insane moment she thought her father had died and she was hearing deep other-worldly rumblings. She stood in the kitchen listening, trying to ascertain where the noise was coming from – the pipes, a fleet of motorcars, maybe a plane?

Then Mary O'Neill burst into the kitchen, carrying Tobias in her strong arms.

"There's a stampede of your cattle after breaking through – they're on the road!"

Mary placed Tobias on the kitchen table.

Tobias's eyes tried to focus on Yseult. His face appeared distorted.

"What's wrong with you, Yseult? I saw you watching him at the window," Mary said impatiently. "Hold him there while I call a doctor."

Yseult seethed.

Later that week Tobias finally expired. He was eighty-six years of age.

CHAPTER FIFTY-THREE

April 1991

Mary O'Neill couldn't help thinking of Lydia when she saw Yseult walking towards her. Even in the distance her face had that startled look. Overnight Yseult appeared to have aged. She used a walking stick. Her movements were cautious. Mary had heard that Yseult spent two months in hospital. It was rumoured that her daughter left her lying in bed for days. It was Brendan, the farm manager, and the housekeeper who called the ambulance. Since returning home, Yseult behaved like Lydia. She had the haunted stare of a woman with her sights on something other than life, her clothes too big for her long thin frame.

Mary was sitting in the garden of the local hotel after eating her Sunday dinner. She was a creature of habit. Every day for the last fifteen years she came to the same hotel for her Sunday dinner with members of her family. Today was a fine afternoon and she sat in the gardens to allow the first of the summer sun to warm her. Mary's youngest grandchildren were playing at the water fountain.

She sat on a bench a few feet away from them with their coats beside her on the bench.

"Granny, can we jump in?" one of them called to Mary.

"You cannot," Mary retorted with a raised voice. "'Tisn't warm enough for that yet."

Mary conceded that her own life was not without difficulty. There were little and large problems that came and went, and some stayed longer. She had to accept that her daughter's husband was a grand fellow but an awful eejit. It was his silly talk that drove her out of the hotel restaurant and into the garden for a bit of peace. He was a problem that wouldn't be going anywhere in the next week. Although the way marriages were breaking down, nothing was set in stone any more. The shame of one of her children's marriages failing had happened already – she could cope with that one again. Her second son's marriage had ended and privately she had to accept that a large part of the blame lay at his door. Of course she'd never say that out loud. She had to accept that he wasn't the best-behaved lad in the parish. Mary tried to find the right word that would sum up Thomas. He was "cracked". There was no incident that made him cracked. He was born that way, as wild as a March hare.

Mary looked back towards Yseult. She noticed she'd stopped walking and was looking in her direction. Mary suddenly felt terribly sorry for her. After all her years of hard work and commitment to her beloved Lugdale, her daughter was talking in the pub about selling the paintings that had hung in the house for centuries. Seemingly, Rachel was all talk about turning Lugdale into a hotel and spa. She also talked about setting up a cheese factory, and they'd have walks around the estate. It all sounded a bit airy-fairy. Rachel's daft talk was light years away from Yseult's attitude.

As late as one week ago Rachel had met Mary's cracked son and asked how much he'd pay for the fields by the river.

"I'll sell them to you at a fair price as we're related," Rachel said.

The DNA samples taken from the skeleton had confirmed that Mary and Yseult were the same blood. It wasn't any secret to Mary, she'd known for years that Tobias was Okeke from Jamaica. His mother Arry and Mary's father Leon were half-brother and sister, Art O'Neill being their father.

Rachel made a reference to her mother's death. "When my mother pops her clogs she might will you a few fields," she'd said, making light of it.

It was all a bit sad, in Mary's opinion, for a daughter to be selling fields and gleefully talking about the mother's death.

Yseult continued to walk, putting one slow foot in front of the other. As she approached, Mary could hear her laboured breathing.

Only today could Mary feel sympathy for Yseult. Two weeks ago when they gave Fonsy a proper burial, the news was still raw. Fonsy hadn't drowned in the sea but had his skull crushed by a blow. The forensics explained that part of his skull had a gaping wound. Every time Mary thought about Tobias Ffrench, her anger returned. She had no doubt that Tobias had killed him. Fonsy was encroaching on Tobias's land and his peace of mind. A few days before Fonsy went missing all those years ago, Mary had seen him more than once hiding on the lawns of Lugdale. Butch Slattery used to pay Mary to trap rabbits on Lugdale. When she checked the traps at night she saw Fonsy peeping in the window of the house. She knew he was watching Tobias.

Then one day she had seen Tobias fleeing the forest with his dogs and his gun. Then Fonsy emerged following him. Mary believed that Fonsy had made his existence known to Tobias. She couldn't say if Fonsy's intention was to harm Tobias, yet clearly it was enough to terrify Tobias into killing the poor soul.

Mary thought of Tobias towards the end of his life, how he'd ramble his estate and always make his way towards the tree beneath which Fonsy was buried. Only when she thought how guilt must have enveloped him in his later years did she soften. At least Mary's father was no longer around to hear about Fonsy's death or his crushed skull.

Yseult arrived at the bench where Mary was sitting. She looked at Mary and then acknowledged her with a nod.

"Beautiful day," Yseult said, slightly breathless.

"'Tis indeed," Mary said. "Grand day for it."

They fell silent, watching the children at the fountain.

Mary had Fonsy's remains buried in the same plot as her parents. On the headstone she had his name etched : *Akeem 'Fonsy' 1881–1923.* The fellow who did the etching knew the story. The undertaker said he knew the story too. So did her eejit of a son-in-law but none of them knew the real story until Mary told them what her father had told her. She showed them an old book that her father had given her when she was a young woman. It was written by Art O'Neill. The pages were too delicate so she had the local stationary shop photocopy each page and gave a copy to all of her children. The day for hiding had long passed.

Mary told them the part of the story that was missing from the book. The story of what happened after Art O'Neill went to the Big House to get his money.

IN THE EARLY MONTHS OF 1891, LEON FOLLOWED HIS FATHER, ART, to the Big House. Leon sensed that trouble was brewing for his father. He'd secretly been forewarned by Henry that Blair was plotting something awful for Art. That morning Leon hid beneath the window of the study. When Art was seated, Blair emptied the pouch of seven gold coins on the desk. Then he said he wasn't going to give him his money.

"Surely you didn't expect me to hand over seven gold coins to a man who has made that and much more from my estate?" Blair said.

Art stood up immediately. "You may not give me the gold but you'll have to hand it out in the long run." As he was leaving he waved his hand around the room. "Your house will be costly to rebuild when its burned, your crops will be costly to resow when they fail. There are many more ways for you to pay."

Leon saw Blair taking the gun from beneath the desk and pointing it at Art's back.

"*Papa!* " Leon cried and began climbing through the window.

Blair fired the gun just as Art moved. The bullet hit him in the back.

Blair began to shout, "Thieves! Thieves! Thieves are robbing me! "

Leon rushed to his father's side.

"Run!" Art gasped. He clutched Leon's hand for a moment before his grip loosened.

Leon looked up to see Blair aiming the gun at him.

"You too," Blair snarled, "or you'll be back to burn me out of my home." Then he shouted again, *"Thieves! Thieves! Thieves are robbing me!"*

A white planter shooting a thief was not questioned, shooting a mulatto thief was applauded. Blair was shouting thief to let the staff hear his cries and justify his actions in the unlikely event he would need to recount his story.

In the stress of the moment, Leon froze by his father's side.

The gunshot came from the door of the study.

As Blair was blasted backwards Leon swung around.

Henry was in the doorway in his wheelchair with a pistol in his hand.

The sight of Henry with red-rimmed focused eyes was the most disturbing scene of hatred Leon had ever seen.

That night some of Blair's friends arrived to comfort Lydia. The story circulating among the white community was that Art and his son had tried to rob Blair, and he shot Art while his son escaped with the gold coins. Lydia told the police she didn't know what happened. She didn't see anything. The staff told the police that Art came to collect his gold. Nobody saw him carrying a gun and he did not look like a man about to rob Blair or shoot him. Their opinions were not considered. The police began to search the area for Leon.

Lydia did not see any of the sympathisers. She remained in her room where she packed luggage for herself and Henry.

That night Leon shared Henry's room.

"They won't search the house for you," Lydia said to Leon as she gave him the gold coins. "These belong to your family."

Lydia didn't wait for Blair's funeral. Their friends thought she was so traumatised by the event that she fled the country immediately. The truth was she was afraid it would be discovered that Henry killed his father. She wanted to take him away as quickly as possible to another country where Blair Stratford-Rice's murder in distant Jamaica would never be speculated upon.

She would take Leon with her, the only witness to Henry's guilt and one of the few people who treated her son with kindness.

Before leaving the following day, Leon gave a small parcel to one of the domestic staff for his mother, Ngozi. Wrapped in the parcel was a letter and five of the gold coins, one gold coin for Ngozi to buy whatever she wanted and the remaining five coins for his siblings to buy land as Art wished. Leon kept one gold coin to help him find Akeem, and another to give to Akeem when he found him. At that age, Leon imagined the yellow gold bringing a little joy to Akeem.

MARY WAS CURIOUS ABOUT HOW MUCH YSEULT KNEW BUT SHE WAS not interested enough to ask her.

She took the children's coats off the bench to make room for Yseult.

"Do you want to sit down and take the weight off your feet?" she asked.

She could see Yseult hesitate. She didn't care if she sat or not but she wouldn't see an old woman left standing either.

Yseult moved the walking stick from one hand to the other, then shuffled closer. Slowly she eased onto the bench and released a loud satisfied sigh.

If that were any other woman, Mary would ask after her health or was she out for the Sunday dinner with the family? They'd have a laugh about walking off the dinner or making room for dessert, but she wouldn't do that with Yseult. She wouldn't open the door to anything personal.

"Granny, please, can we stick our feet in?" one of the children asked.

"You'll have to ask your parents," Mary said.

"The sunshine makes it so much more enticing for the children,"

Yseult commented. "I suppose it's not quite warm enough yet," she added, looking towards the sky.

"I'll leave it up to the parents," Mary sighed. "'Tis dangerous to get involved. The young ones have their own way of doing things."

Mary could see Yseult's hand resting on her cane. They were the same dark hands as her own. They always looked foreign, especially when the Irish sun glossed their waiting skin.

LYDIA HAD TOLD LEON ALL SHE KNEW ABOUT HER HUSBAND'S SLAVE-trading enterprise and he in turn had given her the sparse information his father and the other men had extracted from Nicolas Ffrench: that Akeem had been taken to Morocco and that Okeke's contact in Morocco was a slave trader called Mr. Dockworth.

Lydia promised she would write to this man and all those she felt might be able to throw light on Akeem's whereabouts. And, as soon as they were settled back in Lugdale, she began to keep that promise. Soon she began to receive unwelcome information from various sources. The slave trader Dockworth had by all accounts expired, heart failure being quoted as the cause, and his business had been liquidated. Lydia at length confirmed that this, their one lead, was a dead end.

Leon was devastated at the news and suffered greatly, but he forced himself to focus on his new life in Ireland and began to work as a farmhand for Mr. Falvey, a small farmer at the top of the hill in Mein. All Mr. Falvey's family had left on the boats for America and England and a bond was formed between the old man and his new employee. However, after two years Leon could no longer suppress his desire to find Akeem. He left and worked on the boats travelling the seas between England and Morocco, forever searching, forever hoping. Once a year he returned to Mr. Falvey's farm and visited Lydia at Lugdale. But, as the years passed and he grew towards manhood, his boyish dream was lost. By the age of seventeen, he had little hope.

Leon's only confidantes were Lydia and an Irish girl called

Eileen Kennedy. Eileen worked on the same ship as Leon. Her father was a sailor who died at sea and from the age of twelve she had remained working on the ships drifting between oceans. She and Leon had dreams of a peaceful life far removed from the turbulent life of sailors and ships.

In 1902, Leon visited Ireland. It had been eleven years since they had left Jamaica yet Lydia told him they were still searching Black River for him, believing he had killed Blair. His influential friends were still hell-bent on finding Leon and hanging him.

As a temporary arrangement, Leon moved into Mr. Falvey's farm with Eileen, now his wife. Later their temporary arrangement was extended into a plan to stay longer. They came to an agreement with Mr. Falvey. Leon used his savings to buy two of Mr. Falvey's fields, and for the remainder of Mr. Falvey's life they would look after him, with Eileen cooking and cleaning and Leon working the land. Eventually, they would own the smallholding of eighteen acres.

On the birth of his first daughter in 1902, there was a little fragment of hope from the slave trader, Irish Ignatius, in Jamaica. He wrote to Lydia that he had received some information from Morocco that sounded promising. Leon had been keeping the gold coin to buy Akeem's freedom. He imagined arriving at the gates of an unknown plantation in Morocco and exchanging the coin for Akeem's freedom. Leon gave Lydia one of the gold coins. He asked her to send it to Ignatius, hoping it might hurry matters along. A few months later, Irish Ignatius wrote to say that, armed with his new information, he had contacted Okeke and given him the gold coin on condition that he would verify Akeem's whereabouts. Okeke accepted the gold coin and some months later wrote with precise information of where Akeem could be found. Akeem had been working, not on the sun-drenched plantation Leon had imagined but in the dark bowels of the earth – in a mine.

Leon sailed to Morocco where he found Akeem. At that stage, Akeem could not speak, his body was buckled from overwork and his dead arm hung at his side. Akeem was useless. At the age of twenty-two he was a burden to his owners.

Leon brought him home to North Kerry where he remained until his death, living between fear and pain.

YSEULT BROKE INTO MARY'S THOUGHTS.

"Do they have Irish names?" she asked.

Mary nodded.

Yseult said aloud, "We're only passing through."

Mary looked at Yseult quizzically.

"Poor Nellie Brown used to say that," Yseult said.

Mary smiled when she recalled Nellie Brown.

IN IRELAND, LEON WANTED TO BLEND INTO HIS NEW COMMUNITY. HE knew the Irish were suspicious of those who were not local, Catholic or white. He gave each of his daughters saints' names but the real truth of their identity was hidden in the second names he used in the privacy of their home. Mary Ngozi, Kathleen Oluchi, Bridget Uzoma. When Leon realised that Okeke was the new resident of Lugdale, he spent the first few months plotting Okeke's death. He stalked him constantly, planning revenge. Then one cold December night he realised he was behaving as his father, Art, had behaved towards Blair. He was taking the hatred into his home, into his bed, it was consuming him. Art had told Leon that he regretted wasting years watching Blair and hating him. Leon resolved to learn from his father. He chose to ignore Okeke. It was irrelevant how he lived his life – eventually their past caught up with every man and woman.

"Only a matter of time," he told Mary, "and I can't spend five more minutes waiting for his unhappiness to make me happy."

ONE OF MARY'S GRANDCHILDREN APPEARED AT HER SIDE.

"Granny, we're ordering desserts."

A smaller grandchild appeared at the other side. "Apple tart or ice cream," her eyes were wide with excitement, "or your favourite," she gasped aloud, "a big bowl of different-coloured ice creams with soft chocolate on top!"

"Order that for me, and I'll be in to ye now." Mary stood up and flexed her legs. Yseult remained where she was, looking towards the fountain.

As Mary gathered up the coats belonging to her grandchildren, Yseult extended her closed fist. Mary looked at it.

"This belongs to you," Yseult said.

She opened her hand and dropped one gold coin onto Mary's palm.

Laboriously, Yseult got to her feet and slowly moved back the way she'd come.

THE END

sweeping saga charts the lives of five generations of women, perhaps none more remarkable than Betty Hopkins, whose story triggers the narrative.

Shrewd and ambitious, in 1916 Betty moves to from Tipperary to Dublin with her husband Seamus, a militant republican. With its epic span and multitudinous characters this is a hugely ambitious first novel. A compelling storyline and informed portrayal of Ireland's turbulent political history." Independent

"An enjoyable, deftly written debut, bringing history to life. It shows what the rising and war of independence was like for women." The Examiner

"Engaging and unforgettable," The Post

"A great read" Bleach House Library

AUTHOR Q & A

Author Q & A

Where did you get the idea for the novel?

In the mid-90s I attended a St. Patrick's Day party in Israel where most of us were Scottish, Welsh and Irish. A coloured man from Jamaica joined our crew. He sang along to the Irish songs and even had his own version of the song, "The Wearing of the Green." I assumed the Jamaican liked Irish folk music or had spent some time in Ireland. He told me he'd never been to Ireland however he identified his heritage as Irish.

Most of us born in Ireland pre-1990 will have attended a Catholic school, sat beside a white Irish child, taken a white boy to our debs and had little to no interaction with people other than Irish, Catholic and white. As a "blow-in" to the rural town I was as foreign as it got. At that age I could tell from certain surnames where their family originated. In my home country, families with surnames Ryans, Dwyers and Elys can trace their ancestry back 1000 years. Knowing at least that much, I looked at the Jamaican and noticed the obvious. He didn't look like the Ryans or Dwyers I knew, and most notably he did not look like he had any Irish heritage. I must have appeared doubtful as he went on to tell me his father's family were Irish. The story that was passed down the generations was that his great-great grandfather came to Jamaica in the 1850s from Waterford. I remained doubtful, and without google or android phones in the 1990s, I couldn't check his story. On the rare occasions when I heard "The Wearing of the Green," I thought of the Jamaican's tall tale.

Years later, I watched the Jamaican Movie, "Cool Running." Only when the credits rolled, I noticed the Irish surnames, Roche, McLaughlin, Crowe, Morrison, Maloney and Harris. When the internet became accessible I researched the Jamaican link and found a few staggering facts. The extent of Irish emigration to the Caribbean and Jamaica is so prolific that a staggering 25% of Jamaican citizens claim Irish ancestry, the second-largest reported ethnic group in Jamaica after African ancestry.

How did you develop Art's character?

I had been thinking about this novel for a few years before I wrote it. When I read about the children deported in the 1650s, at least once a week I thought about their journey and their life in a country so vastly different from Ireland. When I eventually began the novel, my nephew was eight years of age, and I found myself looking at the world through his eyes. As I explored Art's character and went with the twists and turns of his life, he became stronger and hopefully I've done him justice.

What was the research like?

In one word - Painstaking! My previous novel was based in Ireland, I had a lot of reference points whereas I had to begin from the very beginning with this novel. I read a lot of history books, academic papers, diaries, novels, old newspapers and didn't stop until I had a sense of the time, place and people. It was difficult to write parts of it, the cruelty and the white man's animalistic attitudes and double-standards towards the slaves appalled me.

I particularly loved writing about emancipation. It was joyous and invigorating to finally see hope for the slaves after 200 years of endless brutality. Even researching that part of history was uplifting. I mention in the book about the slave who galloped widely around on his owner's horse and wearing his owner's hat, and then they killed the hogs and took the rum from the sugar mill – that actually happened. I remember the night I read that account and felt entirely jubilant.

How important is the research for historical fiction?

For me, as a writer – it's as vital as the storytelling and the voice of the characters. I have a loyalty to the reader and it's my duty to present a book that reflects the era. I normally research much more than I need because I like to get absorbed in the era.

Who are your favourite characters?

Art – because I feel maternal towards him and I admire his resilience.

Arry – I would love if she had lived. Initially, I had trouble finding Arry's voice. I kept thinking about her and couldn't settle on anything. Then I was invited to join an underground shop that sold jewellery, handbags and makeup (it was all a bit covert – the shop owner was avoiding taxes!) I met the owner at her home. She was young and beautiful with sallow skin and jet black hair. She was dressed as if she was going to a party with fake foot-long eye-lashes and a sparkling top. She was fantastic at selling her wares. As I pranced around her state-of-the-art kitchen which doubled as her underground shop, she told me part of her life story, I was gripped. In Ireland, there is still a small element of secrecy, this woman had none. She told me about her abusive her teenage pregnancy, her abusive ex-husband and her happy ending. As she spoke in her marble kitchen about her life and passed me handbags to view, I found my Arry.

Yseult – because like Art, she is resilient. She prevailed, she had spirit and in the end she had empathy. And, if I ever reach old age, I imagine I'll be a grumpy old lady like Yseult, defiant and as odd as two left feet.

What are the joys of having your novels published?

I love hearing from readers. I get emails from readers all over the world who tell me they've enjoyed the novel. Nothing beats the thrill of that. I'm genuinely chuffed that I could bring a little joy to someone's life.

What's next?

I've just finished a novel based on an Irish colony in the American West and their interaction with the Native American Indians. A few years ago, a reader from a mining town got in touch with me and told me about her ancestors who left Ireland in the 1860s and moved from the east coast to the American West. Similar to *The Tide Between Us*, I thought about her family and their experience so often that I was eventually compelled to put pen to paper. *The Weaver's Legacy* will be launched in December 2020.

If you'd like to hear more, pleased log onto www.olivecollins.com to receive my newsletter.

Once again, my heartfelt thanks for reading my novel.